Political Morality

POLITICAL THEORY AND CONTEMPORARY POLITICS

Series Editors: Richard Bellamy, University of Reading, Jeremy Jennings, University of Birmingham, and Paul Kelly, London School of Economics and Political Science

This series aims to examine the interplay of political theory and practical politics at the beginning of the twenty-first century. It explores the way that the concepts and ideologies which we have inherited from the past have been transformed or need to be rethought in the light of contemporary political debates. The series comprises concise single-authored books, each representing an original contribution to the literature on a key theme or concept.

Also published in this series:

Love and Politics: Women Politicians and the Ethics of Care
Fiona Mackay

Liberalism and Value Pluralism
George Crowder

Forthcoming titles:

Defending Liberal Neutrality
Jonathan Seglow

Seductive Virtue: The Socratic Art of Civic Education
Russell Bentley

Political Theory and Media
Alan Finlayson

Democracy and Global Warming
Barry Holden

The Politics of Civil Society
James Martin

Political Morality

A Theory of Liberal Democracy

Richard Vernon

CONTINUUM
London and New York

Continuum
The Tower Building, 11 York Road, London SE1 7NX
370 Lexington Avenue, New York, NY 10017-6503

First published 2001

British Library Cataloguing-in-Publication Data
A catalogue record for this book is available from the British Library.

ISBN 0-8264-5067-9 (hardback)
       0-8264-5066-0 (paperback)

Library of Congress Cataloging-in-Publication Data
   Vernon, Richard, 1945–
      Political morality : a theory of liberal democracy / Richard Vernon.
         p. cm. — (Political theory and contemporary politics)
      Includes bibliographical references and index.
      ISBN 0-8264-5067-9 — ISBN 0-8264-5066-0 (pbk.)
      1. Democracy. 2. Liberalism. 3. Political ethics. I. Title. II. Series.
   JC423 .V48 2001
   321.8—dc21   00-066025

Typeset by YHT Ltd, London
Printed and bound in Great Britain by Biddles Ltd
www.biddles.co.uk

Contents

Acknowledgements

Earlier versions of Chapters 3 and 4 of this book were given to seminars at Nuffield College and the Universities of Reading and Keele, and I warmly thank David Miller, Richard Bellamy, John Horton and their colleagues for their criticisms and suggestions. Les Jacobs, Dan Munro and Andrew Robinson kindly read parts of the manuscript and offered helpful critiques, and Leena Grover provided valuable help in preparing the manuscript. I am also grateful to the publisher's anonymous readers.

Chapters 4 and 6 draw in part on earlier work published in, respectively, *Political Studies*, 46 (1998), 295–308 (© the Political Studies Association) and *Ethics*, 106 (1996), 621–32 (© 1996 by the University of Chicago; all rights reserved). I acknowledge the editors' permission to republish this material.

This book was written during a period of sabbatical leave granted by the University of Western Ontario, for which I am very grateful.

Introduction

To count as 'liberal democratic', regimes must meet a certain standard of electoral accountability, and provide some level of constitutionally protected liberty to their citizens. Regimes with some claim to do this – and also claiming legitimacy just on the grounds that they do so – have an important place in contemporary politics. Indeed, some very ambitious assertions have been made about them: they have been seen not just as important but as world-historic and unsurpassable culminations (Fukuyama, 1992). So perhaps the first thing that this book needs to say is that it is not at all a celebration of that kind. It is, rather, an attempt at immanent understanding. Obviously, it would not have been written on the assumption that liberal democratic regimes are either politically negligible, or else quite remote from any significant political values; but one can appreciate the importance of something without making it an apotheosis, and appreciation of the point of something may be the first step towards not triumphalism, but immanent criticism of its practices.

Despite its prominence in the world today, liberal democracy has never ceased to be in question, from the standpoint of political theory. Its justification is often doubted, generally on the grounds that its virtues are too minimal, or else, or additionally, on the grounds that its practices fall short of its claims; and even those who approve of it defend it in very different ways, so that it is hard to find a basic account of it that is shared among its supporters, let alone shared between its supporters and its critics, who are often at cross-purposes entirely. This book is an attempt to outline a basic account of an unorthodox kind. It argues that liberal democracy is the view that one will reach if one accepts a certain elementary conception of politics and the moral constraints that it entails. The point of this account, it is also argued, is that if one accepts it, one is better able to meet many of the justificatory challenges that liberal democracy faces. The cost of accepting it – if it is a cost – is that some standard defences of liberal democracy, and also some of its practices, would have to be abandoned. So this book is directed in roughly equal measure against critics and supporters of liberal democracy. Liberal democracy can survive criticism, the argument maintains, only if it is supported in a different way.

What are the main justificatory challenges that liberal democracy faces? Surely the first that comes to mind is the extraordinarily contentious status of liberalism as a political doctrine. The past three decades have seen an unprecedented flourishing of liberal political theory, beginning, of course, with Rawls's *Theory of Justice*, a book which is generally agreed to have brought analytical political theory back from a premature grave. A stream of revisions have modified its claims; other versions of liberalism, based on renderings of equality, or rights, or ideas of moral development or self-perfection, have staked out rival positions; and central principles of liberalism have been applied to urgent topical issues such as multiculturalism or immigration policy or international justice. We now have a considerable body of theory, dwarfing (in volume) the output of any previous period, internally diverse, and with a sharp practical edge. But every inch of the way has been contested, and the catalogue of objections to liberalism in all its forms, pure or applied, is now immense. It contains, critics say, a false sociology, misrepresenting society as a collection of atomic individuals, recognizing only voluntary ties, and neglecting the basic facts of unchosen human solidarity; a false psychology, locating the source of happiness in lonely endeavours instead of in the success of collective projects, and in the virtues that these projects require; a false geography, even, representing the globe as Euro-centred, not as multi-centred; a false epistemology, exaggerating the role of unaided individual reason, and failing to give weight either to custom and tradition or to the emotions. Above all, perhaps – according to critics – it contains a false morality; and here the objections are many. It is too universalistic, neglecting particular ties; it deceptively claims neutrality, thus effectively disguising its own one-sidedness; it imposes an artificial distinction between the 'right', which all are supposed to acknowledge, and the 'good', about which we can differ; it gives indefensible primacy to the value of autonomy in moral life. John Kekes's *Against Liberalism* (Kekes, 1997) is a recent and particularly comprehensive critique. Despite its obvious attractiveness, liberalism, Kekes maintains, is shot through with inconsistencies. Its moral elevation of the self-chosen life comes into conflict with the values that make life good, and so liberalism is forced either to impoverish life by insisting on the prime importance of choice, or else to compromise this value, thus losing its distinctiveness as a moral and political philosophy.

But, second, there are also objections to the theory's democratic pretensions. Here the history of the past few decades has taken a different form, and the outcome is more complex and less clearly polarized. Roughly speaking, successive waves of critique and counter-critique have left us with two rival conceptions of democracy: an 'aggregative' conception, valuing democracy on the grounds that its outcomes give expression to voters' demands and preferences; and a 'procedural' conception, which values democracy as an expression, in its mode of operation, of some basic value, typically that of equality. Frequently – although the link is often asserted rather than demonstrated – liberal democracy is identified with the former view: it is thought to offer a mode of democracy which allows individuals and groups to promote and defend their interests. Once this link is made, liberal democracy at once becomes vulnerable to a familiar and powerful range of objections. If we favour democracy on the basis of the outcomes that it produces, we have to face the fact that, in general, we have no convincing way to prefer one set of outcomes to another. True, the results produced by majority rule can be shown to be 'special'; but this is the case only if a number of very restrictive assumptions are made (Barry, 1982). We have to assume that majorities and minorities will form and re-form in a quite volatile way on an issue-to-issue basis, or, failing that, that opinion will be spread more or less evenly along the spectrum (or bunched near the centre). On these assumptions, any given voter's distance from the outcomes will be minimized, and we would find it rational to adopt the majority principle. But even then we have to make a further assumption that voters' preferences are equally strong, so that the satisfaction of majorities can be put in the same scale as the dissatisfaction of minorities and be shown to outweigh it. And if we could somehow deal with these difficulties we would still confront a mystery, because, if we assume that politics is based on the promotion and defence of interests, we are hard put to say why it is worthwhile for individuals to vote at all. Hence the paradox that we have a large and sophisticated social science devoted to voting behaviour which cannot convincingly explain the act of voting.[1] Alternatively, one might turn to the procedural account and seek to ally it with liberal democracy. No judgements need be made about outcomes, on this view; democracy is valuable because, by its very nature, it embodies equality (Christiano, 1993). A liberal might find this consideration persuasive because liberalism, too, embodies equality, in a certain sense, in rejecting paternalism, or legal moralism, or other things that privilege one person's view of life over another's. But acknowledging the value of equality, the difficulty is to show why *this* conception of equality is preferable to others. Why, for example, should we give equal weight to individuals, when in fact their group memberships may be of primary importance, and what we may need is a consociational or bi- or multicommunal polity in which equal weight is given to ethnically or linguistically or religiously defined groups? Or why should we opt for a procedural view of equality, when what might be really important is equality of condition? It would seem to be a liberal predisposition to set outcomes aside and to put all the weight on mechanisms expressing a merely formal status, instead of interpreting 'democracy' as requiring a fully egalitarian society.

Here, however, we begin to encounter the third main source of justificatory problems: that of the compatibility of liberalism and democracy – whatever the status of each taken separately. For the very idea of liberal democracy is quite often seen as self-contradictory or paradoxical. Most interestingly, two major histories of liberalism conclude by raising the conjunction of liberalism and democracy as a question. In *The Rise and Decline of Western Liberalism*, Anthony Arblaster writes of 'the importance of sustaining [a] dialectical or, if you prefer, ambiguous attitude towards liberalism,' which, while remembering what is of value in it, also refuses to forget its bourgeois and anti-democratic character (Arblaster, 1984: 347–8). Richard Bellamy, in *Liberalism and Modern Society*, argues that the ethical commitments that have sustained liberalism in the past have become increasingly parochial and insular, and that the task of preserving freedom in a deeply pluralistic society depends on cultivating a more robust kind of democracy than liberals have generally welcomed (Bellamy, 1992: 252–61).

This kind of disjunctive conclusion is supported from a variety of points of view. According to one commentator, the very idea of liberal democracy contains elements of 'paradox', for although it may be true that some features of liberalism are indispensable to the practice of democracy, liberalism has often served as 'a constraint upon the process of democratization' (Beetham, 1992: 41). According to another, the liberal and democratic traditions have been conjoined only for historical reasons, and normatively viewed they may be fundamentally inconsistent or incompatible (Banning, 1986). According to a third position – perhaps the hardest-edged of all – liberal and democratic principles dictate two different constitutions, so that, if we attempted to combine them, we would have not a liberal democratic constitution 'but rather two constitutions, one liberal, the other democratic', and only the most tenuous hope of reconciling their domains (Levine, 1978: 307). For while liberalism demands outcomes which are guaranteed to express individuals' preferences, democracy demands outcomes that respond to shifts in overall preference; and it is hard indeed to see how these two demands could be confined tidily to non-competing spheres.

What have the liberals or the democrats done to clarify the meaning of liberal democracy? Not a great deal, it must be said. A notable essay by Isaiah Berlin appears to drive a decisive wedge between liberalism and democracy, by representing them as responses to two quite distinct questions, and suggesting that liberals' values might be satisfied by wholly non-democratic systems, and wholly unsatisfied by democratic ones: 'Just as a democracy may, in fact, deprive the individual citizen of a great many liberties which he might have in some other form of society, so it is perfectly conceivable that a liberal-minded despot would allow his subjects a large measure of personal freedom' (Berlin, 1969: 129). Other liberals, it is true, would certainly dissent from such a view, for they do not take Berlinian 'negative liberty' to define the liberal programme. Ronald Dworkin, for example, in his essay 'Liberalism', rejects the view that liberty is liberalism's foundational value, and contends that representative democracy is one of the major ways in which liberals would seek to give expression to their belief (which he holds to be normatively fundamental) in equality of respect (Dworkin, 1978). But what is given with one hand is not exactly taken away by the other, but is at least somewhat diminished by it, for it then transpires that democracy contains inherently oppressive tendencies against which liberal rights are the first line of defence. Liberalism calls for democracy, but also seeks to keep the world safe from it. Rawls himself, in *A Theory of Justice*, specifies that a liberal society must be a democracy; the 'original position' from which the contractualist argument begins is one of equality, and this feature should be 'transferred' to the basic decision-making institutions of the polity (Rawls, 1971: 221–2). But critics such as Joshua Cohen complain, persuasively, that whatever Rawls himself would like to see, the argument itself leaves the form that democracy should take more or less indeterminate: there is something of a gap between the quasi-contractual argument that Rawls evolves and the kind of democracy that he thinks we should have (Cohen, 1989: 18–20). The later Rawls, indeed, in *Political Liberalism* (1993) and in the works leading up to that book, shifts his focus much closer to a democratic theory, at least approaching the 'deliberative democracy' of Cohen and Amy Gutmann and Dennis Thompson. He discusses principles and institutions that might help a society to evolve a 'public reason' by means of which people whose views of life differ can govern themselves in a just and stable manner. But it would surely not be unfair to say that what his discussion explains is how democracy can be put to use by a liberal principle of legitimacy; it does not treat democracy as an idea with its own internal requirements, which might turn out to be compatible or incompatible with those of liberalism (Shapiro, 1996: 110).

As for the democratic theorists, some, such as Robert Dahl, bluntly admit that if we value democracy then we cannot prescribe particular outcomes, such as liberal ones, in advance. A democratic process might, from a liberal point of view, go wrong; so, however, might any process that we might put in place to protect ourselves from democracy (Dahl, 1989: 191). Likewise, democracy as defined from a 'republican' perspective is said to resist any prior limiting of its agenda, for where a people enjoys self-governing power then the success of any proposal will necessarily depend on its relation to broadly accepted political views (Miller, 1995a: 447). Others, it is true, are much less unequivocal. Joshua Cohen, for example, argues that the requirements of a deliberative politics can be shown to encompass (some) liberal values. Democratic deliberation naturally requires the existence of political rights, such as equal voting rights and freedom of speech and expression. He claims, however, that the argument for freedom of political expression spills over to protect other forms of expression and perhaps other kinds of freedom too (Cohen, 1989: 29–30). This important claim will need discussion in its place. But one might initially note that it is not obviously compatible with the other claim, presented together with it, that democratic deliberation is a process 'not constrained by the authority of prior norms or requirements' (*ibid.*: 22). That view is bound to give the liberal pause. Surely, if the democratic process itself is going to set its own norms and requirements, it is vain to suppose that *all* the liberal's norms and requirements are going to be accommodated. We can insist, indeed, that democratic deliberators are bound not only by their decisions but also by the 'preconditions' of the decision-making process, the provisions that enable us to say that a valid collective choice has been made. But who, apart from a democratic public, is entitled to interpret those preconditions in an authoritative way?

It is the third kind of objection, based on incompatibility, that this book principally tries to meet. It argues that liberal democracy is a single political conception, not a trade-off or compromise between two independent values, still less a paradox or oxymoron. The context of justification that it outlines leads us to a position with 'democratic' and 'liberal' elements which imply each other mutually. Historically, no doubt, we could give different and partially separate accounts of the development of liberal and democratic ideas. We might recall, for example, Rousseau's view that a sovereign people need give no guarantees against the use of its own power, and Mill's exactly contrary view that restraints are if anything particularly necessary when the majority rules.[2] But even a cursory glance at the world today suggests that the separation between democratic and liberal freedoms, however important it may once have been, now has a certain artificiality. Only democracies provide liberal freedoms;[3] and it has become much harder than it was, perhaps, a decade or two ago to maintain that there are clear examples of non-liberal democracies. A noted Canadian political theorist, the late C. B. Macpherson, deployed a very capacious notion of democracy which placed Western liberal democracies, the Soviet model and one-party Third World states on the same normative footing (Macpherson, 1965). But in the light of intervening experience, I think we would need to be given some very strong reasons before we believed that pre-glasnost Russia was as democratic as post-glasnost Russia, or that Saddam Hussein's Iraq is as democratic as, say, Canada.

In developing the idea of liberal democracy as a single political conception, I also hope to dispose of some of the problems that are thought to disable its component ideas. Even the brief survey sketched above shows that both liberalism and democracy are vulnerable to extremely sharp critiques. I believe that this vulnerability arises from their taking exposed positions which deprive each of the other's support, and that, if we settle on the area of their mutual implication, the objections that they confront lose their force. With regard to the critiques of liberalism mentioned above, I do not believe that the liberal democrat is vulnerable to any of them. To the extent that he or she maintains liberal principles, they do not derive from any of the assumptions that critics find so suspect. They derive from a conception of politics. Within liberal democracy, there is certainly room for movements or ideologies or parties that may be termed 'liberal', and which, within the constraints of liberal democracy, would seek to advance an individualist programme. Some of these may well be vulnerable to some of the criticisms listed above. But in any event, these are not positions defended here. What is defended is a position which, while overlapping substantially with the conclusions of liberalism, is essentially, not contingently, part of a democratic theory.

As for the 'democratic' component, it too is contextualized in a way that (it is hoped) heads off a familiar dilemma. We noted above, and will return to, the distinction between outcome-based and procedural theories of democracy, both of which run into characteristic difficulties. It seems impossible that either can carry the whole burden of legitimation, and it also seems impossible (it will be argued below) that the rival claims of both can simply be combined or traded off. But it will be argued here that liberal democracy rests neither on outcome-based nor on procedural claims, but rather on – for want of a better term – 'processual' ones. It is valuable because it generates a political process in which certain overridingly important constraints tend to be observed.

There is still, however, another source of justificatory problems to be considered. This is the gap between ideal and reality. Perhaps this issue affects any political theory, for no theory is likely to find a real-world embodiment which allows all its aspirations to be fully met. But in the case of liberal democracy, the gap seems especially problematic, for two reasons. First, the term 'liberal democracy' is often used not to name a political theory (however understood), but to label a set of political regimes; it refers to the kind of political system 'currently on offer' (Phillips, 1992: 82).[4] Sometimes the effect of this is to redefine the theory, so that, by a kind of metonymy, it is made to coincide with whatever the main features of those systems are taken to be. Thus, typically, liberal democracy is taken to be a theory of interest group-based politics, even though one would be hard put to find any extant defender of that theory. Sometimes, though, the effect is quite different. It is to drive a wedge between theory and practice, by emphasizing the great difference between the theory of liberal democracy and the practices of liberal democracies, to the obvious discredit of the theory. During the Cold War period, rather the same confusion – wilful or otherwise – impeded the dispassionate study of Marxism. To avoid repeating this confusion, one must bear in mind above all that liberal democracy is a critical theory which offers its own vantage point from which current practices can be assessed and, at least in principle, rejected or transformed.

The second point involves an important special case. When used as a descriptive label, 'liberal democracy' is often taken to embrace not just the political systems of certain countries but their economic systems too, with the result that liberal democracy is thought to refer not only to representative institutions and constitutional rights but to a system of capitalist ownership and market allocation. Sometimes, of course, this is taken as yet another reason to celebrate; that is so in the triumphalist position from which I sought to dissociate myself above – the position that sees 'history' as reaching its 'end' in societies with liberal polities and capitalist economies. But at least as often, it is the basis for critique, since the effects of capitalism so sharply qualify, in practice, both the freedom and the equality that liberal democracy requires. Here several things need to be said. Historically, there can be no doubt about the connections between economic and political liberalisms, the latter having much to do with the emergence of commercial society; but without committing the genetic fallacy – the fallacy of supposing that the origin of something determines its validity – one cannot take that fact to show that liberalism is essentially a capitalist doctrine. (The Reformation was important too; but that doesn't show us that liberalism is essentially Calvinist.[5]) Politically, there are strong reasons not to require liberal democracy to endorse a particular kind of economic organization. How an economy is organized and regulated has far-reaching effects of direct and indirect kinds for the life-chances of citizens, and one can hardly think of a more natural

9

subject for democratic deliberation than that. If a particular kind of economic arrangement is given protection at a basic level, then the system's claim to democracy is negligible, for democratic majorities lose the capacity to determine some of the most crucial aspects of their own society's institutional character (Bobbio, 1987: 23–42).

This book responds to this fourth kind of justificatory objection, suggesting some lines of criticism that bear upon current institutions and practices. It does so, admittedly, only in the broadest terms, for the advocacy of detailed reforms would require a base of knowledge quite different from that provided here. Nevertheless, it will be concluded that two kinds of demands emerge necessarily from the justifying theory that is to be developed. First, on the political side, it is clear that the theory points to a serious deliberative deficit in current institutions, and that a liberal democracy, as defined here, would have to do more than states do now to encourage the uncorrupted exchange of reasons among citizens and between citizens and elites. Second, on the economic side, although I do not believe that liberal democracy issues necessarily in one kind of economic organization rather than another, it is certainly true that it cannot avoid taking an interest in distributive economic outcomes; for some distributive outcomes may impede the kind of citizenship that liberal democratic theory requires. This is not, it should be noted, a demanding kind of citizenship derived from Aristotelian or Machiavellian or Rousseauan political traditions, which 'realists' might dismiss as 'utopian'; it is an idea of citizenship that corresponds to the minimal requirements of political legitimation, in a modern political context.

Neither kind of conclusion is startling; both are conclusions that have struck many observers of regimes termed liberal democratic, from Mill's time to the present. What this book tries to show is that to reach them we do not need to rely on exogenous reasons, but that liberal democracy itself entails them. So in terms of results, the argument tries to show that liberal democracy contains more critical resources than is often thought. In terms of its development, the argument tries to outline a theory which can meet demanding and sceptical objections by making the most minimal assumptions, and drawing conclusions that are defended against alternatives. As the Conclusion will note, the theory has to acknowledge the possibility of stronger forms both of liberalism and of democracy, which rest on more exposed and riskier assumptions; and no doubt, within a liberal democratic polity, these stronger theories will make themselves felt in various demands for legislation or policy. But they are too exclusive, in the assumptions that they require, to impose themselves at the constitutional level, as, it is argued here, the idea of liberal democracy legitimately can.

Those, then, are the concerns that this book tries to address (some, though, as noted, at greater length than others). The first chapter compares some rival background narratives, and settles on one which corresponds to some defensible basic assumptions about the morality of politics. Chapters 2 and 3 draw upon these assumptions to make a case for a particular approach to justifying democracy, and distinguish this approach from the familiar (though problematic) justifications based on outcome or on procedure. Chapters 4 and 5 argue that democracy, thus understood, must be liberal, in that it entails limits to what majorities can do, and also entails personal rights. Chapters 6 and 7 defend this conclusion against some prominent alternative approaches, both liberal and non-liberal. Chapter 8, and the concluding chapter, sketch some examples of the theory's practical implications.

The exploratory nature of everything below will, I hope, be clear. The discussion confronts a number of frequently contested matters, any one of which could be discussed at greater length, if not inexhaustibly; but the objective is to set out a general view in such a way that its scope can be appreciated and its coherence assessed. Along the way, the discussion offers a number of specific judgements which appear to follow from the theory developed here. Whether or not I am right in thinking that they do so is very much of secondary importance, as long as the argument from which they derive is clear. That argument, to summarize, is that liberal democracy is a single political conception; that it is defensible on minimal assumptions; that democrats should embrace it for reasons of legitimacy, liberals for reasons of inclusiveness; and finally, and emphatically, that it is a critical theory, and not a conservative one.

The core of the argument is that it is important to people that they should live as they are persuaded is right. One of the first political theorists to place much weight on this view was John Locke, particularly in his defence of toleration. It is hardly a surprise that Locke's thought should lie behind a theory of a liberal kind; that it lies behind a theory said also to be essentially democratic is, naturally, more of a surprise. But persuasion is important to democracy too; and while there may be little (unambiguously)

11

explicit support for democracy in Locke, what he says about persuasion provides an indispensable starting point for a theory of liberal democracy. The texts that are revealing here are not the *Second Treatise* or even the *Letter concerning Toleration*, but the later letters on toleration in which Locke developed his political case against the resistance of the Anglican hierarchy. What he says in those works leads to two important propositions. The first is that political authority must be politically generated, and not based on extra-political authority for which transcendental claims are made. The second is that in conducting politics we cannot rely on private or incommunicable knowledge, but must try to persuade each other. Whatever Locke's own politics, these two propositions, I shall argue below, provide the most suitable moral framework for a conception of democracy. So if other liberals (such as Mill and Dworkin) are criticized here, and if other ideas of democracy (such as Rousseau's or Habermas's) are rejected, that is because of my view that the 'Lockean moment', when critical thinking engaged the violently authoritarian Church-State, is the best starting point for grasping what liberal democracy is about. It leads to an argument which, like the case developed below, is minimalist, because it recognizes the fact of acute disagreement; which is a theory of legitimacy, rather than of sheer truthfulness, because it recognizes the limits of persuasion; and which is critical, because it recognizes that authority faces a standing temptation to shield itself from politics.[6]

Notes

1. A major critique is that of Green and Shapiro (1994). For some replies, see Friedman (1996). A sophisticated defence by Brennan and Lomasky (1993) is discussed in Chapter 2.
2. Though, of course, Mill, for all his qualifications, was a democrat too, while Rousseau believes that no guarantees are needed just because the process of self-legislation is internally constrained.
3. In discussion, Jan Narveson has suggested to me that pre-1997 Hong Kong might be a counter-example: it enjoyed some liberal freedoms without being self-governing. Although I accept the example, it seems to me significant that the last Governor's attempt to preserve elements of its liberal character led him to measures intended to strengthen democracy.
4. But see also Phillips (1992: 80), where the topic is 'liberal democracy as currently practiced'.
5. Actually, some maintain that liberalism *is* essentially Calvinist; for some critical remarks on this position, see Chapter 1.
6. My view of Locke was developed in Vernon (1997).

CHAPTER 1

Fables about Freedom

Many familiar ideas about liberalism and democracy are shaped by background narratives that highlight some distinctions and obliterate others. Sometimes the narratives are encapsulated in a simple label: the current terms 'Enlightenment liberalism' and 'Reformation liberalism', for example, carry with them very different stories about which events mark off modernity from its past, and what follows from them. In the former case, we are to imagine a transition from superstition to reason, and to think of liberal politics as continuing the impulse to improve and reform. In the latter, the decisive past event is one of disintegration, and liberal politics is imagined, rather, as a continuing process of coping with disagreement. Sometimes, though, the narratives are more evolved, describing transitions and sequences which are clearly meant to dispose us to problematize things in a particular manner. Several different such stories frame the relationship between liberalism and democracy in rival ways.

In a very widely discussed essay – perhaps one of the most contentious works in recent political thought – Isaiah Berlin recommended a sharp distinction between two ideas of freedom, corresponding to two distinct questions that might be posed about it as a political topic. One question is 'What is the area within which the subject . . . is or should be left to do or be what he is able to do or be, without interference by other persons?' The other is 'What, or who, is the source of control or interference that can determine someone to do, or be, this rather than that?' (Berlin,

1969: 121–2).[1] Theorists of negative freedom are concerned with the first question: they see freedom as the area within which one can act without obstruction, and they recommend that this area be extensive. Theorists of positive freedom are concerned with the second question: they regard freedom as the capacity of a person, or group, to be self-determining, and they recommend political institutions which confer self-determining powers upon societies. More than any other text, Berlin's discussion of negative and positive freedom has lodged in political thinking the idea that liberalism and democracy have different conceptual foundations, and promote distinct and often rival projects. Pursuing negative freedom, liberals have sought protection against all authorities, including democratic ones: they have 'little to hope from the rule of majorities', for 'democracy as such is logically uncommitted' to that idea of freedom (*ibid.*: 131–2). Democrats, pursuing the ideal of positive freedom, have often had no time for the restraints on government which prevent peoples or nations from exercising their self-determining power. Interpreters have, naturally, found much to argue about here, and conceptual analysis of Berlin's claim has reached a level of considerable refinement. But note how quickly, in Berlin's own essay, conceptual distinction passes over into story-telling. Only a few pages into his essay, Berlin himself admits that there may be 'no great logical distance' between the two concepts, and that they have been 'historically developed' along different paths. Theorists of negative freedom, for no reason that seems conceptually entailed, took the path of resistance against *deliberate* obstruction by states; theorists of positive freedom – again, it seems, for no reason that their idea required – took a more metaphysical path, embracing forms of monism, and also true self theories, which made the protections favoured by liberals useless or even unintelligible, as dissent came to be discounted as heresy or delusion arising from inadequate self-understanding.

As Berlin constructs his duality, we are to think in terms of two parallel histories, as it were, each offering a series of answers to one of the two foundational questions about freedom. A liberal history is predominantly British, though the Idealists complicate that: a democratic history is predominantly Continental, with Constant and Tocqueville being the great exceptions. We live today with the residues of these two rival traditions, and must ensure that the difference remains clearly understood, despite the 'utopian' temptation to think that we can enjoy all good things at once. But other constructions of history take intriguingly different shapes. Constant himself, for example, while dividing up freedoms in at least a comparable way, thought in terms of the supersession of one by the other (Constant, 1988: 302–28). The liberty of self-determination, or of 'exercising collectively, but directly, several parts of the complete sovereignty', was 'what the ancients called liberty'. It was compatible with

> the complete subjection of the individual. . . . No importance was given to individual independence, neither in relation to opinions, nor to labour, nor, above all, to religion. . . . Thus among the ancients the individual, almost always sovereign in public affairs, was a slave in his private relations.

But this contrasts remarkably with what an Englishman, Frenchman or American would call 'liberty' today: freedom from arbitrary arrest, freedom of expression, freedom to choose a profession and to dispose of property, freedom of conscience, and so on. Political scale has increased hugely; the abolition of slavery has deprived the free population of the leisure to assemble and debate; commerce fills their lives, and gives them a taste for independent enterprise and hence a resistance to intrusive authority. So 'we can no longer enjoy the liberty of the ancients, which consisted in an active and constant participation in collective power. Our freedom must consist of peaceful enjoyment and private independence' (*ibid.*: 311–16).

From the (temporally and politically) different vantage point of C. B. Macpherson, however, we were given a different story again. Democracy, in its modern form, came after liberalism – but the pre-existing liberal character of Western societies has so far prevented the full realization of the democratic idea. 'Before democracy came in the Western world there came the society and the politics of choice, the society and politics of competition, the society and politics of the market' (Macpherson, 1965: 6). This society forced people to be free, in the liberal or bourgeois sense, by compelling them to adopt self-chosen market behaviour. 'There was nothing democratic about it' (*ibid.*: 8). Like Constant, Macpherson recognizes that commercial society wanted and needed a certain kind of responsive politics that would head off tyranny and ensure that important interests were taken into account. But the electorate did not have to be an inclusive one, for participation was not in itself deemed a good. Eventually, though, the excluded demanded a voice. 'Democracy came as a late addition to the competitive market economy' (*ibid.*: 9). The achievements of democracy, however, may have been only to provide a maturing capitalist economy with the welfare provisions and regulatory mechanisms that it needed anyway. They have not altered the fundamental exploitative logic of capitalism, and until that is accomplished, the egalitarian premises of democracy will remain unfulfilled. These premises, it might be noted, seem more closely allied with *self-development* than with the *self-determination* stressed in Berlin's account; and the idea of self-development provides a link between the ideals of democracy and another side of liberalism, a humanistic side which, however, is overshadowed by the dominant market model (Macpherson, 1973: 40–52).

So here we have some stories of different kinds, differently motivated and with different morals, which nevertheless converge on one result: liberalism (in its dominant form, at least) and democracy are distinct political theories which, to varying degrees, are in tension with one another. It may have been stories of that kind, and perhaps those in particular, that have helped to fix that notion as a virtual commonplace of political theory, embedded in textbooks and (presumably) in the lectures which derive from them or accompany them. And that way of thinking of things does provide a usable categorial framework. We *do* broadly distinguish between provisions which relieve us of being controlled and provisions which give us a say in how things are controlled. The distinction lies behind both our readiness to put up with more controls if we have had a say in them, *and* our refusal to accept that just because everyone has had their say, the outcome must be right – two sentiments that are vital to the working of democracy. Likewise, the politics of modern liberal democratic societies often revolve around issues of negative or positive freedom, in some or all of the various senses in which (thanks in part to Berlin's elaborately wrought argument) this distinction might be taken. But intuitive or empirical evidence of a contrary kind would face an uphill struggle against the claims that Berlin, Constant and Macpherson make. They are embedded in broad underlying narratives about modern political evolution, each of which seeks to impose an evaluative context of its own, and thus to frame the terms on which we give assent.

In conceding the importance of narratives, one need not grant the whole postmodern case for scepticism that is supposed to follow from it (Lyotard, 1984: 27–37). There might, after all, be good reasons that tell in favour of some narratives and against others. This chapter will put forward a story which would lead us to see the relationship between liberalism and democracy in a different light. It will then suggest some reasons for adopting it, and for rejecting its main rivals.

It is, of course, a particular challenge to develop a narrative about one's own circumstances, because to locate them within a narrative one must, it would seem, find a way to stand outside them – a self-defeating task. Constant's version of the 'modern', arrived at by way of contrast with the 'ancient', made sense within a classically impregnated political culture in which people could readily define themselves in relation to ancient Athenians and Spartans and their triumphs or failures. But that is hardly an available frame of reference today, and now seems bookish. We need an idea of 'modernity' that relies on more proximate and meaningful contrasts.

There is, however, a background narrative latent in the very way in which political argument is conducted now, and which can thus offer at least a starting point for discussion. A generic assumption of modern political argument is that conclusions are supported *by* argument, by the giving of reasons and evidence – and, beyond that, by the development of persuasive stories which frame and colour reasons and evidence in such a way as to make the best of them. Within the idea of argumentative interchange envisaged here, doubtless there is room for more or less rationalistic and more or less sceptical views (some differences among which will be taken up later in this book). But what is common is the background assumption that it is the formation of opinion that will determine outcomes, and that no appeal to authority can be decisive. We know that this was not always so. A narrative is at once brought into play, then, about the replacement of an authoritarian condition, in which outcomes would be settled by the privileged bearers or interpreters of truth, and a condition in which discursive exchange – however, exactly, it is viewed – is thought to be consequential. This in turn implies the existence of a political discourse which contains its own authority; for otherwise its conclusions could simply be set aside by external appeals, and engaging in it would be completely pointless, since it would not be determinative of anything.

Such a narrative has the initial merit, at least, of relating to one of the most basic features of modern political thought, a feature which governs the way in which legitimation is sought and contested. The distancing of political standards from religious authority is a feature which strikingly distinguishes the states we have now from those of, say, the seventeenth century. Whatever the truth of claims about *general* secularization (or 'death-of-God' claims), the *public* place of religion has been wholly transformed, and, with it, the conduct of political theory itself. It is no longer possible to appeal, simply, to what is authoritatively right (because, for example, it is scriptural, or apostolic); argument has to appeal to considerations which can be communicated to others and which in principle can change their minds discursively.

We may, then, imagine an ancestor society in which political discourse is narrowly confined within other imperatives, which establish its limits and foundations. Of course, these other imperatives can be variously interpreted and their meaning contested, thus becoming effectively subordinate to politics; so the model of the ancestor society also requires authorized interpreters who can give final practical definition to them, pre-empting the alternative definitions that their public elaboration might tend to produce, by telling us what they require us to *do*. Moreover, if authority is to be comprehensive, there would have to be a seamless connection between political and social power, so that the authority to issue binding interpretations of basic imperatives is part of a social order which, it is claimed, also gives expression to the imperatives themselves; social and political relations embody the same basic normative model.

But we can imagine that the authority claims which organize the ancestor society lose their grip. Perhaps, for example, there comes to be insufficient consensus over their interpretation to make politics workable; perhaps socio-economic change disrupts the life-world into which beliefs are woven, so that their plausibility is eroded. Public decisions can no longer be read off fundamental beliefs by ascriptively authorized interpreters; social relations can no longer be based on ranks sustained by sacred or cosmological models; and the private domain is no longer imagined as a microcosm of the public one, the two domains no longer supporting one another mutually. Basic imperatives are taken to be open to interpretation in such a way that privileges are not guaranteed, and cannot be confirmed by a circular appeal to what amounts to a specific political interpretation by or on behalf of the privileged.

A successor society might, then, emerge step by step. Many adjustments would have to be made as a result of the collapse of a whole world-view of the kind that used to ground legitimacy. But at a minimum, the successor society will need to have two things. It will need a defensible way of making public decisions in the absence of ascriptive authority; and it will need a defensible way of regulating the dispersed actions of individuals or families or associations. The first of these will have to be a political mode which is capable of attracting consensus, and which – among those who count politically, perhaps a group smaller than the whole – avoids distributing power unequally. Its rules and methods will have to be robust enough to survive practical interpretation from many points of view and by future generations. As for the second, regulations will have to be generalizable, for the ascriptive differentiation of ranks will have lost its legitimacy; and just as the rules for public decision-making have to survive interpretation from many perspectives, so too the rules of social behaviour will have to be communicable to people with personal differences and independence of judgement.

The point of this narrative, evidently, is to suggest that far from seeing democracy and liberalism as rival doctrines we may see them as two sides of the same coin. They are complementary responses to the circumstances in which a successor society finds itself, and they are similarly motivated. They can be seen as responses to the shortened public reach of sacredness. Collectively and individually, people are compelled to negotiate new circumstances, recognizing that mutually acceptable arrangements must replace what was once authoritatively prescribed. They would opt for some decision rule that would avoid the private appropriation of public institutions, and they would need some mechanism offering a general solution to the problem of conflicts arising from divergent interests and judgements. In retrospect, no doubt, we could if we wished extract from this two different 'concepts' or 'visions' of liberty. For certain purposes that might be a useful step; but it does not help if our objective is to understand the relationship between democracy and liberalism, for in this narrative at least, the two are mutually implicated, as responses to the same evolution. This will serve as a point of departure, in the following chapters, for examining liberal and democratic ideas, in the light of the kinds of considerations that this shared circumstance might prompt. First, however, some other narratives, with quite different political implications, must be acknowledged as rivals, with the potential to undermine the story sketched above.

Another story about secularization bears directly on liberalism, and, a little less directly, has the effect of restoring its opposition to democracy. In this version, we are to see secularization not as the distancing of politics from the sacred, but as the transformation of a certain kind of religious view into moral and political terms. Crudely put, Protestantism becomes liberalism. An individualistic moral epistemology, particularly strong in Protestant versions of Christianity, is taken over by liberals, detheologized, and made into the basis of a new view of life. Essentially, then, liberalism is to be seen as a new religion, making absolutist claims which set it at odds with democracy – especially, of course, with a democracy which, not basing itself on neo-Protestant moral premises, attempts to reassert the values of shared community, accepting and valuing the inherited and the unchosen.

The general claim that important features of liberalism rest on 'Protestantism', understood as a set of beliefs about moral psychology rather than theological tenets, is quite common, though often asserted in passing rather than in full.[2] But an event which provoked its fuller development was the storm arising from Salman Rushdie's *Satanic Verses* and the Ayatollah Khomeini's *fatwa*. Whereas liberals regarded the issue as one of freedom of expression versus religious tyranny, some wished to portray it as at bottom an issue between rival religions. Richard Webster, for example, viewed Rushdie's liberal defenders as promoting a 'creed' derived by a short route from the Protestant notion of a 'bible within', remaining puritanical despite its secular transformation, and responding to enemies with 'religious wrath'. Hence the storm over *The Satanic Verses* was not a clash between freedom and authority at all, but a clash between 'two forms of fundamentalism'. In defending freedom of expression, liberals 'proclaim the superiority of their own revelation' and 'abuse the gods who are worshipped by other, supposedly inferior cultures' (Webster, 1990: 57–9).

A more measured exposition was offered in an essay on 'the Christian connection' by L. A. Siedentop (1989), which is cited approvingly in Charles Taylor's well-known essay on the encounter of liberalism with cultural diversity (Taylor, 1994: 62).[3] Siedentop challenges Western societies' self-description as secular and materialistic. In fact, he claims, the features distinctive of Western society, such as pluralism, tolerance and the state–society distinction, derive from 'Christian assumptions', particularly individualist assumptions that originate in the framework of Christian theology.

'The assumption that society consists of individuals, each with an ontological ground of his or her own, is a translation of the Christian premise of the equality of souls in the eyes of God.' In this sense Western society is like any other, being 'founded on shared beliefs'. What is somewhat different about Western shared beliefs is that they arise not from communal celebration but from 'the privatizing of God', postulating a strictly individual relationship between persons and the 'deeper truth' to which they alone have access. Protestantism raises this kernel of individualism, latent in all forms of Christianity, to a more self-conscious form. Then liberalism secularizes it. Liberals therefore deceive themselves when, confronted with illiberal fundamentalisms, they appeal to secondary values such as pluralism or tolerance, or lay claim to a 'neutral' framework, instead of appealing directly to the core values of their civilization, values which are particularist through and through.

This understanding of liberalism strongly reinforces a more general judgement about its 'cultural particularity', such as Bhikhu Parekh (1992, 1995) offers. Prominent in his depiction of liberal culture is a view that individuals enjoy 'separate existence' and 'seek to run their lives themselves, to make their own choices, to form their own beliefs and judgments, to take nothing for granted as given ... to reconstruct and recreate themselves, and thus to become autonomous and self-determining' (Parekh, 1992: 158). Liberals frame their conception of democracy within these basic assumptions, and the resulting blend of liberal democracy therefore necessarily has features that are objectionable to people with different cultures – people who, for example, 'define the individual in communal terms' and wish to deny 'the freedom to mock and ridicule their sacred texts, practices, beliefs and rituals' (ibid.: 168–9). Whereas democracy as such proves attractive to many non-Western societies, and can be successfully indigenized, the liberal component of liberal democracy is received with more suspicion, as something that 'breaks up the community, [and] undermines the shared body of ideals and values' (ibid.: 172).

The huge claims made and implied by this multi-staged thesis could obviously be approached in many different ways, some historical and some conceptual. There may, for example, be reasons to question the view of Protestantism that is offered, for that movement, after all, was not without 'communitarian' tendencies of its own (Black, 1997).[4] But there is a particularly economical and more direct way to suggest what is wrong with it: we can examine a case which the thesis should find to be an easy one, that of Locke's defence of religious toleration. Locke himself was indisputably 'Protestant' in outlook (however exactly his theology is to be described),[5] and the value in question – 'toleration' – is a quintessentially liberal one. If the thesis works anywhere then it ought to work here; but the turn which Locke's defence of toleration took, in the face of opposition, tells a different story, of a political rather than an epistemological kind.

The opening moves of the *Letter concerning Toleration* look promising for the thesis, with their appeal to familiar Christian virtues, to 'conscientious dissent', and their famous claims on behalf of individual judgement: 'All the life and power of true religion consists in the inward and full persuasion of the mind' (Locke, 1983: 23–6). But this issue very quickly falls out of controversy, as it is shared by both sides, tolerationist and conformist alike. It is upheld, as Locke himself points out, by prelates of the Church and by the fourteenth of the Thirty-Nine Articles (Locke, 1823, vol. 6: 397). What Jonas Proast urges in his polemic against Locke, on behalf of the Church, is not at all a defence of insincere belief, but a view about how best to get people to give their beliefs the earnest 'consideration' that they ought to give them. Compulsory church attendance, he argues, is a proper way for the magistrate to expose subjects to the teachings of Christ (Proast, 1984). That produces a particularly interesting reversal of grounds. It is Proast's argument for conformity, Locke contends, that contains exaggerated requirements for personal consideration. 'You would have men by punishments driven to examine. What? Religion. To what end? To bring them to the knowledge of the truth.' But:

> Would you have every poor protestant, for example, in the Palatinate, examine whether the pope be infallible, or head of the church; whether there be a purgatory; whether saints are to be prayed to, or the dead prayed for; whether the Scripture be the only rule of faith; whether there be no salvation out of the church; and whether there be no church without bishops; and an hundred other questions in controversy between the papists and those protestants. (Locke, 1823: 101).

This would mean that 'the countryman must leave off ploughing and sowing, and betake himself to the study of Greek and Latin; and the artisan must sell his tools, to buy fathers and schoolmen, and leave his family to starve' (*ibid.*: 102). Inevitably, he says, Christians

– no less than 'Turks' – rely on 'prejudice', and on the 'learning, knowledge, and judgment of some persons whom they have in reverence or admiration' (*ibid.*: 298). This is far indeed from 'Bible within' thinking: it is a view based, rather, on community and trust. Locke's position is that there is no standard or public way to measure and enforce sufficiency of 'consideration'. 'Whatever gains any man's assent, one may be sure had sufficient evidence in respect of that man: but that is far from proving it evidence sufficient to prevail on another.' The 'tempers' of people's minds, their received opinions, their capacities of understanding, 'are so various and uncertain' that there is no common measure of sufficiency of evidence (*ibid.*: 297). Punishing people for non-attendance at the state church will not enforce 'consideration'; it will enforce attendance at the state church, punishing some who have 'considered' while providing others with an incentive not to consider seriously.

But this is just an example of Locke's general critique of the conformist position. Again and again, he complains that the position rests on principles that cannot be given public application without absurd or perverse consequences; or, to put this differently, they do not meet the minimum standards of discourse in a self-governing society, which requires principles capable of successful public interpretation. 'If you were to be of the jury,' Locke says to Proast, 'we know what would be your verdict concerning sufficient evidence. ... But whether the rest of the jury could upon this be able ever to bring in any man guilty, and so liable to punishment, is a question' (*ibid.*: 259). Supporters of conformity are among those 'who think all the world should see with their eyes' (*ibid.*: 414). Without of course using that term, Locke condemns the principles of persecution as 'non-neutral', as Gerald Dworkin (1975) was to express the point: we could no doubt reach agreement on a principle like 'sufficiently consider' or 'obey the true God', but our agreement would be purely verbal, and would not lead to a convergence of practical interpretations. Such formulas are a basis for civil war, not for civil order. But Proast and his like, Locke complains, are blind to all this because they cannot grasp the fundamentally multi-perspectival nature of political association and the difficulties inherent in achieving what he elsewhere (Locke, 1975: 476) calls 'civil communication'. Theirs is the perspective of a secure authority, ignorant of the specific needs of *political* legitimation, and unable to understand that public principles must be publicly accessible if they are not to be useless or worse.

This example speaks clearly and directly against the liberalism-as-religion theme, and it also speaks in favour of the rival thesis advanced earlier in the chapter. Not only is Locke's argument not about moral epistemology, it is not even about natural rights, or about negative pre-political freedoms however defined. It derives a case for toleration by measuring the theories of persecutors against the basic discursive standards of a self-governing society, and finding them badly wanting. What was at issue, and what drew from Locke his remarkably ample, choleric and sarcastic replies, was a basic question about political authority: whether it could depend on a bare, privileged claim to rightness, or whether it needed to be formed in a public space, under conditions of reciprocal under-standing, or potential misunderstanding.

The narrative sketched out near the start of the chapter suggested that democratic and liberal tendencies might be seen as comple-mentary responses to the same challenge. Next, this narrative was defended against an alternative version of secularization that sets liberalism, as a new civil religion, against democracy. But there is yet another story about liberalism and democracy, which threatens to make *too much* of a substantive resemblance between them. This is a Promethean story, or a group of rather different Promethean stories, celebrating the release of human powers, and the value of autonomy. It takes self-government not as a predicament, but as a cause. Liberal and democratic tendencies are both said to be expressions of the same underlying idea, that of 'self-determination' (Beetham, 1992: 45, Dagger, 1997: 13–18, Pennock and Chapman, 1983: 412).[6] It may be hard, at first, to see how this story differs from the story sketched at the beginning of the chapter: the reach of authority shrinks, and citizens need to exercise analogously self-determining powers at both private and public levels. But whereas the earlier story takes that merely as a possible description, the Promethean stories take self-determination, personal or collective, as a powerful and normatively charged idea. There are, however, strong reasons to resist the conclusions that emerge if we take it normatively. It does not generate a compelling account of liberalism; it does not generate a coherent account of democracy; and it effectively mystifies the relation between the two.

If we take self-determination – or autonomy in the sense of a self-determining capacity – as the basic or core value, what results is indeed a kind of liberalism, but not a kind that can stand for the whole tradition. It is true that any variety of liberalism will aim to provide autonomy in the sense of a set of objective conditions within which individual (or associated) activities are possible;[7] but it does not follow that liberalism must regard autonomy in the capacity sense – the power to make choices – as a fundamental or overriding value. From the inside, from the perspective of the actor himself or herself, the value may be quite different. Indeed, it would be unusual to see the exercise of self-determining capacity as the reason or point of an action. Belief, as Locke's original *Letter concerning Toleration* pointed out, is coercive; and while we can think of interesting exceptions in which people will acquire beliefs by indirect means, in what may be the standard case of believing something we have no choice in the matter, but are compelled by the evidence as it strikes us (Williams, 1973). Or, under the conditions of liberal freedom, it is surely quite proper to act in ways – at least sometimes – that express concessions to unchosen grounds such as habit or prejudice or sentimentality or desire, or which reflect commitments that one regards as self-constitutive. In none of these cases – which between them seem to cover much of the ground – are we exercising self-choosing powers. We can imagine a liberalism, of course, that would say that we *ought* to, at least more of the time; but that would bring us one step closer to the almost pathological liberalism constructed by critics such as Parekh, in which obsession with having a self-chosen life eats up every other human end.[8]

Could we, more sensibly, keep autonomy as one value among others, as an item on a list – valuing more of it rather than less, but not necessarily more of it than of anything else? The problem is that autonomy has the power to drive everything else off the list, because the power to choose includes the power to make choices about all the other items; otherwise, obviously, it is not a power to choose. We might perhaps try to protect the other items, reasoning somewhat as follows. Autonomy, we might say, is not really an item on a list, but, rather, an underlying condition that gives moral weight to the list of values; autonomy is not, after all, something that one can exercise in a free-standing way – 'today I shall exercise pure autonomy' would be an odd project – but something by the use of which one can adopt something else, such as justice or friendship. When exercised in adopting good things like that, it lends moral weight to their adoption: a person who chooses a just life is more praiseworthy than someone who is coerced into doing so. But an autonomously chosen life of dissolution would not be praiseworthy – it would be more regrettable, in fact, than a dissolute life resulting from unfortunate circumstances (Raz, 1986: 380–1). So we distinguish between two uses of autonomy, some praiseworthy, some not. But this is not a stable solution: we would come back at some point to the problem of the list. If we give protection to all exercises of autonomy, good or bad, then we drive the other values off the list. But if we protect only the good exercises of autonomy, then we neutralize it: if the only choices open to me are morally pre-approved, I can hardly get moral credit for choosing one of them.

At first sight, democracy might seem a rather more promising field for autonomy than liberalism is. If the ideal of autonomy involves very disputable ideas of personal life which impose huge burdens of justification on liberal theory, democracy is surely in some sense an exercise of collective autonomy, by definition: citizens make choices together about matters of public concern. But there are several reasons not to make this definitional element into the basic value. Some of these reasons parallel the individual case above: if collective autonomy is *the* value of democracy, then every other value can be eaten up; and exactly the same ensuing logic applies. Others relate to a set of questions about the justification of democracy, questions which the enthronement of autonomy would simply close off. Some justifications are based on the outcomes (or projected outcomes) of democracy; these make no room for autonomy, for they treat the democratic process just as an instrument for identifying answers which are known, by independent means, to be better than the alternatives. Others, while basing themselves on procedure rather than outcome, still may not treat autonomy as a value, or may treat it only as of instrumental value to something else. They may, for example, focus on the occurrence of public discussion rather than on the act of voting, or they may say that the exercise of autonomy is important because it acts as a check on the arbitrary or corrupt use of power. But even if we did want to make collective autonomy into a justifying value, we would still run into real difficulties. Presumably, if we are making parallels between the individual and collective cases, the reasons for making collective autonomy a value would also extend to individual autonomy:[9] any plausible reasoned argument for letting groups make decisions for themselves would seem naturally to apply as well, or better, to the individual case. But then we would face the problem of reconciling the right to autonomy that one has as an individual with the loss of autonomy that one suffers as a member of a democratic minority. The formal resemblance between the two levels of autonomy would disguise the practical conflict between the two.

But here we begin to enter the third area of consideration, that of analogy between the individual and collective cases. Regardless of questions of value, *can* we regard a group of people as making decisions in the same sense as we speak of an individual as doing so? One kind of theory says that we can: that it makes perfect and important sense to claim that a group of people can exercise control over its own development and destiny just as persons can. In its most complete form, this theory may give us a third fable about secularization, the most ambitious and far-reaching yet. The idea of god, the theory may claim, arises because human beings experience patterns or trends or cycles of change in their common circumstances, patterns which, since they seem to reflect no human will, are ascribed to a non-human one. They are said to reflect a divine will, an explanation which also serves as a justification for obedience and quietism. But actually these patterns reflect the consequences of the exercise of human powers; not, indeed, in a direct or intended way, but as a complex by-product of human actions. The reason that these are unintended by-products rather than intended or planned products is that human actions are undertaken on a dispersed, fragmented and competitive basis: 'what each individual wills is obstructed by everyone else, and what emerges is something that no one willed' (Engels, 1972: 640–2).[10] The solution, evidently, is to remove the social and economic bases on which conflicts of interest occur, so that 'history' will come to reflect a common will; and then ideas of god will wither away. This all ties in nicely with further claims about the interdependence of divine authority and the authority of social and political hierarchies: popular sovereignty is to displace not only god but anyone else's claim to authority over the people.

This model requires that we should eventually be able to identify purposes that can be said to be those of a society, so that we can measure outcomes against them and find that (as predicted) they will match.[11] It further requires that we have some kind of decision procedure that will register these purposes – it is an example of what Charles Beitz terms a 'popular will' theory, which justifies electoral outcomes as embodiments of a collective intention that can be conceived independently of the procedure's result (Beitz, 1989: 50).

But as is now well known, this is problematic. The only way to form an idea of the popular will is to apply a procedure of some kind: and different procedures produce different results. For example, two of the procedures with the strongest intuitive claims to fairness are those devised by Condorcet and Borda respectively (Miller, 1992: 58–9). The Condorcet method involves taking a series of votes on each possible pair of alternatives, until we have discovered the choice which gets a majority over all others. The Borda method involves getting voters to distribute numbers of points among their first, second and third (or more) preferences, and electing the preference with the highest overall score. Obviously, the two will produce different results in cases in which some choices have enough lower-preference support to overcome their relative weakness in higher-preference support. In the absence of some larger theory to tell us which method is better, we do not know what to say the collective will is. We cannot say, therefore, that the outcome has reflected it, and even less can we say that the developments issuing from the outcome embody it.

The argument might try to derive some benefit from David Miller's view that although there is no general superiority of one method over another, each may seem more reasonable for different purposes (*ibid.*: 64–6). For example, when we are trying to maximize overall levels of satisfaction, we might prefer the Borda count: Miller's example is that of choosing a menu for a college feast, when, clearly, we would not want an outcome which delighted a majority at the expense of leaving a minority with nothing on the table that they could stomach. On other issues, where we want to know clearly on which side of a line people stand, we would prefer a Condorcet winner: if we have to decide whether to abolish or restore capital punishment, we would give weight to people's first choices only. A group of voters could in principle decide what was the best way to settle any given issue. But the argument rests on special assumptions which are appropriate to its own context, though not to this one. It assumes that voters would choose the appropriate method on its merits, rather than choosing the one that seemed more likely to favour their own position, and it assumes that once a method had been picked, people would vote in a way that reflected their sincere judgement, rather than in a way that was likely to defeat their first preference's main rival. Moreover, although Miller's approach makes compelling claims about appropriateness, fairness and reasonableness, it is hard to see how anyone could make the further leap from accepting these to the judgement that they give us grounds for thinking that there is a collective will.

Some of these complexities do not, it is true, bear upon simpler situations in which only two alternatives are in play. When that is so, Kenneth May has shown, one solution – simple majority rule – has unique advantages (May, 1952: see Beitz, 1989: 59–62) It produces a definite decision, and it satisfies 'anonymity' and 'indifference' conditions (just overall numbers count, not different distributions of them), and the condition of 'positive responsiveness' (a voter's shift in favour of an option will strengthen the result in favour of that option). Impressed by these advantages, we might perhaps opt for a democratic system which produced a forced choice between two alternatives, as indeed some come close to doing. But, of course, along the way to doing this all kinds of alternatives would have to be closed off, with major consequences for the ultimate fairness or unfairness of the choice which is presented. And even ignoring that, we are still no closer to knowing why that method, just because it uniquely meets a set of conditions – and even if those conditions are important ones – should lead us to suppose that it could identify a popular will, as opposed to just the will of some people, somehow represented.

Beyond these considerations, it is not difficult to think of general reasons for rejecting the individual–collective analogy. Perhaps there are interesting ways in which internal decision-making within an individual resembles political decision-making by a collective. We experience internal conflicts, after all, and go through such things as 'inward debate', and as some psychologists have suggested, the self may have something like a pluralist or even federal unity rather than the unity of a dictatorship (Freud, 1965: 72–3).[12] But all the same, when I trade off one of my desires or purposes against another, it is still my self that is the (putative) gainer, even though also suffering a loss which in less stringent circumstances of choice it might have avoided. It makes perfect sense to say that I can form a will to do something that I prefer to any alternative even though I do it trailing regrets. But in the collective case the losers are other people, and it is no compensation to an individual that someone else is getting what he or she wants. We can speak of individual wills because internal transfers, as it were, are possible, and cannot speak of collective wills because interpersonal transfers cannot be made. Moreover, when I choose between one purpose and another I do not have to justify the choice to anyone else, except when – and the case has already ceased to be an intrapersonal one – I break a commitment to someone else in doing so. But in collective decision-making it is not enough that rival parties should just declare their will: they have to defend and explain their choices to others who, as distinct centres of experience, must make their own calculations of priority and gain or loss. Jon Elster, perhaps for different reasons, supports these conclusions. We can think of selves as being plural, and hence as being, up to a point, something like little polities, but it makes no sense to think of them as being made up of little people (Elster, 1986: 30–1). The argument here is simply the complement of this: if it makes no sense to think of persons as polities made up of little people, then it makes no better sense to think of polities as being like large persons – for polities *are* made up of people, and parallels between the two ultimately founder on this basic asymmetry.

We have, then, three fables about secularization, each of which carries different views about the relation of modern politics to its past, and each of which implies a very different idea about liberalism and democracy and the freedoms that they embody. Fable 1 sees liberalism and democracy as complementary, and draws no bright line between their respective ambitions. They are both doctrines of a society which may have been constituted by tutelary means but which has lost its tutelage, and needs to find reciprocally justifiable ways to replace it. It has to find a way to settle matters of common concern without appealing to higher authority, and it has to find a way to order the no longer uniform actions of individuals according to some generally applicable conditions. Fable 2 sees liberalism as a relic of theological thinking: it rests on ancient absolutes which would be better forgotten and laid to rest, because, whatever their history, they have become divisive and hegemonic. While it says nothing explicitly about democracy, the fable certainly tells us that some democratic projects, such as the public representation of communal values, are impeded and wounded by liberal fixations. Fable 3, in its most developed version, tells us that deep secularization is a political and egalitarian project with radically democratic outcomes: human freedom means collective self-determination. And while this pays individual self-determination the courtesy of an analogical debt, it hardly appears that it is to be (or can be) consequentially made good.

These narratives are termed 'fables' for two reasons. The first and more obvious reason is that it is beyond the scope of so brief a discussion to make claims about their historical truth. But second, to make political claims depend on narrative truth would be to commit something very much like the genetic fallacy: we cannot establish the meaning of modern political concepts by determining where modern polities come from. The value of these narratives is simply that they contain in a usefully compressed form sets of background assumptions about what, in the most general terms, makes democracy significant, and on what basis it can be argued for.

Without any claim to demonstrate a philosophy of modern history – which would, understandably, attract postmodern scepticism – we can apply negative tests, of two kinds. We can point out where the construction of the past seems simply wrong, and we can directly examine the coherence of the assumptions themselves. On these counts, fables 2 and 3 certainly look dubious. Fable 2 is not adequate as an account of the very process that it ought to explain – that is, the withdrawal of religious authority from public life: it does not just oversimplify, it misses the point, and substitutes the banal for the genuinely interesting. It may – as I shall concede below – give us an account of a certain kind of liberalism, but it is a kind of liberalism that is much too optional in its appeal to meet the justificatory needs that are in play here. As for fable 3, it contains utopian requirements which fail the basic tests of meaning and coherence. There *is* no 'macrosubject', to borrow Habermas's term, and whatever the (highly contestable) truth of its diagnosis of religion, the theme has no future because its future makes no logical sense.

Fable 1 comes off better from this comparative encounter. At the very least, it provides a defensible account of what was at stake in the struggle for religious toleration. That struggle, as it is hardly original to say, had many dimensions, which no simple account can embrace. Some were essentially theological, others had a broader epistemological bearing; yet others were brutely political, or ideological in the sense of concerning the justifying beliefs of rival social or economic formations. But all the same, given the question raised here, it is important to recall the political argument to which Locke was driven by the resistance of the Anglican hierarchy: the merit of fable 1 is that it allows us to introduce an argument which has extremely productive consequences. It is in some sense a contractual argument, but it is different from the classical, set-piece contractualism of the *Second Treatise*. It sees political life not as settled by an original contract but as a kind of ongoing contract, in which parties must repeatedly seek to meet one another on mutually intelligible terms. They must advance proposals only if they are satisfied that others will interpret their meaning and extend the principles which they depend on to other cases. And they must do all this knowing that public discussion and interpretation may depart radically from the safer processes of interior dialogue. When 'we talk to ourselves, any words will serve our turn' (Locke, 1975: 476), for we are always in a position to correct for inconsistencies of meaning and implication. But when we 'stipulate with one another' (Locke, 1823: 224), we place our words in others' hands, for them to make of what they can. And as we have seen, Locke's critiques of Proast convey a stern condemnation of the claim to privilege in the interpretation of terms once they have been advanced into public space. They are no longer ours alone, and the assumption that we can continue to control and qualify them as we see fit betrays a misunderstanding of the basic conditions of politics.

This may seem to push Locke's contractualism into a closer relationship with later views of democracy, currently termed 'deliberative', than it is generally thought to have. The difference, baldly put, is that contractualism refers some matters to a hypothetical test of unanimity before other matters are referred to public decision; while deliberative democrats refer (almost) everything to the test of public deliberation, thus applying a democratic criterion where contractualist liberals apply the criterion of reasonableness. But the approach put forward by Locke, whether it should be called contractualist or not, does not involve a once-and-for-all judgement. It demands a continuing ethic of reciprocity in politics, in which claimants must content themselves with claims that they are also prepared to 'allow' to others. This is the only basis on which politics without privilege can be carried on. Though no doubt different in several important ways from the still more stringently rational and open-ended politics that deliberative democrats recommend, it nevertheless concerns what is properly called a deliberative situation, in which a society must come to some reasoned judgement about matters requiring public resolution or a common approach. Neither negative nor positive freedom has precedence here. It is a matter not of maximizing non-interference by the state, but of obliging state action to be defensible on broadly shared terms. It is a matter not of maximizing opportunities for participation either – all Locke's interpreters would agree on that[13]

– but of setting the terms on which the outcomes of political decision would be acceptable.

Notes

1. An abridged edition of Berlin's essay, together with a selection of the most useful commentaries on it, is in Miller (1991).
2. Beiner (1992: 16n) provides a particularly interesting example: the communitarian critique of liberalism needs to be seen in terms of a Jewish–Catholic challenge to 'Protestantism'. Beiner points out, indeed, that some liberals are not Protestants, but leaves the other half of the equation unqualified. David Miller's remarks about the 'protestantism' of toleration (Miller, 1995b: 169–70) refer – less sweepingly – to the British case. See also Walzer (1997: 67, 104) for comments on the American case.
3. Although Taylor qualifies his remark here, that liberalism is an 'organic outgrowth of Christianity', by adding: 'at least as seen from the alternative vantage point of Islam'.
4. On Black's account, it is Rousseau, not Mill, who secularizes Calvin – surely a plausible conclusion if one compares the 'Dedication' of Rousseau's *Discourse on Inequality* with chapter 3 of Mill's *On Liberty*, where the Calvinist view of life is denounced.
5. Waldron (1988) notes the 'protestant' features of Locke's thinking. On Locke's theological reticences, see Wootton (1989).
6. For some criticisms, see Harrison (1993: chapters 1 and 10).
7. Presumably any political theory will prescribe that only certain restraints are legitimate, and in that sense provide for autonomy within limits that are reasonable from its point of view.
8. Parekh (1992: 162): liberal individuals 'define their individuality in terms of their separateness from others and feel ontologically threatened and diminished when ... their selves overlap with those of others. Their constant concern therefore is to preserve their separateness, to construct all kinds of high protective walls around themselves ... They are therefore suspicious of, and feel nervous in the presence of, feelings and emotions.'
9. Of course, there are justifications of collective autonomy that do not draw this parallel; but the argument here concerns justifications that do.
10. The theme appears not only in Marx and Engels but in Proudhon (1868). The project of eliminating 'contingency' is also important to the thought of Castoriades, to be briefly discussed in Chapter 2.
11. Alternatively, we might think in terms of a 'joint intention' which is formed *during* the decision-making process; but as Richardson (1997: 351) points out, this involves bracketing out the question of minorities. See Chapter 4 for a case that what can be said to minorities is crucial.
12. See Elster (1986) for wide-ranging discussion. See also the 'friendship' model of the self in Waldron (1991–2: 791–2).

13. Cf. Dunn (1990: 52): 'Political virtue does not necessarily require an activist disposition. But it does require, in the last instance, a genuine commitment to the public good and a preparedness to make sacrifices on its behalf.'

CHAPTER 2

Democracy as Political Morality

Chapter 1 has suggested that we look for a starting point in the bare notion of a society (a 'successor society') from which extra-political authority has been withdrawn, and which thus confronts the task of governing itself. This chapter turns to the possibility of developing from this the outlines of a 'political morality', a term given currency by John Stuart Mill (Mill, 1910: 83), though put to use more recently in senses that may not all be the same as Mill's own. Sometimes it is taken to refer simply to the conclusions of morality, whatever they are, in their application to politics: political morality would just be what morality requires us to do plus any items that are special to the political domain (or else minus any items that do not belong there). For example, although something might be clearly wrong from a moral point of view, the especially damaging features of coercion – its 'sweeping' character, say – might restrain us from suppressing it, when we weigh evil against evil (Raz, 1986: 418–19). Sometimes, though, the term is taken in a much stronger sense, to refer to a set of distinct political principles, applying specifically to the use of power, alongside the principles that we want to bring to bear on personal decisions. The former must be shared, or at least must overlap extensively enough to make political life possible, while the latter might differ between individuals or groups. Thus understood, the idea of a political morality would seem to belong principally to a context in which there are deep and important disagreements which politics must come to terms with, but which, it is assumed, politics cannot resolve. Its currency in recent liberal thought is thus understandable. The task here, though, is to show its fundamental importance for democracy.

Liberals have come under fire for offering as a political morality what is really (critics claim) a personal one, advancing conclusions that were already concealed in hidden premises. Clearly, there is a dilemma here. If we import strong assumptions at the very beginning, we ensure that any conclusions we may reach will be limited in their appeal to those who share the assumptions. On the other hand, of course, nothing can come of nothing. So there seems to be no alternative to a minimalist strategy – begin with as little content as is needed to propel an argument. One is to begin with reflection on the shared political situation itself, in the hope that its features can be built upon in a way that those who share the situation can recognize and appreciate. The (familiar) corresponding risk is that of importing unjustifiably special features into the description of political situations, in such a way that eventual conclusions are predetermined. Now we cannot avoid bringing in *some* features; but they must be justified – and I hope to show how they can be by examining what is involved in the basic idea of political legitimation.

Like the term 'political morality', 'political legitimation' sometimes has a sense which yields nothing distinctive. Sometimes it is taken to mean the legitimation *of* politics – that is, the activity of giving validating reasons for basic political institutions; and then of course its content is whatever the reasons are that we happen to favour. It has no distinct identity or logic. But it might also mean legitimation *by* politics – that is, a process in which conclusions are given validity because they have been politically reached.[1] Political conclusions do not always receive their validity that way. Sometimes they are held to be valid because of their relation to extra-political appeals: cosmological beliefs, or religious faith, or national mythologies, for example. Even where politics exists, it does not always play a legitimating role. There was certainly politics in Usbek's seraglio in Montesquieu's *Persian Letters*, in the court of Louis XIV, and in Stalin's Russia. But the systems in question claimed legitimation on the basis of religious or traditional or ideological appeals which simply predetermined the question of rightness. Nothing here depends on taking the meaning of 'politics' in any special sense. Certainly it would be disingenuous to define politics in such a way as to privilege a particular way of doing it.

But we can hold the meaning of that term constant, if we wish, while still distinguishing between systems in which legitimation is political and systems which, while containing politics – as perhaps all systems do – are legitimated by other means.

As a first illustration, consider the movement in European political thought from, say, Bodin in the late sixteenth century to Rousseau in the mid-eighteenth: the approach to legitimation is entirely transformed (Vernon, 1986: 15–53). Bodin can appeal directly to an idea of order which was both all-encompassing and widely accepted. There is a 'chain of being' in which items are placed in graded and hierarchical levels of relative dignity. In each component of this universe, the structure of the whole is reproduced, so that 'intertextual' correspondences (to borrow a much later term) serve as guarantees of rightness. The ordering proper to the commonwealth, for example, may be inferred from the ordering of god and man, reason and passion, husband and wife, father and child, and each of these from any other. Social and political hierarchies are thus part of the chain of creation itself, and cosmologically underwritten. Yet hierarchy is both sanctioned and limited by this scheme, which even contains the means of its own adjustment. Everything that exists must exist, or else order would lack 'plenitude', rendering the chain of being discontinuous, as it cannot be; so although sovereigns are indisputably set above their subjects, they cannot dispense with them or annihilate their essential qualities. Sovereigns could not, for instance, abolish the families that they rule over. So we are offered an immense and complex picture in which arguments about authority and its functions and limits can be conducted by means of pre-politically fixed normative points of reference.

Turning to Rousseau, we find a different picture indeed. The human situation, as described in the *Discourse on Inequality* (Rousseau, 1974), can no longer be described teleologically, but is constructed by accidents, deceptions and unintended consequences. It does not contain harmony but paradox: unwanted wants, contentment without awareness or else awareness without contentment, and goodness without morality or else morality without goodness. Politically, legitimacy must be created by exercising 'the art of generalizing' on political circumstances themselves. This art must produce a 'will' which makes it possible for law to be self-imposed, as opposed to being discovered or deduced. Legitimacy, far from being a sort of copy derived from a larger original, is the work of a people who have succeeded in constituting themselves as a political entity by giving representation to their common situation in public acts.

But the issue may go deeper than that. Resulting in foreign wars more terrible than the state of nature could ever be, the very construction of states may be a bad bargain. There may therefore be an essential moral arbitrariness at the heart of politics itself, and states are called upon to justify not only their arrangements but even their very existence. We could hardly have travelled further from the late-medieval world picture of Bodin, in which lines of inquiry appeared not only to have natural conclusions but also to have harmonious ones: political thought comes to carry a radically more stringent burden of justification, with fewer resources lying ready to hand. Politics cannot draw upon pre-existing legitimations; it becomes, rather, the process that legitimates.

But if this first illustration seems too remote, a second is provided by recent democratic transitions, particularly perhaps those undergone by formerly communist regimes. In some ways, in fact, this transition recapitulates – in a very much more compressed time period – the earlier West European example. Frederick Barnard usefully terms it a 'deconsecration' of politics (Barnard, 1991: 58), thus bringing the parallel clearly to light. Here too we have a transition from a closed picture of the political world, authoritatively interpreted, to an open and uncertain picture in which the political process itself must confer authority under competitive conditions. From this point of view, as Barnard argues persuasively, what was of greatest long-term importance was not the rejection of socialism as an economic system, nor even perhaps the rejection of Marxism as a world-view – some, in the Czechoslovak case at least, continued to regard themselves as socialists, and as abandoning only a politically distorted version of Marx. The crucial change concerned, rather, the matter of legitimacy, and, in particular, the recognition of a public space and the distinctive requirements that it imposes – the requirements of 'civic order' (*ibid.*: 122–8). Barnard makes particularly effective use of a remarkable manifesto by the Czechoslovak reformer Vladimir Klokocka on the conditions of electoral competition. Implicitly or explicitly, the new claim was that whatever beliefs enjoy general credence, it is neither what they are nor who holds them that gives them political weight. That they are right, or are declared to be right, is not enough. They must be advanced under conditions in which objections can be made and evidence demanded; and the outcome of public questioning and interchange cannot be constitutionally predetermined, or else it is meaningless. As in the earlier West European case, we encounter a demand that public decisions must not be read off some pre-political text or source, but that they must emerge from a process that is itself public, in the sense of revolving around issues and standards for judging them that are discursively offered and are open to discursive responses.

It is in a similar sense that Adam Przeworski defines democratization as acceptance of 'the contingent outcome of conflicts' (Przeworski, 1988). In an authoritarian regime 'someone has an effective capacity to prevent political outcomes that would be highly adverse to their interests' (*ibid.*: 60). In 'tutelary' regimes, an intermediate form, independent political processes may exist, but only on the understanding that they will not transgress certain limits. What is distinctive to a democratic system is that 'there is no group whose interests would predict political outcomes with a near certainty'. He quotes Adolfo Suarez: 'el futuro no esta escrito, porque solo el pueblo puede escribirlo (the future is not written, because only the people can write it)' (*ibid.*: 62).[2] This acceptance of uncertainty, and its institutionalization in processes which will carry weight whatever they result in, is decisive. Power passes from a determinate group with known desires and interests to a constitution which gives authority to the unknown. And while constitutional democracy denies anyone a guarantee of future success, it may win acceptance only if its institutions are such that groups feel that they have 'a reasonable guarantee that their interests would not be affected in a highly adverse manner in the course of democratic competition' (*ibid.*: 64). Contingency, of course, means just that: it means that we cannot rely on winning, but it also means that one cannot predict that one will lose either (or lose too often, or too badly). A peaceful or negotiated transition to democracy is possible when arrangements can be made which provide for contingency in that sense.[3]

Intriguingly, there is an alternative view of democracy which appears to offer a precisely opposite justification, verbally at least. This is the view that democracy *diminishes* 'contingency' in the sense of the circumstantially or historically given (Castoriades, 1997). Although it is true, Cornelius Castoriades writes, that 'from birth, the human subject is caught in a social-historical field', and subject to the 'infrapower' by means of which societies enter into our being and thus reproduce themselves, nevertheless there is a certain limited human capacity of transcendence (*ibid.*: 2–3). Politically, this capacity is expressed in democratic political cultures and institutions. Through democracy, a society is able to exercise self-rule and thereby to make its own circumstances transparent rather than opaquely given. 'Democratic politics is . . . the kind of activity that endeavors to reduce, as much as it possibly can, the contingent character of our social-historical existence as far as its substantive determinations are concerned' (*ibid.*: 16). Despite appearances, however, this is not the opposite of the previous position, nor even perhaps inconsistent with it. The one contrasts contingency with control over outcomes by a specific group, the other contrasts contingency with human beings' control over their own circumstances. For the present purpose, however, it is the former idea which is more useful, because it is more minimal. The latter embodies a philosophy of history, owing much, clearly, to the more Promethean idea of secularization noted in the previous chapter, by which control over history passes from providence to human beings. Perhaps that is a way to justify democracy; but it carries with it contentious assumptions about the superiority of choice over chance, assumptions for which liberals are often castigated by the more communitarian-minded; it also carries with it contentious claims about the possibility of collective will-formation, some of the acute difficulties with which were noted in the previous chapter. The Barnard–Przeworski[4] position is much better judged as a starting point for thinking about democracy, for it asks us only to consider what is entailed in the very idea of a democratic resolution of disagreement, and can be agnostic on the huge claims that the Castoriades thesis makes.

One thing that is entailed is a certain idea of state neutrality. That idea is disputed in recent political thought, for many reasons. Partly it may be because it seems to be easily confused with other and perhaps even more basically contentious ideas, such as 'impartiality' and 'objectivity' (Young, 1990: 96–121). That seems mistaken and unhelpful: it is possible for institutional arrangements to be neutral in some sense without requiring anyone in particular to attain a state of impartiality; and it is certainly possible to be neutral (and perhaps even to be impartial as well) without laying claim to objective knowledge, however understood. But even without our adding to the difficulties in this way, there are certainly complexities internal to the idea, for there are several quite different versions of it, or models for it (Jones, 1989). One model is that of a state in wartime, adopting neutrality with respect to the conflict. Another is that of the even-handed parent. Yet others are those of the referee, or of the judge, similar in some ways but significantly different from one another. For some purposes, it is urgently necessary to know which model is intended, for they carry quite different messages.

But the idea of neutrality at issue here is so basic that we can skirt these questions. The very idea of political legitimation contains a principle of institutional neutrality; if legitimation depends on what results from an institutionally governed process, then it must be that that process does not predetermine (or even bias) outcomes. If it did, it would become dispensable, for whatever reasons led us to favour that kind of process would also lead us to favour the kinds of outcomes to which it inevitably (or probably) led, and so we could simply (and more economically) replace agreement on that process with agreement on results. Of course – to acknowledge yet another line of criticism – no real-world polity can be wholly neutral, for some things will have been pre-politically settled. Boundaries are an obvious case, since a political process must have a determinate number of participants. The natural language or languages of public discourse must be settled. A sense of solidarity among participants may have to be sustained by the various unreasoned features that seem essential to shared national identity. These are valid, but not weighty, objections. They amount to saying that no polity will be *only* a democracy, as opposed to having democracy as one of its defining features. And they do not touch the point that if a democratic process is to make any sense, it must have *ex ante* neutrality within at least a certain range of outcomes.

That is to say that in a democracy – as distinct from Przeworski's authoritarian or tutelary regimes – public institutions are regarded as no one's private domain. They have the character of a shared resource intended for common use. But that is an idea with considerable (though still quite indefinite) normative power. It requires equality of civil status, in the sense that it rules out privileged connections between public power and assignable individuals or groups; for if it did not, political outcomes would not be contingent ones. What equality is to be taken to *mean*, in a practical sense, is – as we shall very shortly see – a contested matter; but equality in *some* sense is built into the very idea of political legitimation, understood as the process through which demands acquire public authority and a claim to the stamp of collective approval.

'Equality' can no doubt be justified or grounded in many different ways, but the approach adopted here has several merits. The moment of 'political deconsecration' can be located, if one wishes to do so, at any of several historical points; or one need not locate it at all, if one is content to take it as a stylized depiction of the ground of modern politics. One might reach some of the same conclusions by means of the much more formal apparatus of a social contract theory; but then one would have to face much more severe objections. Notably, a social contract model requires us to postulate a prior idea of equality as a background condition. We have to suppose that the parties enjoy some kind of pre-contractual rights, and pre-contractual duties to respect them; and all kinds of familiar objections then arise (Boucher and Kelly, 1994: 1–34). The approach may impose strains and distortions on moral thinking as well as disguising some realities of power. The idea proposed here, however, does not depend on a theory of pre-political equality, and does not have to engage in the sort of counter-measures that might succeed in sustaining that theory. It presents equality not as a background to agreement but as a condition of it – that is, as the only plausible basis on which participants could agree to bind themselves to future outcomes of their agreement under conditions of self-government. Equality results from the shared need to adopt a general rule, not from a pre-existing shared moral status. Conceived of in this way, it is certainly congenial to moral views which give equality a more foundational status. It is quite compatible with a sort of liberal moralism such as one might find in or derive from John Stuart Mill – a kind of liberalism that one might live, in all areas of existence, as distinct from a narrowly political conception. And, at the cost of being accused of surreptitiousness (Ivison, 1997: 156), one might even hope that the narrower sense of equality would stimulate a broader one, and adopt a minimal idea of it with the intention of promoting a maximal one. But these are matters that can be set aside here, for the argument needs only the narrower sense.

A more difficult matter is to decide what follows from this minimalist defence. What kind of political equality would we be trying to provide for? A first approximation might be to say that we would want at least to equalize the chances of being on the winning side. We would therefore opt for a principle of majority rule which, under certain conditions, actually gives us a slightly better than even chance of winning, majorities being larger than minorities. The conditions, it is true, are fairly stringent: we have to assume, for example, that majorities and minorities on different issues are fluidly composed, and that one will not be consistently outvoted because of being in a particular group which lacks status or allies (Guinier, 1994). Perhaps, by means of institutional engineering or constitutional protection, we could come close enough to realizing the condition. But that is not the immediate problem. Having an equal chance of being on the winning side cannot be a good way of stating the purpose of equality, for it is something that we could achieve by obviously undemocratic means. We could, for example, provide for it with some kind of randomizing device: given binary choices, the toss of a coin would give one an equal chance of winning. So might a dictatorship, provided that the dictator was not the puppet of one's enemies.[5] If we think the majority principle is a better way to do things, then, we must restate the objective.

One way in which the majority principle differs from a coin-toss or lottery is that it gives voters an opportunity to influence the outcome in their favour, not just to expect favourable outcomes with a certain probability. So we might say that the version of equality that we want is an equal chance to affect the outcome, as distinct from just having an equal chance to win. Initially it might seem odd that wanting to affect the outcome takes precedence over wanting to win, since one wants to affect the outcome in order *to* win, after all. But we could think of various reasons for preferring a vote to a lottery; perhaps it is more dignified, or perhaps one believes that, given a good cause, one stands a better than even chance of persuading others to join it, or perhaps – standing outside the perspective of rational self-interest – one believes that majority rule is fair, or that (for utilitarian reasons) numbers count. All of these involve taking steps of varying sizes away from the minimalist approach, and invite their own discussion, some of which the following chapter will provide.

But the core problem here is that the idea of having an equal chance to affect the outcome may be beyond rescue by any supplementary means, simply because the effect in question is negligible. By now, a large body of literature has established that the chances of one's vote affecting the outcome, under any conditions that are likely in real-world democracies, are insufficient to motivate the voting act (Brennan and Lomasky, 1993). This is simple to establish with respect to one's vote being the one that tips the balance between one outcome and another. And it does not help to substitute a 'mandate' approach, in which the number of votes cast either way makes a difference regardless of the outcome, in the sense that it increases or decreases the size of the majority: for here, while every vote makes a difference, there is not even a tiny chance that a one-vote difference will have large consequences, as in the 'crucial vote' model (*ibid.*: 70). So whichever approach one takes, having an *equal* chance is neither here nor there, it would seem, since having an equal share in something vanishingly small or indeed non-existent is hardly worth it. Equality in distribution is a good if it is a good that is being distributed, but it is negligible if what is being distributed is negligible, we need to be given an argument, quite independent of equality, for thinking the possession of a vote to be a good thing.

Brennan and Lomasky, in their book *Democracy and Decision*, offer an extremely sophisticated response to the embarrassing circumstance that a theory of democracy seems unable to explain the most basic democratic act, that of casting a vote. They abandon as hopeless the attempt to rescue the claim that a vote is instrumental, in the sense that it is an act intended to bring about a change in the electoral outcome, in either of the suggested ways. To suppose that it is, is equivalent to supposing that one can help one's soccer team by cheering the televised game; that one can improve someone's health by sending a get-well card (*ibid.*: 33), or break one's grandmother's back by stepping on a crack in the sidewalk (*ibid.*: 131). We must, then, distinguish fundamentally between the political act of voting and the economic act of purchasing something in a market, even though the two acts are so often seen as analogous. Whereas a market choice is decisive – if one chooses A rather than B one gets A and doesn't get B – a single vote is typically without consequences: my voting for party A doesn't bring about party B's defeat. But Brennan and Lomasky give this point a most ingenious turn. It is the very inconsequentialness of a single vote, they argue, that is the basis for its normative importance. We should see voting not as instrumental but as *expressive* behaviour, like cheering one's team – that is, behaviour which realizes the good, for the actor, of giving expression to a sentiment or an identification. 'One displays to oneself and to others what sort of person one is' (*ibid.*: 188).

Instrumental behaviour, as in the market, is highly constrained by self-interest: in buying A one expends resources and forgoes B, and one has an incentive, therefore, to examine the personal costs and rewards. But expressive behaviour, like voting, is not so constrained. Knowing that my choice will not be decisive, I can consult things other than personal interest – things such as the public interest. Of course, the same inconsequentialness might free the voter to consult less attractive things, such as whims or hatreds (especially when the ballot is secret); so we need a 'prevailing civic morality' which will encourage the responsible and public-spirited use of the vote (*ibid.*: 174–5). As Mill wrote, in a much-quoted passage, the citizen is called upon 'to weigh interests not his own: to be guided, in case of conflicting claims, by another rule than his private partialities; to apply at every turn, principles and maxims which have for their reason of existence the common good' (Mill, 1910: 217). And whereas this may seem too ambitious a standard to set with regard to *all* the duties of citizenship, it is not too lofty when, as in the case of voting, no personal interest is at stake, other than that of self-expression. So, rather than persisting in trying to attribute some kind of consequential effect to a vote, we should make a virtue of its inconsequentialness. That property enables us to express our identification with what we take to be right, within a civic morality that calls upon us to exercise our judgement about matters of shared concern.

It is surely obvious that at some point in the line of inquiry pursued here, a civic morality (of some sort) must enter in if any progress is to be made. The inconsequentialness of an individual vote is a brute fact which decisively derails any approach based on the rational pursuit of advantage. But it remains to be seen how the idea of a civic morality needs to be filled in. Brennan and Lomasky offer what is in the final analysis a 'good outcome' view – perhaps the best available defence of that view. But if we examine it critically, there is a lack of fit between its expressive and its consequentialist elements, and the need for a different kind of view becomes apparent.

Although the civic morality is introduced as a solution to the inconsequentialness problem, that very problem may come back to haunt it. The morality is to teach public responsibility: but isn't a general ethic of responsibility undermined by inconsequentialness just as much as a single responsible act is? We might seem to have resurrected an error made famous by Anthony Downs, who once sought to rescue voting by introducing a duty to uphold the system – thus naturally inviting the objection that if my vote won't change the outcome of the election, then surely it won't save democracy either (Barry, 1970: 20). As a first response, we might turn to non-consequentialist considerations. Asking 'How can it be the case that a citizen can properly be praised or blamed for an action the performance or nonperformance of which almost certainly makes no difference?' (Brennan and Lomasky, 1993: 176), Brennan and Lomasky reply that people bear responsibility for their behaviour regardless of its effect. People who vote for an evil but hopelessly marginal party can rightly be blamed, because by so voting they *identify themselves* with an evil. Likewise, those who voted for a winning party bear responsibility for the outcome, even if it won by a large majority and no one supporter's vote was decisive. So we are to place voting behaviour within 'a logic of moral discourse appropriate to expressive activity', a logic which is entirely familiar to us in non-consequential (or not primarily consequential) activities such as sympathizing or mourning (*ibid.*: 186–8).

However, although *the individuals'* aims are expressive, *the practice as a whole* might have good consequences. We might turn to the (strikingly Rousseauan) thought that electoral democracy at least ensures that government is not at the disposal of some person or persons dedicated to 'the interests of some subset of society'. Democratic citizens thus enjoy more freedom, understood as 'the absence of deliberate control by others', than those who live under various types of oligarchy. That condition could be achieved, it is true, by other means, such as some sort of randomizing device that would deprive any previously specifiable person or group of reliable control over outcomes. However, unlike a randomizing device such as a lottery, the democratic civic morality gives citizens an incentive to acquire knowledge; and while it cannot be proved that 'aggregation of relatively knowledgeable votes' will produce better outcomes than a lottery, or uninformed voting, 'it seems reasonable to believe that it is so' (*ibid.*: 195–7). So the link between individual expressiveness and good general consequences is produced by the familiar figure of the 'invisible hand'. Intending to secure a personal (expressive) benefit, the voters secure a public benefit – good political outcomes – as a by-product.

But to assess this, we must distinguish between several kinds of 'expressive' behaviour, which is a somewhat lumped category. First, there are expressions of magical thinking, such as not stepping on cracks – thus identifying oneself as a non-grandmother-injuring person – which have no consequences at all. Second, there are such things as sending get-well cards, which are not indeed interchangeable with instrumental acts (like providing medical care), but which all the same have some chance, though slight, of having an effect, by increasing a sick friend's sense of well-being. Third, there are acts which do have an effect, though only a small one when performed by a few people, such as littering. Now it is true that casting a vote *intending* that one should single-handedly change the outcome is just as irrational as wilfully stepping on a crack intending harm to one's grandmother; but the act of voting without that intention does not depend on magical thinking, and we should see it as belonging to the second or third categories. Is it a primarily expressive action which has a very small chance of having a desired effect, or is it an action which makes a very small contribution when combined with the similar actions of others? In one case the good sought is that of the self-satisfaction of having done one's civic duty (with affecting the outcome as a bonus); in the other, the good sought is that of making one's fair contribution to an outcome that one hopes to see.

To invoke the model of the 'invisible hand' (*ibid.*: 172) is to identify it as a case of the former kind. Thanks to a prevailing civic morality, citizens find self-satisfaction in casting a vote reflectively, for performing that action is a feature of the good citizenship held up as a model. The outcome, whatever it is, is a by-product of the way in which voters put their emulation of this model into effect. They intend one thing, and something other results. But this is paradoxical, for what this model tells citizens is that they ought to be concerned about outcomes: casting a random vote, as Brennan and Lomasky rightly point out (*ibid.*: 170), would not count. One has to vote with an informed belief, arrived at after weighing priorities and assessing evidence, that one outcome would be better than another. So the situation is this: the voter seeks the self-satisfaction of being the sort of person who cares about outcomes, yet regards the outcome as incidental to his or her action! This is not, surely, a kind of self-satisfaction that one can have, without self-deception. The outcomes that validate voting behaviour must also motivate it – for otherwise the 'expressive' benefit that citizens derive from it is a delusion. Of course, they might derive psychic benefit even despite the delusion, as long as the ethic of voting were successfully established as a social convention, as 'something the citizen does' (*ibid.*: 195); but we can hardly appeal to this in the course of a moral argument about why the convention would be a good thing to have if it did not already happen to be conventional.

So we must take the alternative route, and regard casting a (reflective) vote as a good thing in a small way – like refraining from littering, or playing one's fair part in maintaining some diffusely important social practice. Because one's contribution is so small, one might selfishly free-ride, relying on others to carry the burden; but one would be constrained by a 'civic morality' which tells one to act on generalizable principles. But what could the relevant principle be?

Three candidates are as follows: (1) 'everyone should vote for the right outcome'; (2) 'everyone should vote for what I think is the right outcome'; and (3) 'everyone should vote for what they think is the right outcome'. Now (1) has to be rejected, as an example of what Gerald Dworkin calls a 'non-neutral principle' (Dworkin, 1975) – that is, a principle which can be given verbal assent but which will not lead to consistent behaviour. It is like saying 'obey the true god' in a situation in which everyone knows that there are severe disagreements about who the true god is. Principle (2), on the other hand, would indeed lead to consistent results, but it is unenforceable. That leaves (3). It is a possible and appropriate maxim of civic morality, but it clearly means, on a moment's reflection, that one must give up Brennan and Lomasky's claims about contributing to the right outcome. From the standpoint of each individual voter, it just is not true that each other person's voting for what they think is right will produce the best outcome. Obviously, being committed to wanting the right outcome – as their model requires – one would want some people to vote, others not to. The best outcome would arise from voting by those who hold the right beliefs and non-voting by those who hold the wrong beliefs. So even with the help of a civic morality, one still cannot come up with a generalizable principle of an outcome-based variety.

But the claim that democracy tends to produce the best outcomes should be abandoned anyway, on other grounds. The idea that democracy is a process which generates public knowledge is bold and compelling; but surely it is to take the edge off it, and to confuse matters, to claim that the maximization of public knowledge will probably lead to better outcomes. First, it greatly weakens its force: to promote something with the claim that it is 'not ... *entirely* groundless' (Brennan and Lomasky, 1993: 197) may be to risk accusations of offering faint praise! Second, it assumes, improbably, that all this increase of knowledge will be accompanied by convergent agreement on the standards for assessing 'better' outcomes, so that we can predict that they will be better from some standpoint acknowledged to be authoritative. This considerably underestimates the depth of political conflict, however. Certainly one can think of cases in which information improves outcomes – for example, cases in which people initially hold mistaken beliefs contrary to their own interests, and abandon them when informed; but it would be a bold rationalism that took such cases as a model, and claimed that knowledge guaranteed rightness.[6] Third, and most significantly, the claim preserves from earlier rational-choice thinking the assumption that the 'outcome' that matters is the *electoral* outcome, and that the rationality of a vote has to be assessed in terms of some relation between the nature of the electoral outcome and the preferences (however defined) of the voters. But there are also 'outcomes' of a processual kind, and it is these (as opposed to electoral outcomes) that can provide a basis for general agreement.

The proper standards for judging electoral outcomes are discerned from the constantly receding standpoint which is constituted by the best available evidence and argument. How things look from that standpoint cannot be institutionally captured. But any standpoint falling short of it – that is, any standpoint which is protected from the best available evidence and argument – is defective, and so is any political system which protects itself by artificially stabilizing the horizon of public knowledge. A democratic polity has the unique merit of creating incentives for openness: in order to win, you must persuade, and in order to persuade, you must generalize the interests that you appeal to and problematize the appeals made by your opponents. If closing horizons is sometimes rational for one party, then reopening them becomes rational for the other. Of course we cannot predict that all this will lead to the best outcome; no institution can, just because it is an institution, and a democratic theory promising the best outcomes is in pursuit of a chimera. But we want to argue about what the best outcome is on the most effective possible terms, and democratic institutions are best fitted to make public argument informed and comprehensive.

Democratic institutions provide an incentive structure which is appropriate to that only if a large enough number of citizens vote, and only if a large enough number of voters think. The knowledge-promoting ends of democracy give one a moral reason to vote, to think about one's vote, and also to vote for what one thinks is right. Of course it is absurd to suppose that one's own vote has enough of a chance of determining the outcome to motivate its casting. What motivates its casting is the duty-based desire to make one's fair contribution to the process, which one can do only by voting one's considered judgement. Only if those who want one's vote know that it will be considered, will they have an incentive to find reasons to influence it. Naturally, when the time to vote arrives, it is too late to play one's fair part in influencing the rationality of the campaign that has already taken place. What motivates the desire to vote reflectively can only be the desire to play one's fair part in influencing the rationality of the next election. It is clearly impossible that the *reflectiveness* of one's vote will influence *this* election – whether it is cast reflectively or with total abandon will have no effect on the tiny direction of influence that it exerts. But the known existence of a political culture in which it is the norm that votes should be reflectively cast will have an effect on the public reasoning of those who seek one's vote. This, not any 'best answer' theory (however tentatively phrased), can give us the generalizable principle that a civic or political morality requires, and which makes the duty to vote intelligible.

This gives us a handle on at least two standard questions that plague the political theory seminar. First, is it democratic to abolish democracy? Suppose the people vote not to have a vote – do we respect democracy by denying their wish or by honouring it? The issue seems to evoke the similar-looking paradox of divine omnipotence with which, it seems, everyone liked to torment their religious education teacher. Can God create something that is too heavy for Him to lift? (Holmes, 1995: 150–2). Likewise, can a sovereign people sovereignly cast off its sovereignty? But the argument above rescues us from whatever by-ways of argument the paradox involves. The point of voting in *this* election is to ensure the continuation of a valued process of mutual public enlightenment; so there would just be no point in voting in the *last* election, for there would be no future process to protect, and its outcome would be meaningless.[7]

The second question is about the importance of '50 per cent plus one'. The answer is that nothing is important about it, and that no theory recognizing the basic durability of the fact-value distinction can claim that it is. But the '50-per cent plus one' rule has consequences which can be defended on moral grounds that are strong enough to give people a reason to vote. It gives rival proposal-makers or office-seekers a reason to generalize the grounds of their appeal, and, if necessary, to modify their appeals for the sake of making them generalizable. A supermajority (for example, a 60 per cent threshold) rule (not to mention a unanimity rule) would give political rivals an incentive to mobilize narrowly distributed but intensely held reasons.[8] If we could not predict non-voting, and if most of those voting did so reflectively, then, given a simple majority rule, political actors would be driven to offer policy alternatives sustained by reasons that they believed to be reflectively sustainable. And that is as far as one can go in justifying democracy as a political system. To go further, and to claim that one reflectively sustainable policy is better than another, is to become a participant. And that is fine, but the hope that the system will produce the outcomes that one personally favours is not something that one can offer, to those who disagree, as a reason to support the system. For – obviously – they will not agree, and we cannot, as it were, agree on their behalf.

That conclusion points back in the direction of an earlier question. Given that the situation of democratic self-government gives a place of privilege to equality, which among many suggested versions of equality should we opt for? The argument above suggests that the sustainable version is the idea of our equality as moral reasoners. Each of us has a distinct point of view – whether points of view are different as well as distinct is another matter – from which we assess rightness. We want this capacity to form a point of view to be respected by the institutional arrangements to which we subscribe. But it makes no sense at all to suppose that our conclusions can somehow be treated equally; that my idea of what is right can be balanced against, or traded with, or compromised by your own idea. Those sorts of notions belong in other areas of human life and social exchange, in which things such as interests or wants are capable of comparison and translation on the basis of some common measure. But when it comes to competing judgements about rightness, it is a category mistake to suppose that such a common measure exists, for the nature of the disagreement itself precludes it. All 'equality' can mean is that our capacity to form judgements is respected by institutional arrangements which prejudge outcomes as little as possible and tend to provide the best available general conditions for informed decision, for those conditions confer privilege on no one. In that respect, then, democracy is a unique solution to the problem of political legitimation as set out above, and a unique candidate for the role of political morality. What it provides – as far as any set of institutions can – is that the winning proposal, whatever it turns out to be, will have been made as persuasive as possible, so that every voter will have had the greatest possible opportunity to understand and evaluate it; and in accepting a set of decision-making institutions on this basis, voters express mutual respect for each other's need to be persuaded.

Notes

1. I am grateful here for many conversations with F. M. Barnard.
2. As a factual statement, this is to be distinguished from the similar-looking opinion of John Dewey, quoted by Ian Shapiro, (1996: 260–1): a democratic philosophy 'will construe liberty as meaning a universe in which there is real uncertainty and contingency, a world which is not all in, and never will be'. This expresses a world-view which some will find attractive, but which is insufficiently minimal for the present purpose.
3. For a critical discussion of this theme, see Shapiro (1996: 84–90).
4. I do not mean to imply that Barnard's and Przeworski's positions are the same, only that they overlap in the way stated.
5. Or, for another alternative, see Estlund (1997) for the 'Queen for a day' model.
6. I take it that Rousseau was seeking to discredit this kind of claim with his anecdote about peasant simplicity in *Social Contract* (Rousseau, 1968: IV.i).
7. Of course, if the last election were held in order to determine whether or not there should be elections in the future, then on the argument here there would have been a point in voting in it.
8. This has a bearing on recent Canadian discussions of the appropriate decision rule for the secession of a province. A supermajority rule would indeed give anti-secessionists an incentive to mobilize minorities (such as Anglophones and non-French-speaking immigrants in Quebec). On the other hand, the general argument in terms of institutional effects might tell against a simple majority rule, if we project its likely effects on the politics of a federal system.

CHAPTER 3

Procedure and Outcome in Democratic Theories

The idea advanced at the end of the previous chapter is more compelling if we consider the alternatives. Standard defences of majority rule divide into two broad types. On proceduralist conceptions, we are to think of the outcomes of democracy as legitimate because they issue from a process which meets certain criteria (such as equality and fairness), while outcome-based conceptions of democracy advance the claim that democratic processes are legitimate because they have desirable consequences. The justifying arguments run in diametrically opposite directions: in the one case, the procedure makes the outcome legitimate, while in the other, the outcome legitimates the procedure.

Both of these ideas have intuitive appeal. If we give weight to democratic outcomes only on the grounds that they are substantively right, by some independent standard, then implicitly we are denying that the democratic process makes any difference: the outcomes would be the right ones regardless of how they had been reached. That seems decidedly odd, and so we might favour the proceduralist alternative. But we would have to approve of the procedure on the basis of some value or other; and we cannot do so if we believe that its outcomes are going to be incompatible with other values that we also hold. On what possible basis could we approve of a system that consistently produced unjust results?[1] So we might shrink from committing ourselves to whatever democracy's outcome is, and decide, after all, to give its outcomes weight only if they are right on independent grounds; but then we seem again to be denying them weight on the grounds that they have been democratically reached, which seems an unacceptable conclusion for democrats.

That, very summarily stated, is the sort of circle in which thinking about democracy often tends to move. Adapting a question invented by Plato (in the *Euthyphro* dialogue) and made famous in subsequent theology, we might ask whether the outcomes of democracy are good because they are democratically chosen, or whether, on the other hand, democracy is good because it leads to good outcomes. What this chapter will argue is that democratic theorists are compelled to evade this choice. The first section, taking Rousseau's theory as an example of an outcome-based view, tries to show that his approach cannot avoid reliance on proceduralist claims. The second section, taking some recent work of Jürgen Habermas as an example of proceduralism, makes the reverse argument: that this approach cannot avoid making claims of a substantive kind. The third section examines and rejects the claims of theorists who, following Rawls, believe they have resolved this dilemma. Finally, I return to the idea of majority rule defended in Chapter 2 and try to show that it removes the need for procedure and outcome to compete for the same normative space, as it were, thus creating unwelcome circularities and paradoxes.

Rousseau's famous argument, in *Social Contract*, may be too refractory to classify, but at several points it takes what seems clearly to be an outcome-based turn. When he makes his especially famous claim, in book IV, chapter 2,[2] that 'when the opinion contrary to mine prevails, that proves only that I have made a mistake, and that what I believed to be the general will was not', he adds an important qualification: that this is so only if 'the characteristics of the general will' are present in the majority. We may take this to refer back to Rousseau's acknowledgement, in the previous chapter, that the 'general will' subsists, 'unchanging, incorruptible and pure', even when the people neglect it, or, in book II, chapter 3, that 'the general will is always right' even though the decisions of the people are not always right. One thing that this might mean is that at any point there is a certain outcome which is right or appropriate because it embodies some specified feature and that the majority's decision is right if it leads to this outcome. A more reasonable-looking version would specify, rather, a set of possible outcomes, all sharing some valued feature. This feature could plausibly be their contribution to 'common preservation and general well-being', which Rousseau describes as the object of the general will (IV.1).

Rousseau's argument sets out to accomplish the important task of explaining why (and when) a majority's view carries weight. Mere numbers mean nothing, and giving weight to numbers of votes alone would just be an instance of a so-called 'right of the strongest', which Rousseau, near the beginning of *Social Contract* (I.3), shows to be no right at all. A majority's vote carries weight if it reflects an interest, which we all share, in 'common preservation', and in that sense can be said to comprehend the minority's interest too. We can regard a will to promote generally shared interests as, in a sense, the will 'of no one' – that is, a will not expressing this or that partial interest, but one which just happens to be recognized by the larger group, or so one hopes. 'The general will derives its generality less from the number of voices than from the common interest that unites them' (II.4). Public decisions are thus no longer to be seen as coercive, compelling some to bend to the preferences of others, for they are arrived at from a standpoint which is potentially accessible to everyone, and, if the decision process is working as it should be, actually accessible to more people than not.

Rousseau prescribes a range of institutions and practices which should have the effect of excluding or at least diminishing the impact of partial interests, thus ensuring that shared interests provide criteria for decision-making. The 'generality' of law, for example (II.6), compels voters to consider matters 'collectively' rather than trying to favour particular groups, which cannot be mentioned in the essentially 'abstract' form that laws must take. Limits on communication and factious activity (II.3) oblige citizens to consider widely shared interests, since exclusive interests shared only by smaller groups thereby become difficult to advance. Much of *Social Contract*, then, might be seen as an effort to give institutional form to an outcome-based principle of legitimacy – that is, to create a polity in which a specified set of criteria becomes the habitual and effective spring of public action.

A reading of that kind accounts for much of what Rousseau says, and may make it both appealing and not wholly implausible. But Rousseau does not leave the matter there. For he also claims that legitimacy arises from the self-prescribed character of laws – that is, the bare fact that they are voluntarily adopted. In addition to 'civil freedom', freedom bounded by the shared civil interests expressed in the general will, he promises 'moral freedom', or 'obedience to a law that one prescribes to oneself' (I.8). As he says later, 'A people, since it is subject to laws, ought to be the author of them' (II.6). He says that 'the general will must spring from all and apply to all' (II.4) (although springing from 'most' rather than 'all' would seem more precise, surely). He occasionally speaks as though the general will *means* what is generally willed, as when he says that popular judgement 'guides' it (II.6). That, of course, would mean that a will became general by virtue of securing a majority, and not by virtue of meeting some substantive test.

How are we to understand this other approach – apparently procedural – to legitimacy, and how are we to see its relation to what appeared to be a substantive or outcome-based theory? If a people, *since it is subject to laws* – which seems, on its face, to state a sufficient condition – ought to make them, what strength can remain in our preferences for outcomes, the origin of law being (apparently) decisive?

Two possible lines of reconciliation offer themselves. One would be to claim that although the core argument was a substantive one, there just happened to be only one way to identify good outcomes – that is, to hold a popular vote under certain stringent conditions, excluding factiousness and so on. This vote does not legitimate the outcome, but is the unique route to its discovery; so we defer to the outcome of the vote because it is the only practical way of identifying the right thing to do. A second line of possible argument organizes priorities quite differently, claiming that the core value is that of a self-governing society, owning no authority but its own, and needing, in order to manage its own affairs, access to a source of good judgement. On this argument, the substantive content of the general will is simply a range of principles conducing to preservation and well-being, principles which members of a self-governing society must apply to their common affairs if their enterprise is to survive. Do either of these approaches successfully explain Rousseau's claims?

The first runs into an impossibility. Rousseau says that 'there can be no assurance that an individual will is in conformity to the general will until it has submitted to the free suffrage of the people' (II.7); but if there were *no* other source of 'assurance', we would be in a bind. If there were only one way to arrive at a right answer, we would have to take it on faith that it was right, since there would be no way to check the answer that we arrived at (Coleman and

Ferejohn, 1986: 16–18). This makes quite unaccountable the deference that the minority is obliged to display when outvoted, as well as making the language of 'assurance' wildly inappropriate. It is certainly hard to read such passages without a sense that a process of voting is not an investigative instrument alone, but adds *something* of its own at least. If the process of voting added nothing, could we make sense of Rousseau's insistence on procedural correctness? Would it really be so important, for example, that *every* vote be counted (II.2, footnote), as long as the number uncounted would not have been enough to change the outcome?

The second approach, which places the value of self-government at the centre of things, might make more unobstructed headway through Rousseau's account of procedures, but it too – though for a different reason – is brought up short by the claim that minorities ought to defer. If the 'general will' *means* 'what is generally willed' (under appropriate procedural constraints), then Rousseau's claim about minority deference becomes absurd. When a law is proposed, he says, the people are asked 'whether it is in conformity with the general will', and those who are outvoted discover that 'what [they] believed to be the general will was not so' (IV.2). But this would mean that each voter, absurdly, would be trying to guess at what other voters were planning to do, and since they would all be doing that, there would be nothing to guess *at*. To rescue this obviously important passage, we have to attribute some substantive content to the 'general will', and refuse to *define* it as, merely, what is generally willed.

We still face the perplexity, then, of being unable to take Rousseau's claims as either procedural or as substantive in nature. Can a hybrid view be sustained? Procedural and substantive views of the general will both seem powerful enough to drive the other out of the picture; but could we, by confining the scope of each of them, make them coexist in Rousseau's account of the voting process? One proposal might be this: one's vote expresses only a conditional preference; on substantive grounds I prefer A to B, but, valuing democratic procedures as I do, I will think B ought to be adopted rather than A, if it turns out that only a minority shares my substantive views. This is like a solution that Richard Wollheim entertains in reflecting on the alleged 'paradox of democracy', the paradox that one appears committed both to A, which one voted for, and B, which the majority voted for (Wollheim, 1962). Wollheim entertains this solution only to reject it, for, he says, if one's initial vote means only 'A if a majority agrees', one might just as well have voted 'B if a majority agrees', for one supports that outcome too. This seems unduly harsh, for, after all, if one has a preference for A one is entitled to do something to promote it (e.g. vote for it) even if as a good democrat one would feel a duty to accept B if A failed.[3] So the solution in question might still perfectly well be useful for some purposes. But these purposes cannot possibly be Rousseau's, because *Social Contract* makes the solution impossible. Immediately after writing 'what I believed to be the general will was not so', Rousseau adds, 'If my particular opinion had prevailed against the general will, I should have done something other than what I had willed.' Now this clearly rules out the proposed hybrid solution, for if my own substantively preferred alternative (A) had 'prevailed' — that is, been the choice of the majority — then I should certainly have 'done what I willed' in aiding in its victory, in a much fuller sense, indeed, than I 'do what I will' in reluctantly accepting B.

Rousseau cannot, then, move from an outcome-based approach to a procedural one, or do without an implied procedural theory to support some of his claims, or explain convincingly how these two approaches work together in his account. Possibly he was the victim of a mistake indicated above, that of confusing the substantive generality of the general will ('applies to all') with the procedural fact of its adoption ('springs from all'), although this leads so quickly to absurd results that it seems quite uncharitable to suspect it. But there is another possible confusion, less egregious, which could serve to conceal the impossibility of the task which Rousseau took on. Two kinds of 'generality' seem important to the self-governing citizen engaged in the task of managing common affairs. One is the idea embedded in the familiar idea of moral generalization, or the golden rule: act only on principles that you wish to be generally acted upon. This powerful idea finds its application in a realm of typical actions whose imagined future repetition provides a critical test for what one proposes to do; and let us accept, for the sake of argument, that an act which passes this test has properties that guarantee its rightness. A second idea is that of a common good in a political sense — that is, a good consisting in desirable future states of affairs in which members of the city will participate together. Here we are not thinking of typical acts, identifiable by some feature abstracted from them, and performed, hypothetically, by an indefinite number of actors; we are thinking, rather, of concrete and complex situations which affect us all because of our objective interdependence. Both of these ideas have something in common – that is, they both require us to step outside narrow considerations of self-interest – and so both can be justified on the basis of a normative ideal of belonging or citizenship. But they do not both require us to step *into* the same thing. And an important difference between the normative contexts that they require us to enter is that the second lacks the guarantees of rightness that are claimed, plausibly, for the first. It is at least a plausible moral theory that tells us that if we will that some act taken under some typical description should be generally performed, then it is right. But it would not be a plausible political theory that claimed that if a proposal were aimed at an objective of general benefit, it would be the right proposal. All that tells us is that it falls within the pale of legitimate politics; it says nothing about its merits in relation to other proposals within the pale.

These two kinds of 'generality' significantly overlap, in that a good citizen must think both about the effects of his or her actions as generally (i.e. typically) defined, and also about the general (i.e. overall) consequences of his or her political proposals. Both requirements impose kinds of self-restraint that may well take psychologically homogeneous forms. And both were undeniably important to Rousseau. If, in certain areas, he neglected the difference between them, that might explain why he made unsustainable claims about the pursuit of a common political good. Rousseau might have thought that by procedural means – requiring the generality of law, inhibiting factious self-preference – he could make people ask the right question; that is, consider only the typical case. And he may have thought, conflating the two senses of 'generality', that this would lead necessarily to the identification of a unique political good of a substantive kind. But only by some error of that sort could one reconcile procedure and substance in the way that Rousseau proposed.

The second, complementary, example is drawn from the recent work of Jürgen Habermas, who has a divided and nuanced view of Rousseau's contribution. He came close, Habermas says, to understanding the immense normative power that democratic procedure would have if correctly understood, but was deflected by his attachment to the substantive or 'ethical' imperatives of particular, historic political communities. He imagined that the members of a political community formed a kind of 'macrosubject' with a character of its own, requiring preservation and nurturing (Habermas, 1996: 101–2). In this he was representative of the 'republican' tradition, as Habermas sees it. That tradition, valuing above all the citizen's devotion to a shared political good, conceives of democracy as a process of self-abnegation in the pursuit of collective ends. Not unreasonably – if his characterization of it is correct – Habermas sees the tradition as imposing excessive and unrealistic ethical demands.

Republicanism is one of the two chief political traditions of modernity, emerging out of the normative crisis induced by secularization, and giving pride of place to one of only two ideals which are sustainable under modern conditions of validation: popular sovereignty. The other chief political tradition, according to Habermas, is liberalism; and that gives pride of place to the other sustainable modern ideal, that of human rights. Kant, the paradigmatic liberal, came close, just as Rousseau did, to solving the problem, but likewise fell short, though for the opposite kind of reason. Far from giving too much unmediated weight to particular local tradition, he sought to impose a morality that was prior to politics altogether, and utterly indifferent to locality (*ibid.*: 105).

Finding both traditions wanting, Habermas advances another approach, which, for the sake of a name, we may call discursive. Habermas himself classifies it as a species of proceduralism, for it ties validation to the exercise of democratic will or 'public autonomy' rather than to criteria of rightness prescribed in advance.[4] I shall argue that it contains problems which are the mirror image of Rousseau's. If Rousseau held an outcome-based view that tried to bring procedures to heel, Habermas seems to hold a procedural view which cannot leave outcomes alone. Some have seen this problem as basic to the whole discursive approach to ethics and truth; it wavers, they complain, between claiming that things are justified because the discursive procedure leads to them, and claiming that the discursive procedure is justified because it leads to the right results.[5] But the argument here is confined to the case of Habermas's democratic theory alone. Is it, and can it afford to be, consistently proceduralist?

The error that is common to both liberal and republican versions of democracy, Habermas says, is that of imposing a false dichotomy between 'private' and 'public' aspects of autonomy – that is, between the liberties enabling individuals to exercise autonomy in their own lives, and the democratic procedures enabling communities to exercise collective self-determination. Fearing majority tyranny, liberals constrain democracy by putting rights first; valuing civic self-determination, republicans make rights subordinate to popular will (Habermas, 1996: 100). The solution is to conceive of both rights and democracy as co-generated by the imperatives of self-rule under conditions of equality. The (basic) rights that we should have are those 'that citizens must mutually grant to one another if they want to legitimately regulate their life in common by means of positive law' (*ibid.*: 118, also 453). These basic rights are due to us either as the 'addressees' of law or as the 'authors' of law – that is, either they give us an entitlement to personal liberty, or they give us an entitlement to participate on equal terms in law-making (*ibid.*: 122–3).

Habermas's account bears mainly on what we might call the ontology of rights and procedures – that is, on what kinds of things they are – and shows their complementarity in relation to a single project, that of association under law. That they may (very interestingly) be seen as having a common origin does not, of course, itself tell us anything at all decisive about their political complementarity – that is, whether or not liberals are correct to fear that the outcomes of procedures will diminish the rights that they favour, or whether or not republicans are correct to fear that rights will constrict the degree of political autonomy that they want. And in fact, rather than responding directly to the liberals' or republicans' concerns, Habermas effectively postpones the answer to an indefinite future. For the basic rights of 'addressees' – that is, the liberties that liberals want to enlarge and that republicans want to subject to democratic will – are a matter of interpretation. Habermas says that we have '[b]asic rights that result from the politically autonomous elaboration of the *right to the greatest possible measure of equal individual liberties*' (*ibid.*: 122). The degree and kind of personal autonomy that one has, therefore, will depend on the outcome of the operation of political autonomy – that is, the democratic process. We may or, there again, may not end up with the degree and kind of personal rights that liberals favour, for liberalism is just one possible 'interpretation' of the first basic right (*ibid.*: 125). As for the republican point of view, basic rights impede republicans' (alleged) project of imposing the polity's substantive ethical values to the full, but it is hard to be clear about the practical extent of this impedance, since there is a kind of circularity between the operation of democracy (constrained by rights) and the outcome of democratic decision (which defines what the rights are). But to Habermas, there is no alternative to this relative inconclusiveness. It is a relic of Platonism to suppose that there must be some ideal disposition of rights and duties, transcendentally lurking, which actual polities must imitate as best they can (*ibid.*: 106). In the modern world, what rights and duties we have depend on the informed and procedurally constrained exercise of political autonomy, for there is no authority that we can appeal to beyond informed and procedurally constrained consent. And so we revert to the puzzle which formed the point of departure of this chapter: given that democracy is a matter of (however constrained) volition (*ibid.*: 100), do not its outcomes become simply untheorizable?

In his essay 'Struggles for recognition' (Habermas, 1994), Habermas confronts directly the alleged dichotomy between rights and democracy. The topic is set by Charles Taylor's famous essay 'The politics of recognition' (Taylor, 1994), which sets out (in a regretful spirit) the difficulties faced by liberal democratic societies which are irrevocably attached to individual equality as a goal, but have to face the challenges posed by cultural groups demanding the means to ensure their survival – means which sometimes conflict with the demands of a purely individualistic model. Taylor's difficulty, according to Habermas, is that he fails to give priority to democracy as the process which at once interprets the scope and meaning of individual rights, and gives deliberated weight to the multicultural realities of modern political societies. Rather than supposing that there is some eternally given set of individual rights, which tragically come into conflict with the local and real identifications which demand recognition, we should rely on the (procedurally constrained) democratic process itself to establish what rights individuals have, in the context of the legitimate demands arising from a pluralist here-and-now reality.

So ultimately, there can be no conflict between legitimate individual claims and legitimate group claims, for a single process – constrained democracy – fixes the respective scope of both, so that complementarity between them is maintained. How, concretely, this is achieved of course depends on the varying circumstances of historically given polities. But however a polity does it, it is not facing a problem of the sort that either liberals or republicans depict, and their depictions both contain false dilemmas.

On Habermas's model we are to see basic rights as very abstract principles in need of concrete elaboration. If it were not for the fact that they are coeval with the state, not prior to it, we might regard them as being like the principles of natural law that social contract theorists postulated; however, since their elaboration takes place concretely, within democracy, and not speculatively, in a natural-law-like theory, they can, it is claimed, accommodate real-world differences. In the democratic process, minorities can – like individuals – press their claims for recognition, and a 'democratic liberalism' such as Habermas describes is not, as abstract liberalism is, biased in an individualistic direction. At any given point a society s will have a scheme of rights adopted in a process through which the unique circumstances of s have been brought to bear on the abstract requirements of freedom and equality. And there is no other, ideal, set of rights with which the scheme adopted by s can be compared.

But it is this that creates difficulties of evaluation. We have to know that the rights of s really *are* interpretations of freedom and equality. Crude communitarian democracy is ruled out, so the scheme of rights cannot just express a community's ethical self-understanding. But how can we tell? We would have to be able to know that it made a difference, or, even, enough of a difference, that demands passed through the filter of procedure and were transformed from crude communitarian assertions into legitimate articulations of rights. To know that it made a difference, or enough of a difference, we would have to be able to compare s with some control scheme (or at least a recipe for one). But if we have a control scheme, or a way of formulating it, then the democratic procedure is not, as claimed, defining legitimate outcomes, but merely discovering them, or failing to.

Habermas himself seems to say as much, especially in the 'Postscript' to *Between Fact and Norms*, where, reviewing his position in the light of various critics' remarks, he adopts a point of view more substantive than procedural. In promoting the most open possible discourse, the democratic process 'grounds the fallibilist assumption that results issuing from proper procedure are more or less reasonable' (Habermas, 1996: 448). Procedural constraints make democracy into a system that 'grounds the supposition that the outcomes of political opinion- and will-formation are reasonable' (*ibid.*: 455). The democratic basis of positive law is a 'procedure of presumptively rational opinion- and will-formation' (*ibid.*: 457). Now 'rational' and 'reasonable' may of course be taken as only procedural terms, referring to the giving and taking of reasons which constitutes open and discursive democracy. But here they must be substantive terms, for otherwise it would not be a matter of 'more or less' or of 'presumption'; the process would *guarantee* rationality.

Claiming only 'presumptive' rationality for the outcomes of democratic discourse, and describing his assumption of reasonableness as 'fallibilist', Habermas stops very well short of Rousseau's view that outvoted minorities should defer to the majority and admit their mistake. Nothing in Habermas suggests that minorities must abandon their judgement in this way. They can form their own judgements about what the rational outcomes of discourse would be, and on that basis put forward their own contributions to it. No doubt they even claim to have 'rights', and with good reason would surely reject any argument that they have no rights until the procedure says they do. Rights claims are advanced as ways of influencing the procedure, after all. Implicitly, Habermas gives full acknowledgement to minorities in recognizing that the discursive process is in principle indefinite in length: we can never say that we have heard the last of any objection to what is generally accepted. Because of 'institutional pressures to decide' we take a vote in which the majority's view is decisive; the discussion may continue, and the vote represents only a temporary interruption or 'caesura' (*ibid.*: 179). But if we ask why the outvoted minority should see the vote as legitimate, we can hardly use the decision's 'presumptive rationality' as an answer, for the minority found some other answer to the question posed to be more rational than the answer favoured by the majority. We can think of various possible reasons for the minority to accede, among them reasons involving 'institutional pressures to decide', the (very Lockean[6]) consideration advanced by Habermas in this passage; but then, what has happened to the discursive approach? If we follow its own logic, we seem to be led inevitably to a demand for substantive safeguards: if discourse could lead to anything at all, we want protection against the brute facticity of majority decision. But if we then back off, for democratic reasons, from claims to substantive rightness, we are led to a kind of proceduralism that has nothing to do with discursiveness. It may well have something to do with stability, or with fairness, but we hardly need a discourse theory to sustain the appeal to those.

On the evidence so far, what are we to say about the choice between procedural and outcome-based approaches? To John Rawls, the moral is that we have to combine the two (Rawls, 1995: 170–80). Even theories that call themselves procedural are really outcome-based, he claims. He employs the analogy of a criminal trial, which must follow a carefully prescribed procedure; we cannot guarantee that its outcome will always be just, yet we would not call the procedure just 'unless it was intelligently drawn up so that [it] gives the correct decision, at least much of the time'. Likewise, when we design democratic political procedures as Habermas does, we shape the procedure 'to accord with our judgment' of what the right outcome is – for example, to secure the expression of generalizable rather than special interests.

But this way of putting things, while successfully exploiting some ambiguities in Habermas's case, seems to conceal a core problem. If it were *only* the (projected or usual) outcomes that justified a procedure, then we would have an outcome-based view pure and simple, and the analogy with the trial would be good. But then, one would be saying in effect that the fact that an outcome was democratically adopted added nothing to its value; and understandably, this would be a point that neither Habermas nor Rousseau, despite their different points of departure, would be willing to concede. Whether or not they are able to do so consistently, they agree – for different reasons – that value attaches to both procedure and outcome, and, it seems, their own arguments drive them to do this.

Rawls's position is advanced at greater length by theorists of 'deliberative democracy', some of whose views we will consider in Chapter 7. But a particularly careful statement is provided by Charles R. Beitz in *Political Equality* (Beitz, 1989). Beitz too argues from a contractualist standpoint,[7] which requires us to take account of the reasonable perspective of every person, as for example utilitarian or epistemic theories would not do. We have to be able to justify democracy from everyone's point of view. We might attempt to do this in a purely proceduralist way. For example, we might claim that some institution such as simple majority rule would treat citizens 'impartially'. But, given that various interests differ greatly in their degrees of urgency, it is hopeless to claim, in abstraction from 'the substantive characteristics of the results that procedures are likely to produce', that meaningful impartiality will be produced by any particular method (Beitz, 1989: 84–91). Or we might take a different approach, claiming that some procedure such as majority rule 'expressed' the equality of citizens in the sense of recognizing them as equal in political status. But again, we would need to know more about outcomes, for if some procedural inequality had the effect of remedying some substantive equality, it would not be seen as 'expressing' disrespect (*ibid.*: 91–5). Beitz concludes that the project of justifying procedures to everyone cannot exclude the anticipation of results. 'The political outcomes to be expected from the operation of a set of procedures are simply too important to be left out of account' (*ibid.*: 95).

How are they to be brought into the account, without banishing the important themes that proceduralists insist upon? Beitz's answer is what he terms 'complex proceduralism', an idea with several components, one of which involves a concern with outcomes. To give form to the abstract idea of equality, we need to accommodate three 'regulative interests of citizenship'. These are our interests in recognition, in equitable treatment, and in deliberative responsibility: 'Each defines a category of interest it would be reasonable to take into account in assessing the arrangements for participation' (*ibid.*: 100). The first of these is quite straightforward: an interest in procedural inclusion. It is the second that brings the anticipation of outcomes into play; people would 'reasonably refuse to accept institutions under which it was predictable that their actual interests ... would be unfairly placed in jeopardy' (*ibid.*: 110). Of course, the terms used in this provision invite disagreement and controversy. Despite this, there is hope for significant agreement since 'the prospects of convergence are greatest in connection with the most vital of human interests' (*ibid.*: 113).

This provision, however, may significantly underrate political conflict. True, we may agree on which interests are vital, but we do not have them ranked. Prime Minister Thatcher once declared that she would rather be dead than Red; now life and liberty would also have been seen as vital interests by her opponents to the left, but that did not make the political distance between her views and theirs any less intense. Moreover, it is one thing to agree in acknowledging the vital importance of some value, and something else to agree in its practical interpretation.

Consider, for example, the range of conflicting policies that can be collected under the shared title of 'equal opportunity', policies ranging from purely procedural fairness to affirmative action. Or consider the practical divergences between different interpretations of 'desert', some treating it as a subordinate conception within some other distributive principle, others regarding it a free-standing merit-based criterion. Given these sorts of considerations, either it seems inconceivable that people should expect the interests that they regard as vital to be protected, or else it seems that agreement on this would be a paper agreement that would be torn up at the level of application.

Alternatively, we might recognize the sorts of basic conflicts just alluded to and weaken the sense of 'equitable treatment'. Perhaps that term does not mean that all the conflicting interests brought under a common label will be accommodated in democratic outcomes; just that they will all be given weight. But that turns the idea back into a purely procedural one: we have no guarantees about outcomes, only about what happens along the way to them.

The reason for insisting on this is that Beitz weakens his third 'regulative interest', which is supremely important, by appearing to treat it as instrumental to the second, which may be a chimera. His fine account of 'deliberative responsibility' cannot be improved upon: democratic citizens will not want their own contributions to be based on mere prejudice, they will want their judgements to be 'the most reasonable ones possible', and so they will want a deliberative process that is open to competing views and adequately informed (*ibid*.: 114). However, Beitz introduces this compelling account with the claim that democratic procedures provide the most reliable means to substantively just outcomes, and concludes it by claiming that deliberative responsibility is the only way to make equitable outcomes more than a pious hope (*ibid*.: 113–14).[8] In the absence of a surer way to predict or identify (consensually) good outcomes than the argument seems to provide, the argument from deliberative responsibility has to stand on its own. But it can stand on its own perfectly well. We can value democracy as the only effective means of stimulating public reason; and if we take that position, we adopt an argument that has no known rivals. However, to argue that public reason will disclose better or more just or more equitable outcomes is to expose the case for democracy to entirely valid kinds of political scepticism, as well as to delegitimate political minorities. No general theory of scepticism is offered here; that would undermine the whole point of political deliberation, for one can hardly deliberate about matters known in advance to be wholly unsettleable. But all the same, we do not know enough.

When democratic theorists (including many of those discussed above) speak of 'outcomes', they have in mind one or both of two (obviously related) things. First, there are the outcomes reached through democracy – that is, decisions about policy or law which are given authority by majority rule. Second, there are the outcomes that are guaranteed despite majority desires – that is, constitutionally protected states of affairs which democratic decisions must respect. But there is a third kind of 'outcome', termed 'processual' above, that is crucially relevant to the kind of justification to be outlined in this final section. When reasoned debate takes place, as theorists of deliberative democracy rightly insist, major consequences of an epistemic kind occur. The need to convince others, as opposed to just reinforcing one's own convictions, creates pressure to root out special pleading from one's case, to generalize one's principles, and to learn what others find important. The need to respond to others makes one consider unanticipated objections, develop new grounds for favoured but contested proposals, and extend initially attractive principles to new and more difficult cases. Both of those needs create a powerful incentive to gather previously overlooked evidence, and to question weaknesses in one's opponents' evidence, thus enhancing the state of public knowledge. And all three of those effects contribute in turn to self-criticism, whether this eventuates in changing one's mind or in discovering new reasons or evidence in support of what one believed to begin with. For drawing attention to all of this, theorists of deliberative democracy deserve enormous credit. But these 'outcomes' are quite enough to justify democracy. If we respect people as bearers of critical reason, we will think it important that they should have a political environment in which their access to others' arguments, to the reach of their own principles, and to publicly useful evidence is maximized. To justify democracy because it does that is to offer a very compelling defence. It is to give weight to a basically important aspect of equality – that is, the recognition of each person as an independent source of judgement, with an interest in judging effectively. Many versions of democracy, some of which we have seen above, draw in part upon a defence of this kind, rightly insisting that a vote uninformed by public reasoning is meaningless.[9] But in going further, and in making claims for the outcome of the *vote*, democratic theories take one step too many.

The substantive version of this mistake is to run together the outcome of the discussion and the outcome of the voting procedure, as though the decision taken followed rationally from the preceding debates. But the outcome of the *discussion* is, as we have seen, the whole body of argument and evidence that mutual critique has generated. It remains open to anyone, by virtue of our respect for critical reason, to assess the direction in which, in total or on balance, it inclines. The vote is no more than a registration of the number of people who think it inclines one way rather than another. There is no reason to think that it better represents the outcome of the discussion than minority views do. Nor, in many cases, is there any reason to think that either view is univocally better. From the (true) thought that we all benefit from better reasoning and evidence, it does not follow that reasoning and evidence are bound even in principle to converge upon a single result. Perhaps, assuming reasonableness, we could predict eventual consensus in a single-valued moral universe or a moral universe in which values could be ranked. But this is remote from reality.

The proceduralist version of the mistake is to claim that majority rule embodies equality in some stronger sense than that noted above. 'Equal respect' is, to be sure, a weak sense of equality, and it is tempting, it seems, to make the stronger claim that majority rule gives equal *weight* to voters' interests. But basic problems, none of them novel, spring up at once.[10] Why prefer procedural equality to equality of outcome, and how could one rationally prefer a democratic polity to an authoritarian one which produced a more equal distribution of benefits? Even given a procedural view of equality, why not opt for a unanimity rule, which gives more equal weight to those who are potentially in a minority? Even given the majority principle, why apply it to individuals rather than well-defined groups? What about different levels of intensity of desire, or of need? And what is it that makes any kind of voting system superior to, say, a lottery, or some other randomizing device that gives equal weight just as well, though in a different way? Note that, without abandoning proceduralism, we cannot claim that voted outcomes are *better* than random ones.

No doubt there are ways to develop responses to these and similar problems. But what is suggested here is that there is a better way to justify majority rule, one which initially may seem surprising, but which lays a number of recurrent difficulties to rest. No significance at all attaches to the fact that more people support one set of reasons or proposals over another. That is a mere fact, which cannot occupy the same space as any value. But the anticipation of the vote will, ideally, have produced 'outcomes' of the third kind distinguished above – that is, a publicly available array of critical argumentation and evidence. What makes majority rule important is that it is the most powerful way to generate this outcome, for it provides the maximum incentive to generalize one's reasoning, in the way that deliberative democrats rightly admire.

The reason for making the decision turn on a vote, a process of counting up how many people have been persuaded by which proposals, is simply to give participants an incentive – as a lottery, for example, would not do – to make their appeals as generally persuasive as they can. That is a reason to distinguish between cases in which majorities and minorities are (at least partially) formed in the process of public discussion, and cases in which already constituted majorities simply use their power to subdue identifiable minorities. Procedurally, the two cases are identical; but if we distinguish quite sharply between the legitimacy of the two, as surely we must, that has to be because in the former case public reasoning was at least in principle consequential, while in the latter the majority functioned merely as a partial group with no interest in increasing the persuasiveness and generality of its case.

By the time the vote occurs, then, all of its benefits have already been secured, and the vote's outcome – as distinct, once again, from the discussion's outcome – adds nothing. It has to take place because otherwise the preceding exercise of public reasoning would not have occurred, and the voter's concern, as the previous chapter claimed, must be to secure the process for the future: one should do one's fair share towards maintaining in existence a public culture in which it is known that votes are cast reflectively by significant numbers of people. On this view, it is entirely understandable that people should cast their votes even though they know that the outcome has been settled (Brennan and Lomasky, 1993: 35), or even though their candidate never stood a chance in the first place.

Nevertheless, the idea that no normative weight attaches to the majority vote is the most counter-intuitive part of the proposal made here. Perhaps, in contexts other than that of political democracy, there is a case to be made. In small groups, for example, policies may need to enjoy the active support, rather than just the acquiescence, of more members rather than fewer, and adopting the majority's desires may make sense for that reason. The familiarity of majority rule in informal contexts such as that may reinforce the sense that in the political context too it must have a certain rightness. But repeated efforts, from Rousseau's time to the present, to explain this rightness are consistently plagued with difficulties.

Not all intuitions can be rescued; and the benefit of abandoning that one is that the way is clear to a better sense of how procedural and substantive features of democracy can coexist.

Notes

1. To avoid misunderstanding, this is not a matter of analysing conceptually the relationship between democracy and other values, such as freedom and justice. Rather, it is a matter of recognizing that we cannot predict the outcomes of the future exercise of majority (or any) discretion.
2. Since readers will have many different editions of *Social Contract*, I supply book and chapter numbers in the text. The edition used is Maurice Cranston's translation (Rousseau, 1968).
3. For criticism, see Barry (1973b).
4. See Habermas (1995), where he particularly stresses the proceduralist character of his argument.
5. See especially Pettit (1992: 212–23), which alludes to the 'Euthyphro' problem alluded to in the introductory section above.
6. See John Locke, *The Second Treatise*, section 96.
7. In his case, Scanlon-derived at least as much as Rawls-derived, but the distinction does not bear upon the matters dealt with here, as far as I can see.
8. Compare, however, his earlier (and I think better) claim that 'the defense of majority rule need not claim more than that, suitably constrained, it enables citizens to reach political decisions on the basis of adequately informed decision and in a way that avoids predictable forms of injustice' (Beitz, 1989: 66). Of course, the last clause here might be seen as accommodating the argument just criticized, but only if (on my view) we assume too much consensus.
9. Cf. Spitz (1984: xiii): 'discussion, not voting, lies at the heart [of democracy]'.
10. For a compact discussion, see Harrison (1993: chapter 11). See also Beitz (1989), especially chapter 1.

CHAPTER 4

Moral Defeats and Majority Rule

In Chapter 3 I tried to show that some basic circumstances, implied in the process of political discussion itself, offer a route to a practical interpretation of 'equality'; that this interpretation picks out, as especially important, the equality of citizens as reasoners; that this will lead us to adopt the majority principle, as a device which respects citizens' need to be persuaded; and that thus understood, the majority principle does not have to meet the dilemmas that confront either procedural or outcome-based views of democracy. These considerations, if accepted, support democratic theory. But what obviously remains to be shown is that a democratic theory, thus constructed, will also be a liberal one. That is the task undertaken by this chapter and the next. This chapter tries to show that the majority principle's own justification sets limits to its scope of operation; the next tries to show that its own logic leads us to a notion of basic rights.

What leads us to worry about the majority principle is, of course, the persistence of differences to which minorities attach importance. Now democratic political systems are likely to be better than others at allowing the articulation of important differences among their citizens; and perhaps they are also better at accommodating these differences, as is claimed by some justifying theories, especially those which focus upon the discursive or deliberative features of democracy. But all the same, no democracy, however ideal, can hope to accommodate differences entirely. It can promote deliberation, or negotiation, or compromise – or even all of these, as responses to different problems (Gutmann and Thompson, 1996: 52–94) – but eventually choices will be made, and some people will lose. Maybe everyone will lose some of the time, and possibly some will lose all of the time; and those who are defeated will have to endure policies which they regard as morally deficient. That they will have been reached by democratic processes will make them more legitimate, but, in the case of severe disagreements of a moral kind, not necessarily more endurable. It may not be easier to bear a wrong performed with full rational deliberation than one performed inadvertently: maybe the opposite is sometimes true.

It is possible, then, that there are some defeats that are just too serious to be endured, and which even ideal democracies should therefore refuse to impose. When only matters of interest are at stake, on both sides of an issue, some theorists are willing to accept majority rule as a workable approximation to equality. There is more resistance, however, to accepting this solution as an egalitarian one when deeply contested moral issues are at stake.

Naturally, those sympathetic to liberalism are particularly sensitive to this issue. Ronald Dworkin, for example, adopts majority rule when ordinary preferences are in play, but argues that a basic principle of equal respect demands that majorities should not impose on minorities their views about how to live: the function of 'rights' is precisely to fend off invasions of this kind in areas in which majorities are likely to find them especially tempting (Dworkin, 1978). Thomas Nagel, discussing issues such as religious requirements, the morality of abortion, sexual conduct, and the killing of animals, once proposed that our views about these matters contain deeply personal and not fully communicable elements; and our respect for the basic moral personality of others should prevent us from imposing our views and compelling others to live lives shaped by ends that they are unable to share (Nagel, 1987). A later work, it is true, partially retracts the argument, but still maintains that whether or not a majority vote rightly settles an issue 'depends on whether the issue is one which it is reasonable to require everyone to put to decision by vote' (Nagel, 1991: 162). So the practice of majority rule runs up against some limit: majorities must not always defeat minorities' moral convictions.

Others, however, reject the very idea of limiting the scope of majorities in this way. As noted in the Introduction to this book, there are tough-minded proceduralists and (some) theorists of republican democracy who, for their different reasons, reject the idea that some things should be protectively removed from the agenda. From the proceduralist standpoint Robert Dahl contends that 'it would be wrong to limit the democratic process solely on the ground that it might be or is in fact employed to harm fundamental rights and interests', for to do so would be to subordinate the democratic process to a non-democratic process, and *that* process might be equally harmful (Dahl, 1989: 191). The republican standpoint, David Miller argues, places 'no limits on what sort of demand may be put forward in the political forum', for in a democratic republic 'the success of any particular demand will depend on how far it can be expressed in terms that are close to . . . the general political ethos of the community' (Miller, 1995a: 447).

It is the latter view that has particular force here, for in effect it trumps the liberals' appeal to equality by taking that notion in a different sense. Whatever the merits of Dworkin's or Nagel's conceptions, they rule out – or at least truncate – another compelling one: the deliberative or republican[1] conception of the equality of citizens as participants in democratic discourse. As a democrat, it might be argued, one is bound to give weight to a society's capacity to shape itself and its environment by the reasoned use of public powers; and no equality could be more important than enjoying equal access to that process of collective self-shaping. To lack it is to lack what a democrat must regard as essential to basic human dignity. It is to lack, in William Cobbett's phrase, 'the right of rights' (Waldron, 1997).

Encountering such views, on either side of the divide at issue here, one may well feel the pull of two plausible but apparently incompatible critical intuitions. On the one hand, to give near-complete authority to democratic processes is to commit oneself to inherently unpredictable future outcomes. We would not do so if we believed that they would be consistently destructive or otherwise appalling. If we believe that they would not be, then in order to make that judgement we must have in mind some evaluative parameters; and if we have those in mind, why should we not specify them in advance – as the liberals propose – as constitutional limits to what majorities can do? The other critical intuition tends in the opposite direction. If we think there are good moral reasons to have democracy rather than some other political system, then we are committed to give some moral weight to its outcomes for the reason that they *are* its outcomes; it must make some difference, surely, that the outcomes have been reached democratically rather than by military force or priestly divinations or inherited authority? But do we not undermine this very basic idea by offering decisive protections, against certain kinds of outcomes, in advance – as though it made no difference how they were reached? If some things are illegitimate for whatever reason they are done, then it makes no difference whether they are democratically determined or not.

This chapter makes no attempt to dislodge either of the above intuitions, which both appear immovable. Rather, acknowledging the appeal of both, it tries to advance a perspective which accommodates them. It outlines an idea of constitutional democracy in which protections for minorities are derived from the internal requirements of the majority principle itself, rather than from independently derived constraints which appeal to liberals but which democrats may see no reason to accept. Its claim is that democracy has a limited moral authority, the limit being set at the point at which defeated minorities would not be able to find compensation – in a particular sense to be stipulated below – for the moral losses that the majority's victory would cause them. It therefore rejects the view that democratic deliberation, even in an idealized form, is an entirely adequate response to the facts of severe moral disagreement, just as it rejects contrasting positions which effectively 'privatize' moral conflicts (Cooke, 1996) by denying democracy the authority to resolve them.

The line of thinking advanced here has at least an approximate classic antecedent, a passage in Locke's *Letter concerning Toleration* which has attracted much less attention than his more prominent arguments; and acknowledging this debt provides an opportunity to make some initial distinctions. Locke contrasts two different categories of loss or injury that states might impose on subjects:

> I would turn merchant upon the prince's command, because in case I should have ill success in trade, he is abundantly able to make up my loss some other way. If it be true, as he pretends, that he desires I should thrive and grow rich, he can set me up again when unsuccessful voyages have broke me. But this is not the case in the things that regard the life to come. If there I take a wrong course, if in that respect I am once undone, it is not in the magistrate's power to repair my loss, to ease my suffering, or to restore me in any measure, much less entirely, to a good estate. (Locke, 1983: 30)

Following Locke, the possibility of 'repair' is taken here as a crucial test as to what can and cannot be demanded. But the kind of 'repair' or compensation to be discussed here is not (except in a special case to be noted below) of the sort to be provided directly, as a kind of gift, by the 'prince' or state: rather, this argument is concerned with the distinction between losses which can or cannot be compensated for by the sufferer himself or herself, within the circumstances of a democratic state. The state is seen here, in other words, not (usually) as providing a quid pro quo for defeats, but as guaranteeing conditions under which individuals can make adjustments, in the context of their allocations of personal resources, for moral defeats of a public kind.[2] In cases in which they cannot – in cases, that is, in which the defeated would wholly lose the capacity to promote a certain good, or act from certain motives – the state must not impose defeats.

Second, this case insists more strongly than Locke does on a distinction between *compensation* and *consolation*. Locke lists 'repair my loss' and 'ease my suffering' as though they were equivalent, but surely this is not so (negligible though the difference is in the case that he is considering). Repairing a loss, defined here as compensation, is a matter of making a return in kind – that is, of substituting the same kind of good (or at least a portion or 'measure' of it) as the one that has been lost. Easing suffering, defined here as consolation, is a matter of offering a distraction from the loss suffered, by means of providing a different kind of good. The latter sets no sort of boundary at all to state action: states could provide (some measure of) consolation for any loss at all – such as the promise of burial with full military honours, or a posthumous medal.

Ordinary language, it must be admitted, does not always support this distinction: what is called a 'consolation prize' is sometimes a good of the same kind as the first prize, though smaller; and the activities that we describe as 'consoling' may or may not provide exactly the good that has been lost – it depends on circumstances. On the other hand, 'compensation' for such things as cruelties committed in wartime seems more like consolation, since the losses suffered cannot normally be made good; and in a legal context, what is generally called 'compensation' is generally a matter of replacing one good with another (i.e. a monetary one). But all the same, however stipulative the distinction made here, experience surely suggests the importance of the difference between getting the equivalent of what one has lost, and being distracted from the pain of having lost it.

Some versions of utilitarianism might find it hard to account for this distinction, if they require 'utility' to be a sufficiently undifferentiated good that losses can necessarily be made up by gains. But such versions of utilitarianism would have to surmount conceptual problems arising from 'contrastive' evaluative languages, in Charles Taylor's expression – languages which contain varied compelling norms that do not seem assimilable to any single standard (Taylor, 1982; see also Williams, 1981: 71–82). And they would also have to surmount evidence that as a matter of fact people resist attempts to translate their values into a single measure, becoming (understandably) abusive when asked what increase in personal consumption would buy off their concern for environmental standards, for example (Barry, 1995: 152–9).

Finally, Locke's case is directed at the legitimate capacities of states in general, and the limits to political authority as such. This discussion, however, concerns the democratic state. The distinction between compensable and uncompensable sacrifices, it is argued, has quite special force given the justifying claims of democracy, and the nature of democratic decisions, if viewed as recommended here, for it derives from the same basic considerations as democracy itself.

The idea of compensation would be entirely out of place in versions of democracy – including some of those discussed above – in which majority decisions are thought in some way to subsume the minority's view, as (for example) Rousseau implied in requiring minorities to change their minds. If we believed that the voting process somehow created or identified a common will, or that the outcome was the right answer, or a proxy for the right answer, or that number as such conferred legitimacy on majorities, then minorities would be no less represented in the outcome than majorities are. But the justification of majority rule defended above was not of that kind. It presented the majority principle as a device that (ideally viewed) leads participants to offer defensible and generalizable reasons for their proposals, to seek plausible evidence in support, and to understand and weigh the proposals, reasons and evidence of others. This does not allow the claim that the *electoral* outcome is improved, a claim that underrates the depth of political disagreement over what a 'better' outcome is, effectively obliterating the minority's view. It enables one to claim only that the outcomes in terms of public reason are improved: participants will have brought the most persuasive considerations to light, and the winning proposal will have been given its maximum chance to persuade. But all the same, if one respects people in their capacity as critical and reflective agents, with an interest in being persuaded by the best possible argument, that outcome is important enough to justify the process, and can do so without making untenable claims.

The case depends, as we saw, on making a distinction more firmly than theorists of democratic deliberation tend to do. When discussion leads eventually to a vote, it may seem natural to describe the outcome of the vote as the outcome of the discussion (Manin, 1987: 359; Benhabib, 1996: 69). But the outcome of a discussion, it was argued, is its actual epistemic product, as it were; whether it supports one conclusion rather than another is a judgement made *about* the outcome of the discussion, and it is open to participants to make this judgement differently, as, indeed, they generally do. This is not at all a subjectivist position. It is perfectly compatible with the claim that any serious discussion must have the discovery of truth as its regulative purpose, an implied purpose without which the activity makes no sense. But just because it is a regulative idea, it cannot be given institutional expression, or a physical location.

This gives rise to an important distinction. On the one hand, a truth-guided discussion has a 'subjectless' character (Popper, 1970: 57)[3] – that is, it aims in principle at discovering an adequate fit between evidence, argument and conclusion, regardless of who offers the evidence, who makes the argument, or who reaches the conclusion; and whatever we take 'adequacy' to mean, it cannot depend on whose minds, or how many minds, experience it. On the other hand, what institutions decide *does* depend inescapably on whose minds, and how many minds, entertain which beliefs. And perhaps the clearest case of all, in fact, is the institution of voting itself, which registers how many people hold what beliefs. That it registers facts in this way enables it to yield the unequivocal results that authoritative declarations – unlike discussions – must have. But for exactly the same reason, *its* outcome cannot be identified with the outcome of a *discussion*, for a process which is in principle subjectless cannot be resolved by applying a distributive criterion. What is right, regardless of what anyone thinks, cannot be established, obviously, by counting up how many people think what.

The consequence for the argument here is this. Disagreeing with the majority about what the outcome of public discussion has been, minorities have to accept policies supported by unpersuasive (to them) reasons, and to live their lives – for the time being – in a society that is shaped by reasons that are (to them) inferior to the reasons that they did find persuasive. Yet the importance of persuasion is a value that is basic to the whole procedure. If we did not think it important that people should be persuaded, we would lack the strongest reason for favouring majority rule as a political principle: its very point is, as it were, to maximize persuasiveness, by giving participants an incentive to justify their proposals on more broadly intelligible grounds than other decision rules do. And that is important, it was suggested above, because it takes seriously the fact of critical reasonableness, and the interest that people consequently have in the existence of a critical and informed public reason. Hence the difficulty: we might approve of democracy as an institution that maximizes the persuasiveness of public reasoning, but as an institution it provides that minorities are by definition unpersuaded.

It does not seem possible to correct for this, as some propose, by limiting the majority's right to pursue morally contestable objectives, so that minorities are protected from measures which they irreconcilably oppose. Ronald Dworkin, as was noted above, proposed that democratic institutions should confine majorities to the satisfaction of 'internal preferences' only – that is, preferences about the circumstances in which they wish to live their own lives – and deny them the capacity to enforce their 'external preferences', or preferences about how others should live. Joshua Cohen has proposed that democracies should deny majorities the power 'to prevent others from fulfilling such demands for reasons that they are compelled – by the lights of a view that commands their conviction – to regard as insufficient', because to do so would be to 'deny them standing as equal citizens' (Cohen, 1996: 103).[4] But such proposals (examined in somewhat more detail in the following chapters) only shift the burden rather than removing it. For in the course of protecting democratic minorities, they prevent majorities from seeking[5] a society shaped by the reasons that *they* find persuasive; and while that is not inherently worse[6] than denying the same benefit to minorities, it leads to a worse form of public decision-making – that is, to one in which there is no incentive to publicize and generalize one's reasoning. If democracy is to be approved of on those kinds of grounds, then it cannot accommodate a general prohibition against taking an interest in how other people live, or against evaluating – and hence, potentially, condemning – their reasons for doing so. It has to be a system in which ideas about right and wrong will clash, for unless it had or could have some effect on the participants' beliefs, it could not be given the sort of justification that was outlined above. Maximizing persuasiveness would be futile, after all, if everyone, being the prisoner of their own convictions, were beyond persuasion (Cohen, 1989: 24).

If, then, we cannot resolve the problem by constraining majorities in that way, it seems natural to turn to the idea of compensation for a solution. When the process of seeking a good necessarily denies it to some, one's first hopeful thought might be that the good may be available to them in some other way. The good in question in this case, however, is an intangible one, rather than an item of a distributable kind; it is the good of living a life in accordance with reasons that one finds persuasive. That in turn suggests that the relevant compensatory changes are to be made not by transfers from the winners to the defeated, but by the defeated themselves in conducting their own lives. What the winners owe to them are the conditions under which they can do that; they owe them self-restraint for the very reasons that legitimate their own victory.

The easiest case for this proposal is – to revert to Locke – that of religious difference, or at least, of some forms of religious difference. The passage from *A Letter concerning Toleration* quoted above makes the point that if an authority prevents some people from practising the religion they believe in, there is no compensation that the authority can provide if it turns out to be wrong. Not only is it too late, but the loss is incalculable, and the state inherently inapt to provide the good in question. But to this we can add the somewhat more generalizable point that the loss of the freedom to practise a particular faith, let alone the imposition of a practice that one believes to be false, is not something that one can satisfactorily adjust one's life to take account of. One must live as one must. There is the Marrano strategy of concealment (or the 'occasional conformity' of Locke's day), but one reason (among others) for rejecting that is that majorities are in no position to judge whether this amounts to a compensation, or only to a form of consolation, in the minority's own life. Religions differ greatly in their require-ments for outward or public observance, and outsiders are ill-equipped to understand how specific and compelling other people's imperatives can be in this domain. We cannot simply assume that what is possible in the private realm makes up for what is forbidden in the public.

Whether or not one can take the case of religious toleration as a model is disputed. Some Locke scholars warn against taking religious toleration as a prototype, for the reasons which bear specifically against imposed religious conformity cannot be assumed to justify other kinds of freedom (Dunn, 1990). Others, such as Rawls, seem inclined to do so, however (Rawls, 1995: xxiv–xxviii).[7] But 'salvation' is so distinctive and paramount a good that compensation for its loss is not merely unavailable but inconceivable. Is it unique in this respect, and the argument therefore ungeneralizable? Moreover, the case may have become too easy a one to be useful, given the modern Western disposition to regard it as unreasonable to impose practices on the unwilling, and thus to find a *suum cuique* solution virtually natural. To a certain extent, sexual preference may have migrated into the same space as denominational belief. In liberal achievements such as the famous 1957 Wolfenden Report in the United Kingdom, basic arguments for toleration, initially developed in a religious context, were successfully put to use in reforming the laws which had criminalized homosexual acts. But perhaps that merely makes the point over again: for here too 'to each his or her own' is available as a solution that is painless to (probably) most people.

For a harder case, which renders 'to each his or her own' manifestly problematic, one could hardly do better than turn to one of Nagel's remaining cases, that of abortion. A solution derived from the classic model of liberal toleration would amount simply to conferring victory on one side – that is, the side that has a principled attachment to the value of autonomy.[8] But the compensability model, while it may lead to the same result, relies on a different line of argument altogether in arriving at it. It would require us to compare the losses suffered on either side, if defeated. Both, if defeated, would suffer the circumstance that an evil was being done, but this is a loss against the possibility of which no protection is available: protecting me would strip you of your protection if we happened to disagree, and vice versa. On the other hand, an uncompensable loss would be suffered by women compelled by state power to give birth to and perhaps to bring up unwanted children on the grounds that they were required to do so by moral beliefs that they reject. Nothing could make up for the sense that one had been treated as an instrument of someone else's beliefs. Hence they would suffer not only the circumstance that legislation was (in their view) unjust – an ordinary risk in democracy – but also the loss of a life conducted according to their own beliefs. It could amount to a loss equivalent to being compelled to have an abortion against one's will. A pro-life advocate who suffered electoral defeat, on the other hand, would not lose the capacity to live according to his or her own beliefs, for there are many ways of combating what one takes to be evil – both private and public ways – which are alternatives to legislative prohibition. One can work for simplified adoption procedures, better child support, more effective education in birth control, and for other measures tending to make abortion decisions either less compelling or less common. These measures make the defeat compensable – that is, they give scope to action directed at the same goods and sustained by the same motives as the goods and motives which sustain anti-abortion legislation. On the basis of the compensation model, and if this application of the model is sound, freedom of choice should be constitutionally protected not by privileging autonomy (or privacy), nor on the basis of contested and ultimately metaphysical definitions of life and personhood, but because of the moral asymmetries involved in the choice between freedom and prohibition.

An unmasking suspicion that immediately arises is that abstract argument about political morality is being put to use in support of positions that liberals happen to regard as right, in terms of personal morality, anyway (Nagel, 1987; Barry, 1990). This suspicion is sometimes advanced on rather a priori grounds without anything like empirical support. Is it really supposed that there are no liberal Catholics whose personal morality forbids abortion but who on the basis of political morality would resist its criminalization?

But to meet this suspicion much more directly, let us turn to Nagel's final example. There must be many liberals, these days, who are vegetarians for reasons of personal moral principle rather than (or as well as) reasons of personal health. Were they to become a majority, they would be in a position to impose a general prohibition against meat-eating, and might seek to justify this on the grounds that adequate substitutes can be found in non-carnivorous diets. But this would be a superficial judgement on the vegetarians' part, resulting in consolation rather than compensation for the minority; for there are revered traditions regarding both the hunting and slaughter of animals, whole cultures based on their domestication, and elaborate cuisines (often closely connected with national or ethnic tradition) involving the preparation of meat.[9] So vegetarian liberals, if they happened to become a majority, should want to be constitutionally inhibited from imposing their beliefs, because those whom they thus defeated could not find compensation in terms of their own beliefs. Vegetarians, on the other hand, would not suffer symmetrically, for there are many ways other than legislative ones to further the good which they value.

It cannot be said, then, that the position merely registers pre-existing liberal commitments. Certainly it dovetails with some commitments shared by liberals – such as religious toleration, and the acceptance of sexual diversity – but it is gratuitous to take the commitment (or at least the considered commitment) to have preceded any argument at all. On other commitments there is scarcely a liberal consensus, and liberals who are, for example, morally opposed to abortion and morally committed to vegetarianism will find an obstacle to their beliefs in the political morality sketched here.

A second objection is that all the work here is being done not, as claimed, by any considerations about 'compensability', but by an idea of external preferences of a Dworkinian kind.[10] In the engagement outlined above, the pro-life advocates and the militant vegetarians were on the losing side; and it might seem that they lose because they are the parties who are trying to compel changes in others' behaviour. The pro-choice advocates do not want to compel anyone to have an abortion. The carnivores do not want to compel anyone to eat meat. So it may appear that the winners are simply those with the less exigent demands as to others' way of life. But this conclusion should be resisted, for several reasons.

First, we have to bear in mind not only the potential loss to be suffered by those whose lives the morally exigent want to change, but also the loss to be suffered by the exigent if they do not get their way. Being morally exigent does not deprive one of citizenship. One has the same entitlement as anyone else – that is, an entitlement to have one's capacity to make adjustments taken into account. What defeats the pro-life advocates and militant vegetarians is not the bare fact that they propose to change others' lives, but the further consideration that their own lives can be changed at less cost than those of others.

Second, there is no reason at all to confine the argument here to the case of external preferences to the exclusion of internal ones. If a majority pursued an internal preference, such as a desire to live in a public environment with certain congenial features, but this desire happened to be deeply offensive to a minority, then that fact should weigh just as much as if the majority's preference were directed towards changing the minority's life. That does not mean that the minority should have to win; it means that balancing issues of compensability should be brought into play.

Third, even though the cases discussed (borrowed from Nagel) happen to work out at the expense of the morally exigent, others do not seem inherently likely to. For example, public opinion in the United Kingdom strongly supports the abolition of foxhunting. A minority objects, casting the issue in terms of a conflict between urban and rural visions of life, and defending hunting on the grounds that it provides inter-class camaraderie, healthy outdoor exercise, local employment spin-offs, and pest control. If those benefits could be provided without the cruelties that the opponents deplore, there is no reason why the majority should not get its way. Nor is there any prima facie reason why democratic majorities should not get their way if they were convinced that pornography (or some form of it) was fundamentally objectionable, if they believed that standards of public decency were essential, or that some marriage practices (such as polygamy[11]) were wrong. How these issues should be settled would depend on a detailed examination of the asymmetries of loss involved, which will not be attempted here. I only want to point to the kind of argument that, in a democracy, is appropriate to their resolution, and to distinguish this from the claim that external preferences are automatically wrong, internal preferences automatically legitimate. The right test, surely, is not what kind of belief the majority has, but what kind of impact it has on minorities.

But we have not yet touched on the most serious objection to the argument. This is the complaint that in the account of compensability and non-compensability above, the pro-life and militant vegetarian positions were, quite simply, misdescribed, and their point missed. Those who are troubled by evils do not simply wish to live lives devoted to diminishing the evil. Their wish is that the evil should not exist; their desires are directed not at the kind of lives they want to lead, but at morally compelling outcomes. They acknowledge absolute imperatives, and regard the murder of fetuses, or of animals, as no more a matter of democratic negotiation than the murder of human beings themselves. And if by virtue of becoming majorities they acquired the power to prohibit murder, what possible considerations should stop them?

A political morality is a set of principles bearing on the claims that citizens can make upon one another through political institutions. It rests on reciprocity, and in considering what is required by reciprocity we necessarily rely on something resembling the 'veil of ignorance' test made famous by Rawls. Not knowing whether one would be the winner or the loser as a result of some arrangement, would one commit oneself to adopting it or not? Let us suppose that this is a good way for citizens to decide upon the claims that they can reciprocally make. One thing that it tells us is that we cannot assert a right to extinguish what we regard as evil. Your right would conflict with mine, if we disagreed about what was evil, and neither of us would know who was going to get their way. So if we end up with a prohibition against some evil, such as murder, that cannot be simply because murder is evil. It is because you and I, both having an interest in not being murdered, are prepared to adopt a general rule. That provides a first answer to the question. From the fact that something is called 'murder', and even properly so called by those who apply the term, it does not follow that it should be prohibited: for the basis of its prohibition is not its sheer evilness but a generalizable interest of citizens.

This approach, however, might backfire badly, as some have argued. True, one might admit, there cannot be such a thing as a right that evil should be extinguished. But majorities can use their democratic powers in order to extinguish what they regard as evil; and should not veil-of-ignorance arguments actually lead us to approve of this? Employing the rational self-interest test under a veil of ignorance, we would want to limit the losses that we would suffer as electorally defeated minorities, and thus want to insist on a scheme of rights. Although doing this would make sense in terms of anxieties about being in the minority, it would also, of course, inhibit our reach when we happened to be in the majority. And while these two risks might appear to cancel each other out, in fact the chance of being in the majority is better, since majorities are larger than minorities. This would seem to make the argument advanced above quite irrational: we would tend to lose more often than we would tend to gain by it; and it is hardly in our interest to propose an institution that works to our disadvantage more often, probably, than to our benefit (De Marneffe, 1994).[12]

Whether or not this objection works, however, would seem to depend very much on what is at issue. True, protecting oneself against the invasive aims of majorities would prevent one from carrying out one's aims as a member of a majority; but everything hinges on the sort of 'aims' that one has in mind. It is one thing to contemplate potential majorities who will favour a less generous cultural support policy than one would want, for example, or a tax regime that would be less than optimal from one's point of view. These may be risks that would be outweighed by the slightly greater chance of being in a majority, and thus of getting one's way. It is something else altogether to contemplate, say, a Shaker majority devoted to the enforcement of universal celibacy. The potential defeats to one's 'aims' are of a different order. And exactly the best way to discriminate would be to employ a compensation test. One would fear falling victim to majorities whose ambitions were, so to speak, total, in the sense that if publicly established they would rule out even the private pursuit of alternative preferences. One would therefore have to accept as reasonable a similar restriction on one's own ambitions if one happened to be in a majority oneself. Given the balance of considerations, the equilibrium point is neither unrestrained majoritarianism nor a form of liberalism in which majorities cannot satisfy any of their external preferences at all, but a constitutional democracy in which minorities are given protection against uncompensable defeats, and in which, subject to that restraint, majorities could advance all their aims, including moral ones.

The underlying point here concerns the asymmetry of gains and losses. If one is unable to get a prohibition imposed by means of electoral success, what one loses is the ability to advance one's ends by that particular use of public resources; one can still seek electoral support for less direct uses of public resources in support of one's aims, and one can adopt private strategies in support of them too. The inhibition that one suffers is thus compensable. But the same is not true, symmetrically, for those who might suffer from a legislative prohibition. Not only might that prohibition very well exclude other public means of pursuing one's aims, it might even preclude their private pursuit. For this reason, it is wrong to make the two kinds of losses morally symmetrical. One kind of loss, while it may well be experienced as serious, compels only a redirection of resources, while the other would require a drastic revision of one's life, for reasons that other people hold.

An especially hard case for this principle, however, is that of beliefs requiring both private and public expression. Where there is a degree of substitutability, the idea of compensation has weight as a basis for both empowering and inhibiting majorities: a defeat in the public realm is less than total if personal adjustments can compensate for it. But two groups may have mutually conflicting practices which both require public acknowledgement as well as personal behaviour. They may, for example, require the Sabbath to be observed on different days, or make other kinds of competing demands on the organization of social time or the disposition of public space. It may be impossible to avoid an uncompensable defeat for both.

If so, then on the present argument a majority victory would be unjustified. The best that the argument can do is to revert to Locke's own solution, and require the majority to compensate the minority, in effect, by accepting a compromise. If the majority imposed its will, it would, like Locke's unjust 'prince', require those subject to it to sustain an irremediable loss: but the loss would become a partially remediable one if the majority accepted a sort of transfer of political resources, adopting a solution in which the minority's interests as well as its own were reflected. Needless to say, to make this more concrete one would need to know a great deal more about the various commitments and costs at stake in particular circumstances (Jones, 1994a).[13]

To return, though, to our principal cases: the objection to the solution favoured here may take a further turn, since veil-of-ignorance strategies are far from universally compelling. One kind of objection is that at least some issues are effectively predetermined. If the participants in the thought-experiment are humans, then the liberties that emerge are going to be human liberties; and any protections that non-humans or unborn humans get will depend on the humans' goodwill. Should we not make the enterprise more inclusive? Perhaps we could bring representatives of non-human animals or of the unborn or of other potential beneficiaries into the picture. Alternatively, we could thicken the veil by denying people the knowledge of what kind of animal they are to be (Van de Veer, 1979), or whether they are to be born at all. While this no doubt magnifies the difficulties that some see even in the more modest Rawlsian version – if an unencumbered self bothers some critics, what about an unspecific one? – it seems an imaginative exercise in moral philosophy. But we have clearly stepped outside the framework of democratic theory. Veil-of-ignorance thinking is one sort of device, of contestable utility, by which citizens can reflect on the justice of the claims that they make upon one another as members of a self-governing community. In that context, it has the merit of enforcing reciprocity – that is, of testing the claims that you make on others against the claims that you are willing that others should make on you, as members of potential majorities and minorities, for example. If it also has the further merit of illuminating the non-reciprocal relations between humans and other animals, or between those who exist and those who may not, then that is a further merit that lies outside the model's democratic use.

But the possible line of objection goes much further. Among the many well-known issues that veil-of-ignorance approaches raise, one is especially relevant here: that of its grip. What is the importance of considerations drawn from what would follow if you did not know your views, when you *do* know your views, and they are near-absolute in their claims? (Miller, 1995a: 437–40). It is not that the considerations may not motivate; what motivates falls beyond the scope of thinking about what is right. Rather, some maintain, it is that they provide no *reason* to act as your deepest convictions dictate, when the veil lifts. But nothing in this section depends on being formulated in a veil-of-ignorance manner. We could dispense with the device, which, in this context, is simply one way of bringing out the inescapable fact that a democratic theory is going to distribute rights on the basis of some interest that citizens share.[14] To do otherwise, and to assign rights which cannot be justified in terms of reciprocity, is to abandon political equality. It is to adopt a stronger notion of equality which, within the model developed here, cannot be binding at the constitutional level, however attractive one may find it.

The case developed here may seem particularly vulnerable to conflicts of interpretation. In this it resembles other attempts at drawing lines, such as (notably) the so-called 'harm principle' offered by Mill (1910) in *On Liberty*. While we might all give general assent to the principle, one objection runs, once we try to apply it we quickly run out of clear cases and find that whether or not something is harmful is highly contestable (Horton, 1985).[15] Similarly, agreement on a ban against uncompensable losses might be merely formal, given the level of disagreement about what is compensable and what is not. Who interprets it, it might well be objected, is the key to what it will actually mean. Now the case developed above points in the direction of safeguards, to be given some form of constitutional protection, in the areas in which the threat of moral defeats is particularly likely; and unsurprisingly, these will correspond to some of the areas covered by liberal rights. We can acknowledge rights of this kind, and hand off their interpretation to courts; but eventually the political moment will arrive, in one forum or another, for rights may be hard to interpret and may conflict, and liberties may be important even though they fall through the net of rights which constitution-makers specify. So in addition to schemes of rights, we need a principle of interpretation.

If I claim that as a follower of Odin, I have a religious duty to wear a sword at all times, and that I suffer uncompensably as a result of laws against carrying dangerous weapons, do I get the protection of this theory? Or if we claim that it is essential to our culture and identity as Orangemen to celebrate the Battle of the Boyne by marching to Drumcree and back – thus outraging a Catholic community with a different feeling about what happened in 1690 – then does the theory confer a right on us? It seems impossible that uncompensability should be wholly self-defined, for anyone could then hold the majority hostage. But do we not then immediately face the equally unacceptable alternative, that majorities get to say what minorities should and should not suffer, thus undermining the whole position advanced here, in practice at least?

Initially it may seem tempting to cast about for a philosophical solution to the problem, a way of judging what is and is not essential to a person's life. On the one hand, a tradition of what is termed 'insider epistemology' (Fay, 1996: 9–29) would tell us that only the subject himself or herself can tell us what particular items of experience mean, from within the form or way of life or paradigm in which that person lives and which constitutes his or her self-understanding. On the other hand, T. M. Scanlon has pointed out that in assessing the relative urgency of preferences or needs we do as a matter of fact employ an outsider or objective standpoint, inquiring not just into subjective urgency but into reasons capable of translation into 'familiar general categories' (Scanlon, 1975: 660). But it is not either epistemology or moral philosophy that can provide the solution here. The problem arises within a conception of political morality, and considerations of political morality must provide an answer.

The idea advanced above was that political democracy is justified by its effects on public reason, in particular by the incentives that it gives to citizens to clarify and to generalize the appeal of their proposals and to bring to light evidence that may support them. The point of a majority vote, it was argued, is not to demonstrate that more people favour one set of proposals – a fact which simply cannot compete for normative space with any value – but to give participants an incentive to persuade more people, with the consequences just noted. If that is so, then the question at hand virtually answers itself. Ultimately, when the clear cases run out, it has to be majorities who assess what is essential and uncompensable and what is not: for if any group could make its claims impervious on demand, that would defeat the point by removing incentives to explain and persuade. The theory also tells us, however, that the articulation of minority claims is crucial to the process. It is important that the neo-Viking be given every opportunity to explain why Odin would not be satisfied by some more innocent item (perhaps a Swiss Army knife). It is important that the Orangeman be given every opportunity to explain why his culture and identity depend *essentially* on a provocative choice of route.[16] It is important that the foxhunter be given every opportunity to explain why all the pleasures of the hunt would vanish if it ended not in the death of a fox but in the ritual destruction of, say, a bag of kibbles. Democracy as justified above must provide these opportunities as a matter of course, but particularly if there are grounds for thinking that some groups have reasons which majorities are chronically likely to overlook; but to go beyond this would be to neutralize the case for democracy.

Like any similarly abstract theory, this one is open to uncertainties of interpretation at the level of its practical use. What it offers is a criterion, as it were, rather than a standard – that is, it tells us what kind of thing should count as a consideration, but it does not give us a way of measuring it that others can reliably replicate. However, the view advanced here does not seem inherently more accident-prone in this regard than others are. And it is no more than realistic in recognizing that any limits to political action depend on a sense of self-restraint on the part of those who hold power, without which all constitutional restraints amount, in the last resort, to paper. A democracy can have effective limits only if there is an ethos of self-restraint among a majority of its citizens. This chapter has suggested a principle on which this ethos should be based – that is, the principle that persuasion has its limits. To demand more than that is to exaggerate the role of political theory. In *On Liberty*, Mill advanced his own 'principle', which he said was 'entitled to govern absolutely the dealings of society with the individual' (Mill, 1910: 73). He was perfectly well aware that it was not up to him, but up to 'society', to apply this principle; that principles were hard to apply; that even when applied correctly they would sometimes underdetermine outcomes. Nevertheless, he believed that there was a point in putting forward considerations which ought to modify the use of power, hoping that, by influencing the ways in which issues came to be framed, they would exercise an effect on society's 'likings and dislikings'.

Notes

1. I believe Habermas is unusual in contrasting these two terms; if there are differences between them in current usage, they are not important for the argument here.
2. James Fishkin (1979: 30) also uses 'compensation' in this sense. But Fishkin speaks of compensating for damage to one's 'personal life plan', a category which includes non-moral commitments and excludes other-regarding beliefs; and damage to them can be 'compensated for' by substituting a different good altogether. In these respects the definition stipulated here is different.
3. The point does not seem to depend on accepting Popper's theory of knowledge. It holds true as a fact about discussion even if one adopts a more 'interpretive' view of knowledge and insists that all discussion takes place within a community. To be a discussion, in the unstrained sense of that word, it must still be 'subjectless' within that community – that is, claims cannot be accepted or discounted because of the identity of the person making them.
4. What Cohen terms the 'stringency' of others' moral views functions in a similar way to the uncompensability criterion outlined below, but the two ideas are different. Some stringent requirements are compensable, others not: see the text below. Non-stringent compensable losses would embrace ordinary market behaviour. An uncompensable non-stringent loss would be something like losing an object of sentimental value.
5. Dworkin (1977: 357–8) protests against being misunderstood as saying that majorities should not pursue external preferences, when his position is, rather, that they should be prevented (by constitutional rights) from getting their way. See Chapter 5 for a critical discussion.
6. Not inherently worse, that is, in a political democracy. Different

considerations might support the majority principle in smaller groups within the polity. For example, when it would be important, for the successful execution of some policy, that a majority of the group concerned should actively support it, that would be a reason for making its adoption depend on majority approval. Yet other considerations support the use of majority rule (rather than unanimity) by juries in criminal trials. I see no reason why justifications should be the same across the board.

7. See also Lukes (1989: 139): 'Liberalism was born out of religious conflict and the attempt to tame it.'
8. Nor can those who support that side claim (convincingly) that even those who do not value autonomy should accept the more libertarian position when values conflict: see Barry (1995: 88–93).
9. Some of these practices might, of course, be condemned on other grounds: see below for the case of foxhunting.
10. Or 'public-regarding' preferences, as Fishkin (1979: 27–8) phrases it.
11. Mill, of course, discusses this matter in *On Liberty* (Mill, 1910: 147–9). Since he resolves it on the narrow grounds that Utah was not yet an incorporated territory, we may assume that wider grounds would be less decisive against intervention: see Baum (1997).
12. See Vernon (1998) for some criticisms of De Marneffe's very sophisticated paper.
13. It should be noted that the argument of this book would not support resorting to compromise until such limiting cases were reached. That is because an earlier resort to compromise would work strongly against the deliberative case for majority rule set out in Chapter 2.
14. The following chapter returns to the issue of non-citizens.
15. Mill's argument is discussed in Chapter 5.
17. Assuming that the Northern Ireland Protestants count as a minority within the United Kingdom. If we view them as a local majority, then the considerations of 'social morality' noted in Chapter 5 come into play.

CHAPTER 5

How Rights Come In

The approach developed in the previous chapter establishes the protection of (some) individual interests by an indirect route, claiming that the very idea of political legitimacy puts limits to the scope of political decisions. And obviously, this approach can be questioned from the standpoint of an alternative and much more direct route. Why should we not just say that individuals have rights, regardless of the decision-making process of the political regime under which they happen to live? That view, after all, has enormous normative appeal, and corresponds to some of the more persuasive claims made in the history of political thought, as well as to intuitions which many will find compelling. Moreover, the very idea of rights reinforces the counter-proposal here. A right arises from an interest that is sufficiently important, regardless of other considerations of (say) a public interest kind (Raz, 1984). To decide that someone has a right is to remove the relevant interest from the process of weighing and balancing through which the public interest is established – it is to say that the interest is important enough that countervailing interests should not weigh against it. So if we are to talk of rights at all, do we not have to establish their proper domain before we consider modes of public decision-making? That is, I take it, the traditional liberal view: we are to establish the scope of rights before we set about establishing the modes of state activity; and the scheme of rights that we endorse will then set limits to, and also at least in part structure, the kind of state activity that then becomes permissible. Rights pre-define what politics can do. This traditional approach is so well entrenched, and (if observed) offers so strong a protection to the important interests of individuals, that it should not be lightly abandoned by anyone sympathetic to any of the liberal freedoms.

Moreover, doubts may well arise about the effectiveness of the protection argued for in the previous chapter, for two reasons at least. First, the agenda of democratic politics is limited, that chapter argued, because democracy rests on persuasion, and persuasion has a limited reach. But the interpretation of those limits, it had to be conceded, must itself – in the last resort – be democratic, for otherwise the justifying process is undermined. Thus the protection that individuals enjoy against majorities, it would seem, is ultimately in the majority's own gift, and therefore precarious.

Second, limits to the reach of democratic politics get their support from the reciprocal obligations among citizens, particularly their respect for each other's desire to live as they are persuaded is right; so no protection at all is extended to non-citizens, such as potential immigrants, citizens of less advantaged countries, the unborn, or non-human animals. For those who are worried by either of these two deficiencies in the argument, the direct appeal to rights will naturally be attractive. It will say that democratic majorities are among the things that we need protection against, not agents that should effectively define what protections we have; and it will provide a basis for arguing that at least some non-citizens deserve protection against the democratically concluded decisions that citizens make among themselves.

While recognizing these attractions, this chapter will make a case, nevertheless, against a rights-*based* approach. This is not at all because the argument dismisses rights – it will conclude with an argument for believing in them – but because it rejects the case for making rights fundamental. It rejects that case because, it will be argued, there is a more compelling way to secure them, one which builds on democratic premises themselves, rather than setting itself up as a rival to them, thus risking destruction at the hands of some of the most inescapable arguments that modern political theory has to offer – arguments connected with the very idea of political legitimacy, and with the basic morality that regulates political life.

Chapter 1 acknowledged the need for a basic justifying narrative which would pick out the background conditions assumed by the normative argument. No argument can be wholly self-supporting:

arguments reproduce assumptions; and background narratives are particularly condensed and efficient ways of making assumptions transparent. The 'basic justifying narrative' adopted above depicted a shift in the logic of political argument: rather than seeing politics as a way of registering truths that could be non-politically established, we should see it as a way of establishing standards which are binding because they have been politically determined, under conditions that confer privilege on no one. The importance of that way of setting the context, it was argued, is that it is binding upon anyone who is likely to deploy critical argument for any purpose, since it is implied in the very activity in which they are engaged.

Now the idea of 'rights' might perhaps have been introduced directly into the basic justifying narrative by the following attractively simple route. In that narrative, the need to establish agreed criteria of legitimacy arose from the contraction of authority and the exclusion of extra-political truth. But that same contraction, it could be argued, would lead also, and no less immediately, to rights. The background regime was one in which received truths governed not only public decisions but also the obligations and expectations that comprised the proper conduct of private life. When the background regime collapses, we need something to replace its hegemony in the private domain as well as its hegemony in public affairs. And the idea of rights does this for us, by offering equal and reciprocal obligations as a replacement for the extra-politically justified hierarchy of the background regime. What each person can reasonably expect depends on what he or she is prepared to extend to others. So we will be led – it might be argued – to a scheme of mutually acceptable expectations which could in turn generate a set of constitutionally protected rights. We do not need to arrive at rights by way of the conditions for self-government; we arrive at rights as soon as we sweep away social authorities who can treat other people's lives as means to their own ends. When we do that, individuals acquire a right to determine ends for themselves. Historically, moreover, it is hardly far-fetched to suppose that it was such a demand for personal self-determination, however formulated, that was itself part of the battery of demands that led to the contraction of pre-modern authority. So why should we not treat rights as basic? Let us consider two quite familiar objections, the first of which, I shall argue, fails, while the second carries weight.

One kind of objection to making rights basic arises from a set of problems concerning the indeterminacy of rights.[1] It is difficult to suppose that people could have a coherent and compatible set of rights before there existed a legitimate collective procedure for settling rights conflicts. This does not of course depend on accepting a literal-minded story about a state of nature and the making of a social contract. If the contractualist story is used, that is just a way of stating conceptual priorities, not chronological ones. But even taken as a conceptual claim, it is argued, the primacy of rights is impossible for the reason given: until there is a way of defining and assuring rights and resolving boundary problems between them, we do not know what rights we have; so rights cannot 'come first' – they are essentially derivative. This line of thinking may incline us in favour of a 'communitarian' position in which common interests, such as the maintenance of shared values, 'come first'. And there is a real risk that if we are led in this direction, we will deny rights their essential critical function. For while there are many things that rights are supposed to do, we could hardly think them very important unless they provided a way to resist and undermine the ethos of communal understanding, however arrived at, if and when it became oppressive.

But the arguments in support of this critique seem quite inconclusive, and raise many questions. First, there is a question about the very idea of a right. It may perhaps be true in the context of *legal* rights that one has no right to something unless there is some procedure to render one's claim both assured and determinate. In that context, there is a sense in which what I have a right to is the same as what is assured and determined by a court; though even here – as, for example, in Canadian jurisprudence, in which a court may determine that one has a right, but that it is 'reasonably' overridden[2] – there are reasons to query the claim. Outside that context, however, matters become even more unclear. Suppose there is no way for me, in an imaginary state of nature, to establish that I have a right (for example) to subsist despite someone else's rightful appropriation of the means of subsistence. Does it follow that I have no right to subsist? Perhaps, from the standpoint of moral theory, my claim is good, even if there happens to be no way publicly to declare its goodness. Or perhaps we have a case of the conflict of rights, rather than of the extinction of a right, and I have a right to subsist even though it conflicts with someone else's right to appropriate, so that my right is 'overridden'; it does not follow that my right is 'undermined', to borrow Charles Taylor's useful distinction (Taylor, 1967). What to do when rights conflict is a vexed question; but conflict does not extinguish the very existence of rights (Waldron, 1993: 202–34).

Second, we need to establish whether a right confers a protection only against certain kinds of impositions or burdens, or against all impositions or burdens. If it is the latter, then the state-of-nature hypothesis does indeed tell against the primacy of rights, because the fact of their non-compossibility prevents us from assuring rights-bearers that any claims protected by their rights will be immune from any contrary burden – just because other people's rights might impose one. But this is to place a needlessly stringent requirement on the theory of rights. That theory need only claim that rights confer protection against certain kinds of impositions, such as things imposed in the name of other people's interests. It need not claim that some rights will not have to be limited because they conflict with other rights. What will settle this matter, after all, is discussion about what rights *any* individual has – that is, discussion about what claims unassigned individuals have upon each other in general, rather than a decision about whether one particular person's interests should be preferred to another's, or whether a group's interests should be preferred to an individual's.

So communitarian objections of this kind are, at the least, not decisive. But that does not mean that the rights-based position survives, for there is a quite different objection to it. The problem that it faces, in the context of the present argument, is that it is insufficiently minimal to figure in a basic justifying narrative. The point of rights, to repeat, is that they foreclose upon political deliberation; they confirm the importance of some interest regardless of possible competing concerns. Liberals believe that there *are* interests that have that kind of importance, and they define them in a certain way. But, with any familiarity with recent critiques of liberalism, one can think of at least three important alternative points of view.

From the political right, one can imagine a 'Confucian' position, as it might be termed, which would place the stress upon obligations.[3] Undesirable and outmoded social hierarchies are not the only source of immediate obligations. Other and more attractive ones arise from the concrete circumstances of life: the mutual obligations of parents and children, of spouses, siblings and friends. To say that there is any individual interest which is so compelling that it predefines and limits all such concrete ties is to make a radical claim, and one that leads, it is maintained, to sadly atomistic consequences and to the destruction of community. The self is not in the first instance right-bearing. It is in the first instance 'encumbered' with affections and loyalties that together make up the core of its moral experience, and what we make of the practical force of these affections and loyalties is too complex and concrete a matter to be settled by, simply, ascribing a right to anyone, an ascription that short-circuits the consequentialist reasoning that acknowledgement of one's encumbered state requires.

From the political left, one can imagine a 'socialist' position which would find the rights argument not egalitarian enough (Nielsen, 1978). Rights provide that people should be treated equally in certain ways. But they do not ensure equally good lives, only equal entitlements, which might of course be deployed with very different degrees of success. Why should our aim not be to equalize actual life-chances by a variety of political and social measures, as opposed to providing standard moral or legal entitlements which are quite compatible with enormous material inequalities? This is at least as good a response to the moral collapse of privilege. If what is objectionable about privilege is that it causes inequalities, then the most egalitarian alternative to it would surely seem, at least prima facie, to be the best.

From the standpoint of a stronger democracy, one can imagine a 'republican' alternative, which, rather than placing resources at the disposition of individual judgement, would emphasize the resources of collective judgement (Pettit, 1997). The liberal idea of reciprocal interests, on such a view, is a poor substitute for the deeper reciprocities of dialogue, through which we come to understand ourselves and others differently, not just to affirm pre-existing wants or needs. Political society should be organized in such a way that it is transparent to public dialogue, individuals defining themselves not as bearing essential rights against one another, but as co-participants in a common enterprise, and as having the identities disclosed by the enterprise itself.

So there are several possible ethical responses to the collapse of privilege, and deciding between them would obviously be a matter of sustained and elaborate moral argument. The reason for the disanalogy with the political case is not hard to see. In that case, one solution, that of self-government, was unique, because its adoption was a clear precondition for the legitimacy of any subsequent decisions on matters of policy or substance. Nothing else *could* legitimate those decisions, except a politically unsustainable return to privilege. But in the ethical case, the 'rights' solution, like its 'Confucian', 'socialist' or 'republican' alternatives, requires an immediate substantive commitment. In the political case, we can arrive at substantive conclusions (it was argued) by a mediated series of steps made intelligible by the prior acceptance of a procedural value. But in the ethical case there seems to be no way to do this, for the good reason that here all the alternatives take us at once, without mediation, into contested domains which compel basic choices about life. In making rights basic, the liberal view draws attention to the importance of human agency, to the need to see people as originators of projects who therefore must have resources which enable them to give their lives a self-chosen shape and direction. The Confucian view tells us that our starting point is not self-reflection (Who am I?) but a given context of obligations (What reliance are others placing upon me?). The socialist view confronts us with human solidarity, as something over and above either personal entitlement or social particularity. The republican view stresses collective self-fashioning. It is impossible to discount the force of any of these visions; we are responsible agents, we are morally embedded, we acknowledge equality, and we are dialogical animals. Much of modern political and moral thought tries to find ways to accommodate these contrasting truths. One is entitled to find one solution compelling and to support it with critical argument; but there is a difference between finding a position compelling and making it compulsory. Within a 'basic justifying narrative' the rights argument has to take its chances; it cannot expect to write the story in its own way.

How, then, can rights come more firmly into the picture? If we want them to have some purchase in the face of the community's expectations or the prevailing ethos of value, what basis can they have? One proposed solution is to ground them in the requirements of democracy itself. This route is favoured by political theorists who want to ground liberty not in some pre-politically established scheme which precedes and controls what citizens deliberate about, but in that very process of deliberation. Two articles by Joshua Cohen explore this approach with both ingenuity and care (Cohen, 1989, 1998). It is quite clear, Cohen notes, that the requirements of democracy support Constant's 'liberties of the ancients' – that is, the various liberties that have to be protected if there is to be a democratic process at all, notably, freedom of political speech and association. What is harder to show is that 'liberties of the moderns' are also to be protected; for if democracy is the basic justifying principle, what is to protect personal freedoms if they get in the way of what the democratic process concludes? Cohen's discussions offer two different though not incompatible answers: an instrumental argument that focuses on non-political expression, and an intrinsic argument that takes religious freedom as the paradigm.

The instrumental argument builds upon the fact that political life is affected by more than political thoughts, and that it may be a legitimate political objective to want to influence non-political beliefs and attitudes as well as political ones. So the desire to change people's non-political attitudes, by means of expression that is not in the first instance political, may deserve protection for the same reason as does directly political speech.

> Forms of expression that do not address issues of policy may well bear on the formation of the interests, aims, and ideals that citizens bring to public deliberation. For this reason the deliberative conception supports protection for the full range of expression, regardless of the content. (Cohen, 1989: 30)

But this argument seems very double-edged (Vernon, 1998). Perhaps the first instance of politically relevant but not directly political attitudes that comes to mind is that of attitudes about gender. Much recent feminist thought concerns the ways in which 'the formation of interests, aims and ideals' of a non-political kind affects the political interests of women. And the example suggests that it is far from clear that this causal connection tends to support the case for freedom of expression. On the contrary, what it provides is one of the most compelling current reasons for censorship, on the grounds that pornography is part of a system that structures the interests, aims and ideals of women and men in such a way that the political equality of women is undermined. Moreover, if it is hard to make a case for non-political expression by extending the case for political expression, it would seem even harder to extend the case outside the realm of expression altogether so as to cover non-expressive freedoms too. It becomes even harder, in fact, to the extent that we recognize a political interest in personal attitudes and behaviour, an interest which would appear to recognize no natural limit, and would tend strongly to undermine the reservation of 'private' elements from politics.

The second article, however, traces a different and much closer connection between democratic deliberation and 'modern' liberties such as religious liberty. That connection is discerned in a 'principle of deliberative inclusion' (Cohen, 1998: 203). The principle tells us that laws and policies ought to be based on reasons that are generally acceptable – that is, the reasons offered in support of proposed laws and policies should not depend on contestable, comprehensive views of life that some accept but others do not. Now we know that some people hold religious beliefs that from their point of view are entirely compelling, and cannot be regarded as things that are optional or 'chosen'. So if we were to compel them to do things that violated their beliefs, we would not be treating them as deliberative equals, because we would not be offering them reasons that they could accept. The idea of religious liberty is supposed to follow. To deny people the right to practise the religion that they believe in is to neglect the 'stringency' with which religious beliefs impose themselves upon their adherents.

There is an interesting juxtaposition of arguments here. On the one hand, in order to enter the public and deliberative realm, one has to prescind from beliefs that, however deeply held, cannot be communicated to others, and offer reasons for one's proposals that can be accepted by people with other deeply held but publicly uncommunicable beliefs. When it comes to advocating laws or policies, communicability is king: if you can't say it, then it doesn't count. But when it comes to the question of the limits to law or policy, then *in*communicability is king: if you have 'stringent' but intensely personal beliefs, then they get protection. One view is Rousseau-like: only reasons pertaining to a general or shared interest are admissible to the public realm. The other is Locke-like: the public realm is limited by the fact that some reasons contain uncommunicable elements, and what one person finds convincing will leave another cold.

This could be entertained if there were a clear or even a workable separation between the domains of two sets of reasons, between (1) reasons for legislating or policy-making, and (2) reasons for limiting legislation or policy-making. The idea that we can do so could be defended on an assumption that religious liberty is a matter of securing entirely private practices which make no demands on the use of shared space, the disposition of public arrangements, or the tolerance of others. But the requirements of religion cannot be contained in this way, for claims may be made for the use of public space, for sabbatical and vacation arrangements, and for educational provisions, and religions may involve practices that others regard as cruel or oppressive. When any of these things happens, the theory seems to leave us in something of a bind. On the one hand, religious reasons do not give a group valid claims against others, because they cannot be publicly communicated, yet on the other hand the group does have claims against others, precisely on the grounds that it has strong but non-communicable beliefs.

The main objection, however, is that the 'argument from belief', as it is sometimes termed (Passmore, 1978), goes too far. For while it was the religious case that introduced that argument into the history of political thought, the argument itself is quite general in form. It states that we cannot help believing what the evidence leads us to believe. While coercion by others may change our voluntary actions by altering our will, belief is not something willed or voluntarily adopted. Thus its control is not something that falls under the scope of state power, and we must take others' beliefs as we find them. That is true of beliefs other than religious ones. Some people believe, on the basis of the evidence as they see it, that foxhunting is humane; that bullfighting is an essential part of national culture; that the corporal punishment of children is crucial to their upbringing; that arranged marriages are better than voluntary ones; that female infanticide falls within the scope of parental choice; that the mutilation of women improves their mental health. Some of these things evidently fall within the scope of public deliberation, and what should be done about them will depend on the evidence as the majority sees it; others raise basic issues of personal security of the kind to be discussed in what follows. But the fact that, in either case, minorities see things differently is, in itself, neither here nor there; and it is entirely unclear why, if a minority believes some practice to be wrong, it should be protected if it is supported by religious reasons but not otherwise.

The consideration of 'stringency' seems additional, and somewhat different. It is true that religions often impose requirements to which believers attach tremendous importance. This is a forward-looking consideration, which is to do with what will happen to them if they cannot do what their beliefs require, rather than a backward-looking consideration about how they came to have the beliefs in the first place. Perhaps religious belief is the paradigm case to which this argument applies; but again, it is not the only case.

For many people, stringent importance attaches to quite secular things, such as, for example, the maintenance of a local culture in which one's family has lived for generations, and which provides a powerful sense of community and self-respect. Maintaining this would give rise to a serious political demand; but we would not give automatic protection to, say, a fishing village or coalmining community made unviable by economic change, even if we would give a good deal of weight to its pleas for survival. So just why religious forms of stringency should be given automatic protection does not seem to be established, for if every stringent need had to be respected, the scope of democratic politics would shrink to next to nothing.

In the previous chapter a different line of inquiry was outlined, in terms of the compensability of losses. This, rather than either the argument from belief or the consideration of stringency as such, might encounter fewer difficulties in dealing with the religious case, which may more typically involve subjectively uncompensable losses than many other kinds of case. However, the present point is not to return to the defence of that position, but simply to argue that the case for deriving liberty from democracy, in terms of the requirements of deliberation, is not a clear success. Let us consider, then, an alternative approach.

As a parallel – not as a foundation – this approach draws on H. L. A. Hart's well-known argument in his article 'Are there any natural rights?' (Hart, 1955). In explaining the idea of a right, Hart draws a distinction between 'special' and 'general' rights. The former 'arise out of special transactions between individuals or out of some special relationship in which they stand to each other', and include, most obviously, the rights created by promises. By making promises, 'we alter the existing moral independence of the parties' freedom of choice in relation to some action' by conferring on one party the right to demand something of another. General rights, however, 'do not arise out of any special relationship or transaction', and consist in (valid) claims to be free of another's attempts to interfere with one's choices. Clearly, rights of the former kind depend on the existence of at least one right of the second kind – that is, a right to moral independence; for a special right amounts to a justified claim to limit the independence of action of another, and would make no sense unless a justification for limiting the other's freedom were required.

The constructive merit of Hart's argument lies in its showing that given some familiar and accepted practice, a background value can be demonstrated, as a necessary implication of that practice. It is something which the practice shows us to be – consciously or otherwise – committed to. A similarly structured argument is available here. The previous chapters developed a case for accepting that under suitable conditions democratic majorities are justified in making decisions that bear coercively upon minorities who dissent, thus compelling others to accept their judgement on contested issues. This is, obviously, a 'special' entitlement, arising from a series of activities performed against the background of certain institutional provisions. And as in the case of Hart's special rights, this special entitlement necessarily implies a general liberty. If the use of compulsion were not something requiring justification, there would be no need to give one; so the claim that majorities have this entitlement implies a general background prohibition against compulsorily substituting one's own judgement for another's. In the realm of social relations, each person must retain his or her own capacity to judge what is and is not a compensable loss to that person; and we know this because, if it were not so, there would be no need to give an account of the different requirements of political democracy, as, evidently, there is.

The difference between the political and the social realms is not, perhaps, at all surprising. Political morality takes as its subject the relationships between citizens as mediated by public institutions and the publicly sanctioned use of power. These relationships, and the obligations connected with them, have to be justified by considerations which bear upon the political community as a whole, as in the general argument, developed above, about the functions of majority rule. Social morality, however, takes as its subject the relations of unmediated reciprocity among co-citizens, and it is their interests, considered severally, that count, rather than considerations about the political needs of the community as a whole. So the conclusion that we arrive at is not an arbitrary one, but makes sense in terms of elementary differences between political and social interactions.

This argument is abstract in form, and the need for practical interpretation has to be acknowledged in several respects. First, although it was claimed that in social morality it is the subjective judgement of loss that counts, in reality what has to count is some standard assessment of what a subjectively uncompensable loss is.

This is simply because social relations are not intimate ones, in which one can learn about the actual subjective desires and judgements of each other person.[4] We have to make assumptions. Nevertheless, our standard assessments of what we owe others contain some attempt to understand what they will regard as an uncompensable loss. Personal security is the pre-eminent example. When, in a celebrated passage in chapter 5 of *On Liberty*, J. S. Mill says that we may seize a person who is about to step on to an unsafe bridge (Mill, 1910: 151–2), he is assuming an assessment of this kind; we are not substituting our judgement for the bridge-walker's, but simply assuming what the bridge-walker's subjective judgement would be, if he or she knew the facts. So this is still quite different from the political case, in which we are prepared, when necessary, to override express minority judgements: we try to reproduce, as well as we can, others' own conception of their needs, and base their entitlements upon this. In the social case, as Mill's example makes clear, once we know that the person has non-standard preferences, we should act on the basis of these.

Second, the requirements of social morality are potentially contestable, for a variety of reasons. It may not be clear what the standard case is; or some may have subjective needs that seem insignificant to others; or there may be agreement on what needs are, but disagreement over their priority. Certainly it would be naive to suppose that a social morality could be defined without disagreements. But all the same, there has to be a difference between politics, which is permanently contested, and the norms of social conduct, which are potentially contested. Only in reign-of-terror situations do we lose the ability to form comparatively stable expectations about our security against other citizens. These may or may not be termed 'rights'; they may be defined constitutionally, or by the slower track of a 'two-track' politics, or simply by culturally embedded conventions. But whatever form they take, their modification must be the work of something other than ordinary democratic decision.

Third, the requirements of political and social morality may conflict. There is no impermeable boundary between them. Suppose, within political morality, we establish a right of freedom of expression, as a way of giving weight to the principle of equality; and suppose, as is now the case, that some people form the view that freedom of expression damages women's right to personal security, the most basic right that social morality provides; then we will have to engage in the difficult processes of weighing and defining that such conflicts give rise to. But the fact that we cannot keep the two moralities separate does nothing to suggest that they are not distinct. They follow different logics. Political morality arises because some things – public institutions and processes – are no one's; social morality arises because some things – such as expectations of security – are everyone's. The criteria for deciding on their content, then, are very different.

So several kinds of qualifications have to be made in order to avoid simple-mindedness. Despite these, the argument shows that legitimate democratic authority is limited in two important ways. It is limited by the need to avoid public policies which impose losses upon minorities that are found uncompensable by external judgements. It is limited by the need to prohibit social practices found uncompensable by their victims. A political system that fails to meet either of these needs falls short to that extent of the justifying criteria of democracy. The first need is definitional; the second is implied.

These may seem to be much too slender grounds on which to base a theory of rights – especially when much more generous ones are available. The grounds employed here are duties arising, by implication, among co-citizens whose relations are governed by the requirements of political legitimacy. But some attractive theories of rights, needless to say, are both wider in their scope and less mediated in their approach. We need look no further, for one example, than Hart's discussion cited above. If there are rights, then there is a right of a kind once termed 'natural', which one enjoys not by virtue of a special status (such as citizenship) but as a person. To be sure, Hart's argument is both scrupulous and tentative. He acknowledges that there may be languages and cultures in which the idea of a right is inexpressible. He points out that even in our own experience, there are moral phenomena (such as the Ten Commandments) that do not generate rights. Moreover, the conditional nature of his case ('if there are rights, then . . . ') might conceivably confine its scope to co-citizens, for someone who believed that although there *are* rights, co-citizens are the only people who have any, could presumably evade the conclusion. But all of these hesitations are cast aside by more assertive theories which attach rights, unconditionally, to the simple fact of personhood or to one of its attributes, such as the possession of agency, or of inescapable needs. Many such strong theories are now on offer (Gewirth, 1978; Shue, 1980).

To those who are persuaded by any of these theories, the case above will be objectionable because it confers a privilege. It confines our obligations to those with whom we share political space, excluding those beyond it. That would be much less objectionable if all political societies were roughly equal in their advantages, or, if not roughly equal, at least were all above a threshold of well-being considered genuinely adequate. Then, if we believed that there were human rights, we might accept a world regime of citizen-based rights, in which each country took care of its own, as a reasonably effective way of ensuring that universal obligations were met. But in fact countries are very unequal in wealth, and many are below any acceptable threshold. So citizen-based rights serve in effect as guarantors of global inequality. As theorists of international justice have pointed out, the side of a certain political boundary on which one is born, or gets to reside, is the principal determinant of one's life-advantages (Barry, 1973a: 128–33; Beitz, 1979). Confining rights to co-citizens provides that those who live in poor countries have no right to a share of the wealth of rich countries, and also that they have no right to migrate to better-off countries in order to meet their needs, even when the better-off countries could afford to let them do so.

It is not a good argument to say that one recognizes this right on the part of non-citizens only by way of copying, or extrapolating from, the rights of co-citizens, and that because the non-citizen's right is derivative, then it is in some way deficient. Just possibly the factual claim here is true (though I shall suggest reasons for doubt in the Conclusion below). But even granting it, it would seem to be a version of the genetic fallacy to claim that the supposed consequence follows. How we get to learn something does not affect its validity. One might have learned arithmetic in a repressive elementary school, but it does not follow that its rules rest on physical violence. One might have learned about human beings by observing fellow Canadians or fellow Somalis or fellow Scots, but it does not follow that one's conclusions about what humans need, or what their agency requires, is inherently local in character. Once one has arrived at a sense of what a human life is like, it should be open to revision in the light of new experience, but it can hardly be declared false for the bare reason that its experiential basis is partial – for if that were so, we could never be said to have true beliefs about anything, all our experience being partial.

So it would be a mistake to try to undermine the idea of a human right in this way. And it seems quite unnecessary to try to undermine it. The argument above is entirely consistent with recognizing a full conception of human rights. It is consistent, too, with accepting that, among the various approaches to international justice and other distributive issues affecting non-citizens, the rights-based approach is best. But the argument developed here inserts a distinction between the possession and the enforcement of rights. It is one thing to acknowledge that x has a right against y, and something else to claim that some third party, z, can properly compel y to recognize it. Within the political process, what anyone can be compelled to do is governed by the considerations outlined in the chapters above. At the constitutional level, where the scope of compulsion is set, basic considerations of reciprocity apply.

One might fully acknowledge that humans, just as humans, have interests which are important enough to create duties, immediately, for others; and that these duties reach across political boundaries and attach to whoever is in a position to fulfil them, by personal or by political means. Those who acknowledge this will recognize a duty to promote the interests of the non-citizens in question, by whatever means is compatible with their other obligations, and to the extent required by their own interpretation of the duty's entailments. Since collective responses are far more effective than personal ones, the duty would lead principally to support for parties or organizations committed to internationally redistributive programmes. The form that they should take, the relative effectiveness of different approaches, the distribution of the costs – all these are matters which justice requires us to explore. But within the argument developed here, the rights of non-citizens do not have the constitutional (or equivalent) protection that co-citizens have against each other and against their government, as a condition of their government's legitimacy.

Observance of these rights can be compelled because they form part of a scheme of reciprocal obligation. To pursue aims within a democratic framework is to make use of publicly sustained decision-making institutions, and to rely on widespread habits of compliance. Those institutions and habits draw upon background assumptions and entailed limits that make them legitimate to those who have to accept the outcomes that arise. So those who are called on to respect these limits are required only to accept that they are entailed by practices in which they themselves are already engaged. They are not required (politically or legally speaking) to accept the outcome of moral argument wherever it goes; they are asked only to comprehend what they are doing and to accept the implications of that for the scope of their own conduct.

We revert, then, to a basic proposition of political morality: that compulsion has to be justified by principles that are implicit in the conduct of those on whom compulsion is used. It can hardly be denied, however much it is regretted, that this privileges co-citizens over non-citizens: a *political* morality can hardly avoid doing so. But political morality, while setting limits to the demands that one citizen can place upon another, does not tell us what ends should be pursued *in* politics: it provides a framework within which the choice among competing ends is argued out. And the case for the just treatment of non-citizens is so strong that one can hope it will succeed, politically, on its merits.

Notes

1. Here I draw from Charvet (1992) and Bellamy (1997) – without holding either author responsible for the composite argument that I outline.
2. Section 1 of the Canadian Charter of Rights and Freedoms provides that rights are subject 'to such reasonable limits prescribed by law as can be demonstrably justified in a free and democratic society'. Section 33 provides that a legislature may declare that a law may have force 'notwithstanding' the rights (including the 'fundamental freedoms' listed in Section 2) prescribed by the Charter. Pressing hard on the requirement of determinacy risks ruling Canada out of the realm of intelligible rights discourse.
3. A convenient brief statement is provided by Rosemont (1998). For another view of Confucianism, see Sen (1999).
4. It certainly seems doubtful that intimate relationships could survive if one party repeatedly made demands on grounds of uncompensability that the other found unreasonable. This is a reason to accept Aristotle's view that friendship involves similarity in judgement about the good: see Aristotle's *Ethics*, viii.3 (Aristotle, 1953: 233).

CHAPTER 6

The Scope of Liberty

Theories of liberalism present various and rival ways to justify the limitation of politics that they defend, and the justification developed in the previous chapter not only must be plausible, but must offer advantages that other approaches lack. There are two positions which inescapably demand attention, as one or other of them, in some form, is often taken to be a standard feature of liberalism. The first is the 'harm principle' which J. S. Mill is usually thought to have offered in *On Liberty*. The second, still recognizably Millian, though different,[1] is Ronald Dworkin's distinction between the 'internal' (or personal) preferences which democratic majorities may pursue and the 'external' preferences that are closed off by the imposition of rights. Both might be said, with caution,[2] to express a rejection of 'legal moralism', if that doctrine means that law should express the moral beliefs of the lawmaker. This chapter, however, defends the view that liberal democrats should not reject legal moralism. It does so by arguing, first, that the idea of a 'harm principle' does not capture what Mill was attempting in *On Liberty*, and, second, that Dworkin's category of 'external preferences' should not be ruled off the agenda of liberal democratic polities; it is too important to them.

Near the beginning of *On Liberty*, Mill makes his famous statement that

> the sole end for which mankind are warranted . . . in interfering with the liberty of action of any of their number,

is self-protection. That the only purpose for which power can be rightfully exercised over any member of a civilised community, is to prevent harm to others. His own good, either physical or moral, is not a sufficient warrant. (Mill, 1910: 72–3)

Since, in the immediately preceding sentence, Mill announces that his object is to assert a 'very simple principle', it would seem right to accept Joel Feinberg's coinage, 'the harm principle', as a label for what Mill is saying in the three sentences just quoted (Feinberg, 1973: 25). But what is he saying? Many commentators have taken the 'harm principle' to be a principle in the sense of a criterion that can be directly applied to actions in determining whether or not they fall within the state's jurisdiction. 'Harm', however, as has often been pointed out, is not a term well suited to functioning in this way. To refer to just one perceptive commentary, 'what is thought to be harmful depends on what is held to be valuable, and in so far as what is thought to be valuable is a matter of disagreement and controversy, so is what is conceived as harmful' (Horton, 1985: 115). It might seem that there are at least some clear cases, even if others are controversial; but even the clear cases are not clear enough. Bodily harm looks like a clear case, but what about the voluntary acceptance of ritual mutilation? Even if some cases are relatively clear, there is no reason to think that they are more important than some relatively unclear ones. And the desire for clarity has the effect of biasing the discussion to cases of physical harm, at the expense of all the other kinds of harm that people might plausibly be thought to suffer. 'Are we to believe that the real and deep moral differences that divide humanity will not be reflected in different conceptions of what is harmful? If this is what the liberal believes then liberalism is in bad trouble' (ibid.: 133).

To this we may add that Mill's own use of 'harm' in On Liberty apparently falls short of consistency. It would, for example, be of great importance to know whether or not to regard offensiveness as harmful, either because 'common sense' itself suggests that to be shocked and distressed by something is to be harmed by it (ibid.: 115), or, if this may not be quite so clearly the case, because this is one of the areas in which common sense yields different lessons to different people. But if we expect On Liberty to tell us, Mill leaves us very disappointed. On the one hand, there is the case of the offence caused by violating someone else's religious prohibitions, for example by eating pork, or permitting clergy to marry (Mill, 1910: 141–2). Mill offers this as an example of the way in which the public is tempted to 'invest its own preferences with the character of moral laws' and 'to extend the bounds of what may be called moral police, until it encroaches on the most unquestionably legitimate liberty of the individual'. Since preventing such offensive actions would violate a harm principle, presumably we should regard the actions in question as harmless. On the other hand, there is the case of public indecencies, of which he says that they are 'a violation of good manners, and, coming thus within the category of offences against others, may rightly be prohibited' (*ibid.*: 153). In neither case does Mill use the term 'harm'; but it would certainly be difficult to identify a meaning of the term that would discriminate one of these cases from the other. In both cases equally, distress is caused only because the sufferer holds certain views (Honderich, 1982), and in that way both cases equally are distinguished from the standard case of physical harm.

Moreover, the way in which Mill conducts his argument is perplexing if we are assuming a harm principle as a criterion of intervention or toleration. Immediately after the introductory section that announces the principle, Mill launches into *On Liberty*'s longest chapter, defending a freedom for thought and discussion that he calls 'absolute'. 'Harm' is nowhere mentioned. Mill's familiar argument is that free thought and discussion is an essential ingredient of human progress, and the only basis on which claims to knowledge can reputably be made. These goals are of overriding importance. It would be entirely consistent with this argument to admit that discussion, or even the bare knowledge that other people entertained certain thoughts without discussing them, *did* cause harm, in some strong sense that everyone would agree to be significant. Perhaps what is thought or said by some makes others incapable of self-respect, and hence of enjoying meaningful lives; or perhaps, to adopt W. B. Gallie's more fanciful example, the thrill of discussion leads people to neglect other important interests (Gallie, 1955–6: 179). But, since the freedom is held to be absolute, none of this would matter. So 'harm' seems to have nothing to do with what may be *On Liberty*'s most famous point. Of course, some *speech* (not 'discussion') causes harm, as when we incite an angry mob in front of a profiteer's house; but Mill detaches this issue cleanly from the argument of chapter 2 by classifying such words as 'acts' (Mill, 1910: 114).

The result of all this is to render the application of the supposed 'harm principle' not just indeterminate but more or less promiscuous. In keeping with Mill's own line of thinking in chapter 5, where, by discussing some difficult cases, he encourages the reader to participate in thinking through the essay's claims, we want to know how *On Liberty* bears upon live issues of intervention or toleration. What, for example, does it have to say about pornography? We find interpreters on both sides of the issue entirely convinced of Mill's support. Perhaps we can associate pornography, as a form of 'expression', with the 'expression of opinion' defended in chapter 2, in which case, of course, we could slam the door on all forms of censorship. Or, alternatively, but with the same effect, we could insist on a narrow construal of harm, and resist censorship because no evidence connects pornography with demonstrable harm in a sufficiently direct way. On the other hand, we might just as plausibly accept the offensiveness to women as at least equivalent to assaults on good 'manners', and thus approve of restricting pornography. Or we might – without any decisive opposition from the text – take 'harm' to embrace the more diffuse kinds of effects which diminish the life-chances of groups who suffer broadly from the effects of other groups' practices; for otherwise the position would be unable to accommodate other cases in which there are no direct victims, but which are usually criminalized (Vernon, 1996).

One way to cut through all this might be to insist that whatever 'harm' *might* mean, and admitting its vagueness, we should assume *On Liberty* to be assuming a narrow meaning. We might admit that the term could be stretched to cover any kind of negative effect, major or minor, directly or indirectly caused, of one person's or group's action upon another person or group. But then *On Liberty*, if advocating a harm principle, would be advocating something approaching a totalitarian state, which we know to have been the opposite of its purpose. So let us consistently take the term in its narrowest sense at every point, so that a libertarian purpose is achieved. This would of course mean that the harm principle would become incapable of lending any support to libertarian purposes, since its libertarian implications would simply have been predetermined, and the idea of harm would no longer have any independent weight. Moreover, that approach is clearly incompatible with Mill's own practice. In chapter 5 Mill discusses several cases of harm in which, he says, people consistently damage one another's interests, although, considering the balance of harms involved in intervention or toleration, there is no case for intervening. That he concludes against intervention is not to the present point, but that he regards them as cases of 'harm' certainly is. One of his examples is 'trade', in which, of course, people constantly suffer losses, often devastating ones, because others are more successful at promoting their interests. Another is the competitive examination for places in employment or institutions of advanced training, for here, too, one person's success means another's failure (Mill, 1910: 150). What is remarkable is that the losses suffered in both of these cases are not losses of things to which the loser can be said to have been entitled: I have no entitlement to success in my business, or to a place in law school. If I did, those who deprived me of it could be said to have harmed me, but not otherwise. Mill himself elsewhere subscribes to this position (*ibid.*: 50). Yet in *On Liberty*, where, according to the thesis at issue here, he should have wanted to take 'harm' in as narrow a sense as possible, he actually abandons the other (and better) view in order to extend the sense of the term. He *could* have arrived at a case for a market economy and for competitive examinations just by stipulating that neither causes harm; but in fact he arrives at his case by saying that although market transactions and competitive examinations indeed cause harm, more harm would be caused – given certain assumptions – by intervening in their operation.

In view of all this, might we not want to revisit the idea that Mill employs a 'harm principle' as a criterion? Let us go back to the original passage. First, the sentence setting out 'the sole end' which justifies intervention refers to the much broader end of social 'self-protection'. A society's capacity to protect itself would seem to be a good, though somewhat vague, thing (if it is a good society); it does not immediately suggest that society's good can somehow be broken down into discrete acts of harm (however defined) caused to its constituent individuals. The following sentence, however, does mention 'harm to others'. But perhaps we need to read it together with the next sentence: 'His [i.e. a citizen's] own good . . . is not a sufficient warrant.' In his essay on Bentham, Mill notes that some authors (like the subject of that essay) cannot bear to say a little more than they mean in one sentence even though they have an opportunity to correct it in the next (Mill, 1965: 286). No reader of *On Liberty* could place Mill himself in this atomistic and literal-minded class. And it is reasonable, I think, to take the two sentences together to mean something like this: 'Power can be used to defeat the will of individuals when the interests of others are concerned, but not when only their own interest is.' In other words, the point of those two sentences is basically an anti-paternalist one, more precise in excluding 'harm-to-oneself' arguments than in explaining what exactly it *in*cludes. If we want to know what Mill included, we might just as well revert to the social 'self-protection' of the previous sentence – rather than to 'harm' – and a good reason for doing that is that it gives us a rather more comprehensive perspective on the various recommendations of Mill's essay. For example, it accommodates integrally, without adaptation or stretching, the acceptance of an 'equitable' share in duties the neglect of which has no direct victims, such as smuggling or tax evasion; society can surely 'protect itself' against them, whether they turn out to count as 'harms' or not.

So we might wonder about the whole idea of a 'harm principle' reading of Mill, since it leads to indeterminacy and special pleading. An account of what Mill himself does in *On Liberty*, after all, is plainly much more complex than applying a simple criterion, even if he believes that the underlying principle – reduce harm – is a 'very simple' one. Even a sparse account of Mill's approach would require three elements. First, following J. C. Rees, one needs to give weight to the importance of rights (Rees, 1985: 173–4). Mill states that we can be called to account for conduct which 'consists in injuring the interests of one another; or rather certain interests, which . . . ought to be considered as rights' (Mill, 1910: 132). Harm or 'injury' is thus a subordinate notion here, coming into play only when we have established what a right is. Although natural rights have no place in the argument, Mill believes that rights can be given a utilitarian foundation: in *Utilitarianism*, he says that to have a right is 'to have something which society ought to defend me in the possession of'. If asked why society ought to do so, 'I can give . . . no other reason than general utility' (*ibid.*: 50). The right to freedom of thought and discussion, as defended in *On Liberty*, provides a very clear example: the 'general utility' of society, its capacity to progress and its very contact with reality, depends on this freedom. In *Utilitarianism* the example offered is basic personal security: we have a 'claim . . . on our fellow-citizens to join in making safe for us the very groundwork of our existence' (*ibid.*: 50).

But the sphere of rights does not exhaust the sphere of protection. Mill says that there are in fact two kinds of injury to others, one being 'encroachment on their rights', the other 'infliction on them of any loss or damage not justified by [one's] own rights' (*ibid.*: 135). A right, then, does two things. First, obviously, it defines and prohibits injuries of a certain kind; second, it licenses the right-holder to impose injuries of a certain kind – that is, those that are inseparable from the exercise of a right. So I have two kinds of liberty: there is a sphere in which I am protected from others' actions by direct considerations of general utility; and there is another sphere in which general utility applies less directly – that is, a category of acts that I can legitimately perform without having to surmount the right-based objections of others. We can think in terms of a core and a penumbra of liberty. In the core are actions deemed so valuable that they are protected by rights; in the penumbra are actions that are protected only because they are consequences of rights and inseparable from their exercise.

In neither of these cases, we may note, is the definition of 'harm' at issue. We need to know what general utility requires, how to express this in terms of rights, and how to assess the scope or reach of rights in the context of social interdependence. It is true that there may well be yet another level of assessment, one, that is, of right-indifference, as it may be termed. We may reach this level either because at some point the connection of an act with a right becomes too attenuated to count, or because two rights with competing requirements are in play. (The discussion of prostitution and gambling, in the last chapter of *On Liberty*, could be seen as an example of the latter.) Here, finally, we would have to define harm and weigh kinds of harm against each other. But that is hardly where the distinctiveness and originality of Mill's text lies, or where we should locate the centre of his argument.

If this approach has merit, Mill's theory – while still facing large issues in the course of its application – is at least not guilty of the vacuousness that so open-ended a criterion as 'harm' would seem to threaten. The questions move to a different and more productive area. But the cost of this is that it is opened to revisions which are potentially less liberal than Mill, or many of his readers, would want. 'Harm' becomes a residue of 'rights'. Rights depend on an interpretation of 'general utility'. And utility, in turn, is opened up to readings of a kind that Mill, as a passionate moralist, wished to insert into it. *On Liberty* takes its stand on 'utility in the largest sense, grounded on the permanent interests of man as a progressive being' (*ibid.*: 74). *Utilitarianism* gives us a vivid idea of what these interests are. Altruism and a sense of the common good are constantly encouraged and extended by 'civilisation' and 'political improvement'. 'The smallest germs of the feeling are laid hold of and nourished by the contagion of sympathy and the influences of education; and a complete web of corroborative association is woven round it.' He continues, 'In an improving state of the human mind, the influences are constantly on the increase, which tend to generate in each individual a feeling of unity with all the rest' (*ibid.*: 30). Remarkably, here and in his essay on Auguste Comte, Mill wholeheartedly endorses, as a moral project, the idea of a 'religion of humanity' as the binding ethos of progressive society. That idea, he says, 'has superabundantly shown the possibility of giving to the service of humanity . . . the psychological power and the social efficacy of a religion; making it take hold of human life, and colour all thought, feeling and action' (*ibid.*: 31). This is no longer the Lockean separation of church and state, obviously, but the alternative mode of secularism, noted in Chapter 1, in which society becomes a kind of church.[3]

Equally firmly, Mill rejects the authoritarian politics which, in Comte's hands, accompanied the religion of humanity, and there is no question of illiberal guilt by association. The principles of *On Liberty* put a stop to political Comteanism. But all the same, one wonders about the kind of liberalism that Mill opens the door to here. It is still individualistic, for the altruism is of the kind that recognizes the worth of others rather than submerging individuals in some collective project. But the 'individuals' who are recognized are, it seems, increasingly idealized. As progress occurs and civilization deepens, would we be concerned with the utility of protecting people as they are, or of people as they are becoming, might be, and should be, given the manifest superiority of the civilized state? As we have seen, that will determine what rights they have, and that in turn will determine what can be said to harm them.

None of this touches the ban on paternalism, which, it was suggested above, may be the central point of the 'simple principle' passage. It could remain Mill's point, even as 'civilization' advances, that personal improvement must still be principally a matter of self-improvement, that virtue must be assumed and not imposed, and even that some weight attaches to choices even if they are mistaken choices. But what could change, as civilization advances, is the level of harm-avoidance that one can be required to observe in relation to others, as a more refined and demanding sense of general utility affects in turn the rights that people ought to have. Of course, one might well approve of this refinement, or much of it anyway; but the nature of Mill's argument seems to have removed any inherent obstacle to the process of improvement. One might, in principle, be held to vanishingly higher standards of concern for others, and vanishingly higher standards of respectful conduct. For paternalism is one thing, legal moralism another, and the barriers which Mill sets against the former leave the latter an open field.

A better approach, drawing upon the previous chapters, would be to embrace the moralistic character of liberal democracy, but to develop limits to what otherwise would be a logic of potentially total control, against the liberal instincts of Mill himself. The criteria set out above seem more secure than the 'harm principle' in this respect. But before accepting this conclusion, we need a more complete statement of the case against legal moralism.

Dworkin's approach differs from Mill's by – among other differences – introducing a basic 'right to moral independence', an alternative formulation of the 'right to equal respect' which he has put to such impressive use. A 'right to moral independence' is a right to exercise one's own judgement in contested moral matters, and hence a right to do wrong – a right to do what someone else believes is wrong, or to do what one regards, oneself, as morally risky. An important example of the right, thus defined, again involves the issue of pornography (Dworkin, 1985). If governments or majorities proposed to ban or censor or restrict access to pornography on the sole ground that consuming it was morally wrong, then they would run up against the right to moral independence. (Dworkin's argument here does not address other grounds, nor, for his purposes, does it need to do so.) It is a right not to be coercively prevented on the grounds that one's tastes are declared by someone else to be unworthy or degraded. Of course, this right is perfectly compatible with the belief that some practices, such as the consumption of pornography, or at least of some forms of it, are unworthy or degraded; but as a component of *political* morality, the right only requires us to think that it is not a good thing that states should act on judgements of this kind, even if we agree that some of them, at least, are right.

We may contrast this with what we assume Mill's argument to make of the pornography issue – 'assume', because *On Liberty* gives us nothing explicit to go on. Recalling the three stages outlined above, we would first need to ask whether the production or consumption of pornography was directly protected by any right. The only plausible candidate would seem to be the right of free 'thought and discussion' defended in chapter 2 of Mill's essay, but a moment's thought rules this out: pornography is not 'discussion', or, if one is unwilling to settle the matter on semantic grounds, it would be hopeless to try to defend it in terms of the functions that Mill attributes to the forms of expression that he *does* defend. Second, we would need to ask whether pornography benefited in a second-order way from a covering right. Might it, for example, be protected by a privacy right, or, alternatively, might we need to protect it because we cannot adequately define the boundary that it shares with, say, adventurous artistic expression? This goes somewhere, but not all the way. Respect for privacy would eliminate certain invasive kinds of seizure, while boundary problems would doubtless protect some pornography, though surely not all of it. Third, we would need to look at the balance of harms; and given the increasingly sensitive calibrations of harmfulness that Mill predicts (and hopes for), it cannot be said that prohibition or censorship must be ruled out.

So by introducing a right to moral independence, Dworkin stops a slide which Mill's argument, as interpreted here, seems to permit or encourage. But a 'right to moral independence' can hardly be an absolute thing. It is no part of Dworkin's programme to license liberty of judgement in the case of acts causing harm to others. But if we need to contain his right within a harm principle, or something resembling it, then we just resurrect all of Mill's own problems, and we are no further ahead. Over a certain range, the 'right to moral independence' has an indisputable appeal to anyone inclined to dispute the identification of the state with a parent, or to anyone recognizing the contestability of (at least) some moral issues. But 'over what range?' is the question. If, as Dworkin himself points out (1985: 336–7), the area of 'harm' is inherently contestable, then the residual and complementary area of moral discretion is contestable too, and, in a democracy, subject to majority definition.

Dworkin believes, however, that we can put a stop to the majority's potential intrusiveness at an appropriate point. Majorities might seek to impose two kinds of preferences, he says (Dworkin, 1977, 1978). On the one hand, there are 'internal' preferences – that is, preferences about the kind of life they themselves would like to lead, and the kind of environment that they would like to lead it in. On the other hand, there are 'external' preferences – that is, preferences about the kind of life that they would like to see *others* lead. Majorities can use their political power to advance the first kind of preference, on a broadly or loosely utilitarian principle that numbers count in this sort of case. But when it comes to a question about which side is right on a contested moral issue, the majority view has no special merit. So majorities founded on the first kind of preference rightly have weight, while majorities founded on the second kind of preference do not. But unfortunately, real-world majorities typically express both; so we need to put in place a scheme of rights designed to protect outvoted minorities against the majority's belief about how they ought to live. The difference between internal and external preferences does not always lie in their effects. By voting for what they want for themselves, majorities might in some cases change minorities' lives just as much as they would if they were trying to accomplish that. What is crucial is the difference in the implied attitude, the former preference not implying, as the latter does, disrespect for the moral judgement of minorities.

But, Dworkin insists, we must not think that this means that democratic politics cannot be about moral principles. People 'will vote their external preferences; they will vote for legislators, for example, who share their own theories of political justice. How else should they decide for whom to vote?' (Dworkin, 1977: 358). The point concerns not how majorities vote (or should vote), but what it is that justifies giving weight to the majority's view. Suppose we take a utilitarian approach to justifying it (the only approach discussed in Dworkin's essay 'Liberalism' (1978)). Counting each person once in a utilitarian calculus, we will satisfy more people's preferences by satisfying the majority than by satisfying the minority. But this is true only if each person states his or her personal or internal preference, rather than altruistic ones. If he or she states a preference for improving the life of a friend, Sarah, then Sarah's preferences will be counted twice, unfairly, thus distorting the outcome of the calculus.

To the objection that *not* counting Sarah's friend's altruistic preference will eliminate the friend from the calculus, also unfairly, Dworkin replies that as far as the calculus goes, people can express any number of preferences, so the friend can express her personal preferences too. But to the extent that external preferences continue to skew the net result, the calculus will not be accurate.

The upshot of this is that the outcome of a democratic election will carry moral weight to the extent that it corresponds to the outcome of a non-skewed utilitarian calculus. But voters will inevitably mix such things as 'theories of justice' in with their pursuit of personal goods; and while the outcome will necessarily be right to the extent that it contains a true reflection of personal desires, it is a matter of chance whether or not it is right in the judgements that it contains about matters of justice, matters that cannot depend on how many people hold which view. By means of 'rights', as noted above, we predetermine or constrain the outcome in areas in which majorities are predictably likely to try to enforce their moralistic preferences.

But surely it is only their *bad* moralistic preferences that need to be constrained? No problem arises if their moralistic preferences coincide with the just outcomes that we want to secure, in part by means of a scheme of rights. One may wonder, then, why moralistic preferences as such pose a threat. They have to be warded off in order to secure the utilitarian benefits of democracy; but these benefits would seem to be decisively corrupted already by the co-presence of those judgements about justice that are held to be inseparable from democratic politics. The provision of rights, indeed, prevents some external preferences from being given effective expression, but it cannot prevent all of them, for, as Dworkin insists, some kinds of external preference are left over, for democratic publics to argue about, after some have been precluded by constitutional rights. If they were not, democratic publics would be in the impossible position of being encouraged to vote according to their moral purposes while being systematically prevented from realizing *any* of them.

We are left, then, with a somewhat questionable justifying argument for democracy. A utilitarian justification is offered, but does not work because the democratic process, as described, corrupts it. It would not corrupt it if rights took up the whole potential ground available to external preferences – but then the democratic process could not take place as described. There is the alternative justification that democratic majorities might sometimes hold views which coincide with what justice prescribes. This justification would carry weight if we were somewhat confident that the coincidence would be a frequent one, yet the very idea of rights amounts to a warning against the mistaken external preferences of majorities. We have to take the idea this way, I suggested, because in democracy (as opposed to utilitarianism) there is no reason to fear external preferences as such, only unjust ones.

None of this touches Dworkin's true and never-to-be-forgotten point that the degree of support that a just claim receives cannot change its moral weight, only its chances of success. The just claims of a disadvantaged minority have as much moral weight in a society which happens to have a selfish majority as in a society which has an altruistic one. Only a hopelessly confused or cynical relativism could confuse the majority's desires with justice. But with this we seem to have exhausted all the conventional paths of justification. The majority does not define what is right. It is not particularly likely to reach conclusions antecedently defined to be right. It is not able to give most people what they want, in the sense that counts for a utilitarian, because politics corrupts the aggregation of personal preferences.

So what does justify majority rule? On Dworkin's argument, majority rule has weight only in a realm of preference satisfaction, alongside but distinct from decisions about justice, made by 'officials' (such as legislators or judges), with whose judgements majorities may possibly agree, although whether or not they do so does not seem to matter. But this is unworkable for at least two reasons.

First, we cannot thus separate preference satisfaction from justice: not because we cannot distinguish between the net effects of the two – let us accept that we can – but because the two are much too highly interdependent. The officials cannot conduct their task of justice-seeking if they also have to accommodate preference-satisfaction, unless they make a compromise according to some as yet unknown formula. If a majority wants to live in a society in which, say, sexual relations are decorous, while a minority claims that its self-respect depends on public expressiveness, the officials have to decide between the two positions, and whatever their decision they cannot be said to be accommodating both.

Second, it just cannot be the case, in a democracy, that it is an indifferent matter whether power-holders agree with popular majorities or do not. That would nullify the difference between authoritarian regimes in which officials occasionally solicit the people's views, and democratic regimes in which officials are essentially the servants of a process. In favouring the second, we might seem to be veering back in the direction of the view which

Dworkin properly rejects – that is, the view that the outcomes of the democratic process acquire rightness. As we have seen, however, there is a way of avoiding this conclusion. We can give weight to the outcomes not on the grounds that they are right – grounds that inevitably offend some among the various rival rightness-claimants – but on the grounds that how they were reached maximized everyone's access to relevant evidence and argumentation. As we have also seen, that may be the only way to give force to Dworkin's value of 'equal respect'. We can provide the conditions under which everyone has the best possible chance of getting access to the body of facts and principles that are relevant to their decision. Once they have made their decision, however, there simply is no meaningful way in which we can be said to observe equality among them. Although nothing much hinges on the use of a word, it is in this regard that the term 'external preferences' has the potential to mislead:[4] personal preferences can, of course, be given equal weight, but it is wrong to suppose that beliefs about justice can be analogously treated. If I believe that *a* is *b*, while you believe that *a* is *not-b*, in what sense can an adjudication between our views be *equal*? The adjudicator can of course be required to be unbiased, but if he or she finds that the truth lies wholly or even principally on my side or yours, in what further sense has he or she treated us equally? Treating people equally as moral agents can only mean giving equal consideration to their reasons, not equal weight to their conclusions.

But although it makes no sense to say that their reasons are equal, it remains true that they are, equally, reasoning agents, and it is a hallmark of both liberalism and democracy to take account of that fact. In the manner outlined in the previous chapter, we can do so by recognizing that the outvoted continue (normally) to hold the reasons which motivated their vote, and must continue to live their lives in an environment shaped by the reasons that they reject. Proposals for legislation or policy should give weight to this, and the need to do so acts as a limit to what majorities should propose to do. Rather than constraining the role of 'external preferences' in democracy, therefore, it would be better to embrace 'legal moralism', so that the limits to one person's moral claims upon another can be explicitly addressed and recognized.

Recognizing democracy as a site of moral confrontations allows us not only to investigate its limits, but also to acknowledge its foundations. *On Liberty* treats democracy as a fact, a background condition against which the topic of liberty must be set, rather than as a value requiring defence. (*On Representative Government*, of course, says more.) In 'Liberalism' and elsewhere, Dworkin discusses a utilitarian defence of democracy, although, it was claimed above, its utilitarian credentials are highly compromised, given that democratic citizens persistently stray so far from the personal preference model. In Chapter 2, however, a defence more congenial to moral conflict was put forward. We should value democracy, it was argued, because it exposes our convictions to the reasoning of others and to the evidence that others' reasoning unearths. That case bears upon convictions of all kinds, but its relevance in the case of moral convictions – as opposed to, say, purely value-free theoretical ones – is especially acute. No doubt all our convictions would benefit from the critique of others; but that in itself is a reason to take philosophy courses rather than to subscribe to democracy. We have a reason to subscribe to democracy because some of our convictions bear upon how we should behave to others and how others should behave to others and to us. If we are conscientious, we will want such convictions to take account of how others see things, and so we will want institutions which promote that condition, or which promote it better than alternative arrangements can. Above, it was argued that this is the only viable case for majoritarianism; and evidently that case would be devastated, or at least trivialized, if majorities and minorities did not form around the most crucially relevant reasons – that is, moral ones.

The case rests on the reasons for approving of democracy. If principles describable as 'liberal' emerge from it, that is because the reasons for approving of democracy are self-limiting – that is, their own logic points to stopping-places, or to places beyond which the reasons run out. No special or additional set of reasons termed 'liberal' has been invoked. The problem that we have been considering is that of finding justifiable ways in which a society can manage the task of self-government that it confronts, and not that of finding ways of satisfying some list of requirements ('autonomy', 'self-realization', etc.) that is held to comprise a liberal view of life. For that reason, while legal moralism is embraced, another view, the idea of liberal 'perfectionism', is rejected.

'Perfectionism', in its political sense, must refer to a set of beliefs which have in common the proposition that institutions ought to have as their object the perfecting or improving of those who live in them or with them. *Liberal* perfectionism must be the belief that liberal political principles entail the creation of institutions which are justified by their (predicted) capacity to perfect or improve people, according to the standards set by beliefs termed 'liberal'. This view of liberalism is developed largely as a critique of 'neutralist' approaches which claim that liberalism can accommodate the diversity of belief in modern societies only by refraining from promoting one idea of perfection at another's expense. And certainly there is a good deal in the perfectionist critique of this claim that is congenial to the position developed here.

For example, it certainly seems right – in the light of the argument of previous chapters – that some ways of defending neutralism should be opened to basic questioning. In particular, 'perfectionist' critics such as Joseph Raz (1986) and William Galston (1991) are right to question the idea that in liberal polities a sort of 'epistemic abstinence' (Raz, 1990) must be practised – that is, that political actors are not to put forward their full views, but can advance only those views which fall within a range that other actors can accept.[5] Against this, Galston develops a defence of democracy as full dialogue, in which participants do what they can to explain themselves and to persuade others to change their minds. Not only is dialogue of that kind consistent with the view developed here, it is required by the basic defence of democracy offered in Chapters 2 and 3. Only under conditions of full dialogue does the logic of disclosure take effect, and if dialogue were less than full, it would be hard to see what merit the democratic process could have. There are, as we saw, some reasons of political morality which would lead us to exercise restraint in the kinds of laws or policies that we advanced; but to make these restraints epistemic – rather than moral – seems, for the reason just given, self-defeating. Likewise, it seems self-defeating to defend neutralism by giving overall priority to one value, that of negative freedom, for that too would defeat the purpose of democratic discourse, by pre-establishing so many of its potential outcomes.

Other lines of criticism, however, seem rather wide of the relevant mark, in that what they show is that liberalism has to be a moral position, not that it ought to be a perfectionist one. That it is a moral position has never been in doubt, and neutralist liberals do not offer the claim that the principles of neutrality must themselves be neutrally justified, a claim that would lead political theory in a rapid downward spiral. Clearly, one can hold views about how it is right to treat other people without necessarily holding views about how other people ought to be (MacCormick, 1982: 19–20). Or perhaps the term 'perfectionism' is to be stretched to include any belief in rules of conduct and any project to teach, promote and enforce them; but that would no longer be the perfectionism – the aim 'to maximize the achievement of human excellence' (Rawls, 1971: 325) – that neutralists reject.

But, it is sometimes argued, there *are* specifically liberal virtues, so that liberalism amounts to a perfectionist project in the relevant sense (Galston, 1991: 213–37). Galston is particularly clear and explicit in listing the virtues which, in his view, are instrumental to a liberal society, economy and polity, and the virtues that liberals, he believes, attach intrinsic value to. Reflection on his list, however, casts doubt on the argumentative role that it is meant to play. Many of the virtues, such as tolerance, moderation and patience, are of what we might call the 'procedural' sort, or, following Alasdair MacIntyre, the 'secondary' sort (MacIntyre, 1967: 24–5). MacIntyre usefully distinguishes between 'primary' virtues 'which are directly related to the goals which men pursue as the ends of their life', and secondary virtues which 'concern the way in which we should go about our projects; their cultivation will not assist us in discovering upon which projects we ought to be engaged'. We could not, for example, place patience or tolerance among the 'ends' of life in MacIntyre's sense, for to be patient we would already have to have other goals, and to be tolerant we would already have to disapprove of something. So these are not virtues of the sort that neutralists need deny being in favour of.

Others, particularly perhaps the economy-related virtues, while sometimes falling into the 'primary' category, simply seem contentious. There is absolutely no reason why 'the work ethic' (Galston, 1991: 223) should not be challenged and overturned within the framework of a liberal democracy. It is in fact a good example of exactly the kind of far-reaching topic, with general implications, that would be the subject of contestation in a society reflecting publicly on its own basic institutions and way of life. The same goes for the (alleged) virtue of being adaptable to technological change (*ibid.*: 223–4); it would seem, on the face of it, absolutely desirable that there should be democratic scrutiny of the limits of adaptability. Nothing rules out a neo-Luddite movement (or a neo-Thomist movement promoting leisure as the basis of culture). Outside the range of economic virtues, it is certainly questionable whether belief in rational self-direction and the flowering of individuality are beliefs essential to liberal democracy; for a political system which gives weight to the ideals that people actually do have will try to accommodate traditional ways of life when these are important to people.

Yet other virtues on the list look more like features of any non-tyrannical society than features of, specifically, liberalism. Is the acceptance of diversity (*ibid.*: 222) an essentially liberal practice? A liberal society, it is true, puts obstacles in the path of doctrines (such as some religious ones) which require 'control over the totality of individual life, including the formative social and political environment' (*ibid.*: 277). But the only society which would *not* set obstacles to one's views, if they were of that kind, would be a theocracy in which one happened, luckily, to be on the winning side. Here 'liberalism', it seems, is being made to do much of the work of 'politics'. One gets civil war, not politics, when rival groups demand exclusive total control, and it seems unnecessary to say that *liberal* politics places obstacles in the path of militant theocrats – for *politics* does.

Perfectionist liberalisms like Galston's, or Mill's in chapter 3 of *On Liberty*, are best seen as trends of thinking that appear in various national or historical contexts *within* liberal democratic politics; they are poorly suited to defining what a liberal democracy is. Mill himself contextualizes his plea for 'individuality': 'In this age, the mere example of non-conformity, the mere refusal to bend the knee to custom, is itself a service. . . . That so few now dare to be eccentric marks the chief danger of the time' (Mill, 1910: 124–5). It is not impossible that in other 'ages' the level of nonconformity might be at least adequate, and that the lack of some other good might constitute 'the chief danger'.

Notes

1. One interesting difference is Mill's rejection of the 'likings and dislikings' of majorities (Mill, 1910: 70), as compared with Dworkin's acceptance of the majority's internal preferences.
2. 'With caution', because as H. L. A. Hart (1963: 1–4) pointed out, there are many different possible questions about the relation between law and morality.
3. Elsewhere I explore a contrast between Lockean and Millian liberalisms (Vernon, 1997).
4. Barry (1990: 51–2) offers somewhat different objections.
5. This is an abbreviated statement of a range of positions developed by Galston (1991: 103–11).

CHAPTER 7

On Disagreement

The earlier chapters have developed the idea of a political morality, finding its origins in the basic conditions of self-government, its content in the idea of public reason, and its limits in the notion of uncompensable harm. The outcome, it was argued, is a theory of liberal democracy which, however, is critical of both liberal and democratic theories that enjoy currency today. But the very idea of a political morality, in the sense assumed above, is contestable. It is an idea that claims to be useful in contexts of widespread moral disagreement, in which no other general basis for political association exists, or, at least, can be sufficiently relied upon. Typically, then, a democratic political morality will coexist with other views, including views which also have moral weight, that are less widely shared. The point of the political morality is, of course, to govern what people can properly *do* about their other moral beliefs, rather than to change those beliefs themselves, and so it does not challenge those beliefs directly. In this respect it follows the model of 'toleration'. Nevertheless, one can hardly regard the resulting situation as unproblematic. Can two sets of beliefs, both making moral claims, *simply* coexist? As Ronald Dworkin notes, the idea

> seems to ask us to become, in and for politics, people we cannot recognize as ourselves, special political creatures wholly different from ordinary people who decide for themselves, in their ordinary lives, what to be and what to praise and whom to love. (Dworkin, 1990: 15)

The theory proposed here offers to explain how this is possible, as well as giving some guidance as to what is to be done when the two sets of claims conflict. But we must take note of and respond to some of the important objections to the 'two moralities' thesis. Let us consider two opposed but complementary objections that, if successful, would be particularly damaging. The first is the view that no political morality can take adequate account of the depth and pervasiveness of 'difference' in the beliefs and ways of life that people value, and will inevitably be hegemonic, privileging some ways of life and marginalizing others. The second, diametrically opposed to the first, is that instead of separating a political morality from other moral beliefs we should have a rational and deliberative politics in which the holders of rival moral views seek dialogue and consensus, so that the terms on which politics is conducted are themselves politically set, not pre-politically set in a sort of meta-constitutional way. Finally, this chapter argues for thinking about difference in terms of a theory of *political* disagreement, one that focuses on the asymmetries of political conflict, rather than a *general* theory of disagreement, whether postmodern *or* rationalist.

In addition to the evils of distributive injustice, the evils of non- or misrecognition have attracted much recent attention. These are evils, as Charles Taylor and others have pointed out, that survive even the honest and scrupulous application of individual rights, for they are harms done to particularist features of the self rather than those universal features which schemes of rights typically protect (Taylor, 1994). To recognize or be recognized is no doubt a many-faceted event, but at a minimum to be recognized is to be understood as having a perspective of one's own, which makes it inappropriate that one should be merely subsumed within someone else's. One is a subject – and a subject with a particular kind of character – not an object to be summed up in terms of someone else's view of life. Experience and intuition both suggest the force of this point; or, if one wants a theory, there are various sources of philosophical anti-universalism, ranging from Herder, to whom Taylor appeals, to the postmodern points of reference favoured by Iris Marion Young. But however, exactly, the position is elaborated, it will suggest that claims to universal validity are perilous, and always open to subversion by the 'differences' that they exclude. And the idea of a political morality is a prime target for subversion of this kind, claiming as it does to overlie differences in a generally justifiable and non-prejudicial way. It is an attempt to explain why and on what basis public institutions *are* 'public', as opposed to instruments of someone's hegemony.

The appeal to postmodern sources, such as the work of Jacques Derrida, is, however, curiously double-edged, or even, one might think, self-defeating. It confers the prestige of a stylish and inventive mind on the theory of 'difference', but with results that are distracting at best and hopeless at worst. It is not, indeed, simply wrong to suppose that Derrida's complicated idea of *différance* has something in common with 'difference' in its social and political sense. Against a view that the world is somehow ordered in such a way that things (such as groups) belong to stable categories objectively assigned, 'difference', Young writes, 'names both the play of concrete events and the shifting differentiation on which signification depends. Reason, discourse, is always already inserted in a plural, heterogeneous world that outruns totalizing comprehension.' This totalizing comprehension, termed 'the logic of identity', always 'flees from the sensuous particularity, with its ambiguities', whereas the idea of difference embraces these features of a diverse and complex society (Young, 1990: 98). So Derridean 'textuality', the recognition of the inherent instability of a text and its resistance to a privileged reading, finds its counterpart in a non-oppressive politics which refuses to expel or marginalize what does not fit into standard, hegemonic conceptions of things (*ibid.*: 102).

But in a Derridean view, first of all, no particular importance seems to attach to *group* difference. Unlike diversity theories such as Herder's, which attach so much importance to cultural and linguistic differentiation, Derrida's theory may not lend itself to any clear line between communications across languages and communications *within* a language (Derrida, 1974: lxxxvii). If anything, the view would seem to point towards a radical individualism, perhaps too radical to be entirely accommodated by saving remarks about the need for groups to be sensitive to internal difference. Why, one might ask, give prominence to groups at all – let alone giving them formal political presence – in the context of a theory which seems to leave lines of demarcation quite indeterminate? There is at least a lack of comfortable fit between postmodern schemelessness and the listing of targeted groups that multiculturalist law and policy require.

Second, the theory seems to be – for want of a better word – too cognitive, in the sense that it bears upon how some groups might understand or fail to understand the beliefs of others; how large or powerful groups will fail to understand marginalized ones, for example, or whether marginalized groups will manage to achieve enough mutual understanding to be 'together in difference'. Those sorts of questions are primary when differences are above all *cultural* – when, that is, societies are riven by deep differences which flow into basic ways of living and thinking. But are they primary when the paradigm cases are differences of *identity*? While the two are often confused, it is surely very important to distinguish between group memberships which spring from different ways of life and group memberships which spring from whom it is that people want to identify with. A century ago, as has plausibly been argued, the United States was a society with enormous cultural diversity combined with a predominant desire to identify with America: now it is a much more culturally homogeneous society which is characterized, however, by the assertion of multiple identifications (Appiah, 1997). These do not have anything decisive to do with 'difference' in the cultural sense, and certainly do not mirror differences in ways of life; they are built on the fact that (some) groups entertain separate (not necessarily different) ambitions, and these would not have to be undermined even if difference approached the vanishing point.

But third, and most important, the image of 'textuality' is just massively wrong from a political point of view. The Derridean thesis is that texts yield an indefinite number of meanings and critics can range freely over them, uninhibited by the restrictions that their authors might have wished to place upon how they should be taken. Anything, quite properly from the standpoint of literary theory, can be seen as a text, including a society; thus we might arrive at a picture of society as a constellation of endlessly shifting relations and meanings, resisting subordination to some fixed and authoritarian doctrine. That lends initial support to a 'politics of difference', but only in a metaphorical way; if we dwell upon the ground of the metaphor, quite the wrong results emerge. The theory undermines the perspectives of the social actors themselves, just as, in the literary case, it discounts and refuses privilege to the perspective of the author. Just possibly some of the groups comprising the social text might themselves be postmodern, celebrating the same poly-morphousness as the critic; but the perspectives of Catholic pro-life groups, or unions of welfare recipients, or defenders of Islam, or believers in aboriginal religion, are falsified by the way in which they are represented within a theory that they cannot possibly share. Here one may begin to see the force of Foucault's complaint that the Derridean vision itself lays claim to a sort of interpretive sovereignty (Foucault, 1972). One is reminded of the joke about 'irregular verbs' – in this case, perhaps, 'I have imaginative insight', 'You have a theory', 'He has a totalizing comprehension.' If we want a position that gives weight to the views which comprise social diversity, just about the first to be ruled out would be postmodernism, which gets in the way of understanding that we live in a world in which people make mutually exclusive claims and must find a way to coexist despite stubborn and unironic self-righteousness.

But Young's vigorous and influential book *Justice and the Politics of Difference* does not need Derrida's or any other postmodern thesis to support its main claim: that the different (and especially the oppressed – if the two are distinct categories at all) inherently evade comprehension by a theory of justice which, imposed from above, assumes standard cases. These cases will be standard only to some, not to others. Two alternatives are offered. The first is a recipe for dialogic interchange, in which a premium is placed on 'listening' for the distinctive voices of others (Young, 1990: 4, 73). Norms arising from this dialogue will be just if everyone has had an effective voice in their formulation (*ibid.*: 34), if the process is characterized by sympathy and nuanced understanding (*ibid.*: 96), and if the conclusion incorporates different perspectives (*ibid.*: 187). Yet there is to be no assumption of natural consensus. Habermas (*ibid.*: 7, 106) and 'republican' theorists of democracy (*ibid.*: 97, 117–18) are criticized for supposing that points of view, rationally understood, will necessarily converge. Hence, perhaps (I infer this connection), the second recipe, for a group veto against the outcomes of the democratic process, when it issues in 'specific policies that affect a group directly' (*ibid.*: 184). Here, then, we have two complementary rivals to any idea of a standard political morality: a requirement that norms must arise from actual dialogue, and a provision for excepting oneself from them. At first sight these two ideas might seem ill-assorted, the one calling for sympathetic engagement with others, the other for protection against them. But given the premise of mutual opaqueness, they both make sense. Opaqueness can, after all, be a matter of degree, sometimes yielding to nuanced under-standing, sometimes resisting even that. Let us consider the two provisions in turn.

First, it is a standing possibility that any standpoint presented as neutral will turn out in fact to reflect the self-absorption of privileged groups who have succeeded in getting their own partial outlook installed as a universal one, against which the perspectives of the oppressed and of minorities figure as irrational and other. One response to this would be to insist on keeping the issue open, by both liberal and democratic means, so that, through the challenging of false closure, one can identify more genuinely neutral principles. However, the 'politics of difference' response is to demand a change of direction, and to abandon spurious neutrality for democratically generated conclusions, reflecting the full range of articulated group preferences and perspectives. But what does it mean to say that these conclusions would *reflect* articulated differences? That very idea, it will be argued below, requires a political morality, and while any particular political morality is always open to challenge, the idea that one can do without any at all seems to lay a false trail.

According to Young, the idea of 'an impartial general perspective is a myth. People necessarily and properly consider public issues in terms influenced by their situated experience and perception of social relations.' This considering of public issues is not, however, to be confused with interest-group pluralism, or particularistic self-interest, of the kind that theorists of citizenship rightly reject. For 'it is possible for persons to maintain their group identity and ... at the same time to be public spirited, in the sense of being open to listening to the claims of others'. This openness to others may seem, perhaps, to veer back in the direction of impartiality, for, Young continues, 'it is possible and necessary for people to take a critical distance from their own immediate desires and gut reactions in order to discuss public proposals'. Two features distinguish this self-critical state of mind from the (forbidden) state of impartiality. First, it is still partial, for people cannot be expected to 'leave behind their particular affiliations and experiences to adopt a general point of view' – that requirement effectively reinforces a privileged perspective which passes itself off as neutral (Young, 1989: 257–8). Second, the idea of justice is arrived at through the process of group interaction, rather than preceding it by virtue of enjoying some kind of pre-democratic authority. 'In the absence of a Philosopher King who reads transcendent normative verities, the only ground for a claim that a policy or decision is just is that it has been arrived at by a public which has truly promoted free expression of all needs and points of view' (*ibid.*: 263).

Three features of this important claim demand critical comment. First, the alternative presented is a false one, for the claim to impartiality is different from the claim to objectivity represented by the figure of the philosopher king. The philosopher king, after all, is hardly impartial, in the sense of having to give due weight to the articulated views of others; famously, he discounts their views altogether. The person who *does* claim to be impartial would claim to be so, surely, by virtue of a disposition rather than a theory of knowledge. Moreover, the relevant (non-fanciful) alternative is effectively disguised – that is, the possibility of a critical political theory in which demanding tests of justification are advanced and challenged; that activity is simply obliterated by the proffered choice between epistemic authority on the one hand and the politics of difference on the other.

Second, the middle ground sketched out here between interest-group pluralism and standard theories of justice is very unstable. I am supposed to 'take a critical distance' from my own desires without, however, abandoning my 'particular affiliations, experiences and social location' (*ibid.*: 258). Taking a critical distance from my desires can only mean suspending my spontaneous belief in their validity, an interpretation surely supported by the fact that I am called on to do so in order to listen to the claims of others. If I assume that what I want is valid, I will be unable to give weight to what other people think is valid, or perhaps even to 'listen'. So my absorption in my particular affiliation or location is an obstacle to my reaching a just outcome in which all claims are given accommodation – just as theorists of citizenship often argue. But what seems impossible to understand is why my taking a critical distance has to stop short just where it does. If, for example, I belong to an immigrant culture in which women are consigned to secondary roles, and my views on that matter are put on the table along with rival views from groups of women within or outside my own cultural group, it may well be that I ought to think about the public defensibility of my view, as theories of justice maintain. Or, given a kind of politics that interest-group pluralists advocate, I should, rather, advance my view and hope to win, or to win something. But what sense does it make to say that I should be self-critical enough to listen to others' views, but not self-critical enough to abandon my own?

The third criticism, however, is the most serious, for it casts doubt on the intelligibility of the democratic process which is advocated. It can hardly be enough, for an outcome to be just, that it has been preceded by a process which has 'promoted free expression of all needs'. We could promote their expression – even 'truly' promote their expression – but fail to do anything at all about them. More charitably, of course, we could regard as implied the point that mere expression is not enough, and that the needs expressed should find recognition in the actual outcome of the process. They must be 'taken account of' (*ibid.*: 263). But that is not enough either: Elster (1986: 115) gives the example of the child who has taken half a cake and who then offers to divide the rest equally with his brother. While his brother's claim would indeed 'find recognition' in the outcome, one-quarter of the cake would hardly represent a just outcome for him, even though he had been 'taken account of'. So we want the outcome to represent not just *some* recognition of each claim, but a *due* recognition of each claim. How do we assess that? To avoid the standard theory-of-justice view of the kind that Rawls or Dworkin or others put forward, we would have to say that the participants in the process put forward not only claims reflecting their group affiliation but also views of justice reflecting their group affiliation, for otherwise the views of justice proposed, if different, would demand assessment from a non-group-based point of view. We would then face the following puzzle: if people are obliged to take a critical distance with respect to the desires arising from their group affiliation, why would they not be obliged to distance themselves similarly from the ideas of justice arising from their group affiliation? It would, after all, be deeply hypocritical to profess distance from one's desires while clinging to an idea of justice which happened to favour them. Moreover, if there is any reason to differentiate between one's desires and one's idea of justice, it would surely work the other way around: for while it makes some limited sense to say that one desires something because of one's affiliation and social location, it makes no sense at all to say both that something is just and that one believes that to be so only because one happens to belong to a particular group. To say that is simply to undermine the validity of a claim that is meant to have some influence on how other people conduct their lives, and which one must therefore support by means of reasons which could become *their* reasons. 'Because it reflects my social position' is not among those reasons, being explanatory as opposed to justifying.

Finally, even if we could somehow make our way through these fairly considerable difficulties, we would still face a problem of inclusion and exclusion. If theories of justice were simply to represent the best available arguments, participation in their formulation would matter only to the extent that it affected the availability of good reasons. It would be important that every good reason be heard, rather than that everyone be heard from; I would be content if my point of view happened to be put forward by someone else, even if I were not heard myself. If, however, the representation of difference is essential to arriving at a good theory of justice, then who is represented in its formulation is obviously of crucial importance. Can we determine who is justly represented? If we can arrive at a view of justice only after a process of group participation, then justice cannot tell us which groups should participate. And if the outcome depends on which groups did participate – as would seem clearly implied by the rejection of an impartial standpoint, potentially attainable regardless of who participates – initial decisions about inclusion and exclusion are crucial.

Young recognizes this dilemma in part, but responds disappointingly. There is, she says, 'an origin problem' which 'no philosophical argument can solve'; we cannot sensibly resolve the problem of who should decide the question of who should decide, 'because politics is always a process in which we are already engaged' (Young, 1989: 20). This seems to miss the point of 'origin problems'. If they are indeed insuperable, then that normally casts doubt on what is supposed to follow the origination. If, for example, there is no way for philosophers to become kings, given the way Plato organizes the initial situation, then that undermines the model of political justice that he gives us (or else suggests that we read it more elliptically). Likewise, if we want the terrain of politics as well as the process to be fair or defensible, and do not want it to be a terrain predetermined by some earlier decision about who should have access and who should not, but there is no way to achieve this – then we are pursuing a false trail. On the other hand, if the problem is not insuperable, then thinking about the terms on which we would originate a political system is one of the radical ways of criticizing the system that we have, and to rule it out of court is to deprive critical politics of one of its most potent devices.

Turning to the second provision, the group veto, one can understand why a respect for difference would make it attractive. Obviously a political morality has a point only if it defeats or constrains other objectives that one has, and if, instead of accepting such constraints, one could pursue one's objectives in an uncompromised fashion, that would be to the good, from one's own point of view. That consideration is even stronger if we assume, as the politics of difference does, that the possibility of genuine consensus, while not to be ruled out, is pretty tenuous.

But even if we make that assumption, the idea of a group veto poses immense problems. First, even if (as argued above) the dialogue idea and the veto idea complement each other in a conceptual sense, they are unlikely to work together functionally. For those who are below the level of average scrupulousness, the prospect of using a veto could serve as an incentive to transform the dialogic process into a bargaining game; while for those who are above the level of average scrupulousness, having taken part sincerely and sympathetically in a dialogue creates a strong sense of obligation not to undermine its results. The danger of unintended consequences seems quite overwhelming here, and while that danger is an across-the-board one, there is a point at which neglect of it becomes a political liability.

Second, the idea of a group veto seems to imply a quite unrealistic separability of issues. If a policy 'affect[s] a group directly' and adversely, the group can veto it, but what could be more likely than that it would affect more than one group? To employ a Canadian example, policies concerning the right of children of mixed unions to live on Aboriginal reserves impact differentially on women's and Aboriginal interests. A veto by either group would damage the other's interests, thus defeating the very point of a veto, as defended above; and a veto by both groups, the vetoes tending in different directions, would produce absurd results.

Third, a group veto obviously requires that a group should speak with a single voice: yes or no. But as Young herself is acutely aware, identity is not summed up in group membership: it is just as 'essentialist' to say that someone is summed up by their gender or race as it is to say that they are summed up by their citizenship. So what happens to those who dissent from the 'yes' or 'no' that is issued, *in their name*, by their group? They might want to appeal to the larger society for defence against patriarchalism, denial of autonomy, or physical mutilation; and in such circumstances, that anyone could see a group veto as liberating or radical is quite beyond belief, for it consigns dissenting minorities to oppression with full public sanction. True, we should not romanticize the enlightenment of majorities. We should not romanticize the warmth or sympathy of minorities either. The solution, surely, is to romanticize neither of them.

Quite another approach, while still stressing 'difference' in a sense, takes a primary interest in differences which can be regarded as rival claims upon our belief, as opposed to distinctive characteristics requiring protection and nurture; and where the politics of difference stresses the uniqueness of perspectives, this approach stresses, rather, the common ground that reason can often discern. This is 'deliberative democracy', a set of ideas with which the position developed here obviously has much in common, in conceiving of democracy as essentially a discursive process. Interestingly, deliberative democrats can also claim a point of departure in (a certain reading of) the political theory of toleration (Gutmann and Thompson, 1990). Locke posited an idea of validity – that is, he recognized the importance of believing that one's views can be sustained, not merely asserted; and he believed in deliberation as a means to the testing of claims. Both of these ideas translate quite readily into a view of democracy in which public deliberation is the means to the development and defence of validity claims; but whereas toleration theorists saw the private quest for validity as a reason for *precluding* some things from the political agenda, democratic theorists, Amy Gutmann and Dennis Thompson argue, will see public deliberation as a way of *accommodating* disagreements once they have reached the public forum. And just as Locke's theory of toleration was entirely distinct from a so-called toleration of the 'anything goes' variety, so this view of democracy is resolutely opposed to any form of relativism or subjectivism. Deliberation is a cognitive instrument, or a way of coming to know.

Whatever values it may broadly share with liberalism, deliberative democracy has a view of constitutionalism which seems quite different from the view typical of liberals. For while constitutions do indeed specify the terms on which accommodations are to be reached, liberals have taken at least an equal interest in their capacity to preclude; they are ways of pre-committing future majorities. Social contract arguments or theories of rights pre-establish the terms within which majorities and minorities subsequently form. But deliberative theories of democracy sometimes prefer to bring constitutional arrangements themselves under the control of deliberation, so that the democratic process sets its own terms, rather than being confined within a pre-democratic framework. That is not to say that deliberation theorists are hostile to the liberties which liberals want to protect. But, against the typical liberal idea of constitutional protection, Gutmann and Thompson make three points. First, rights may be better protected by informed and politically aware majorities than by paper barriers (Gutmann and Thompson, 1996: 34). Second, constitutionally protected values – such as 'basic liberty' – are essentially abstract, and require politically informed interpretation (*ibid.*: 35). And third, if for some purposes courts are better guardians of liberty than majorities are, then that is the conclusion that informed majorities will reach – but whether or not to place something beyond the reach of public deliberation must itself be a subject *for* public deliberation (*ibid.*: 48–9). For such reasons, the deliberative public becomes, as it were, fully sovereign. As opposed to a 'politics of difference' view that offers the shelter of a veto against democratic outcomes, deliberative democracy opens everything, in principle, to discursive inspection. Everything goes on the table; and groups which cannot persuade others of their case will pay the price. Public reason cannot reach those who refuse to press their claims in terms accessible to others (*ibid.*: 55).

It is certainly no part of the theory, however, that democratic outcomes have to be accepted as right (*ibid.*: 17, 49–50, 368n). The outcomes of the process are only provisional ones, always open to further criticism by those who have been outvoted. Each person reaches his or her own conclusion about the justice of outcomes, by applying, for example, the 'original position' test of Rawlsian liberalism. This, of course, brings into being two standards of rightness: the personal judgement, based on internal dialogue, and the public decision, based on democratic dialogue (*ibid.*: 37–8). The two may lead to opposed conclusions (as Locke may have been among the first to point out, in distinguishing between 'talking to ourselves' and 'stipulating with others'). But Gutmann and Thompson believe that this split may be repaired, over time. Internal and public dialogue supplement each other: on the one hand, reflectiveness should inform the proposals which citizens bring forward in their efforts to make or change policy or legislation; and on the other hand, the decisions actually made by a polity, informed by reason and observing basic deliberative values, serve as a check on the conclusions that one has reflectively reached. No general priority can be assigned, they claim. There is a mutual or interactive or 'dynamic' process in which private and public reason reinforce and correct each other. But it seems clear that in fact it is public reason that is the dependent variable here. 'We can say that the more nearly the conditions [of deliberative reasoning] are satisfied, the more nearly justifiable are the results likely to be' (*ibid.*: 17). But that judgement must be made, evidently, from the standpoint of private reason, or else it is circular. It is a reflective standpoint that judges between the conclusions of reflection and the outcomes of democracy. The process is one in which the views of others serve as a source of information and a constant spur to self-critique, but the truth is all on one side.

Perhaps, though, we could regard the reflective standpoint as providing us only with such things as basic rights, while some interactive process fills in, by reasoned consent, the space which abstract reflection necessarily leaves between theory and practice. In a polity that values equality, deliberation is the appropriate way to give practical meaning to abstract rights in particular concrete circumstances. Deliberative democracy, as Gutmann and Thompson put it, must have the authority to deal with moral conflicts which neither pure proceduralism nor constitutional principles are capable of settling (*ibid.*: 41). But here a basic difficulty arises in the understanding of moral conflict. From what standpoint is some matter said either to involve or not to involve the direct application of a basic right? We might grant, for the sake of argument, that there is some neutral standpoint of that kind; but it has no practical relevance to democratic deliberation – except as a regulative ideal – for there is no way to give it institutional embodiment. From the standpoints of the participants themselves, there are various possibilities, some of them asymmetrical. A or B might not agree with each other that a basic right is involved, or A and B might agree that a basic right is involved, but disagree about which right it is; but in either case, the two parties would simply regard each other as wrong.

Suppose that I, a pro-choice advocate, base my position on some manifestly weak reason – for example, that abortion should be permitted because there are too many people in the world. You, a pro-life advocate, maintaining that a basic right was at stake, would quite justifiably dismiss my construction of the issue, which, by making the decision an optional one, simply misses the point. Or, to make it slightly more complex and realistic, suppose I hold a better reason (I believe in autonomy) and recognize that you have a relevant reason (one should promote respect for life); I may still think you have got it quite wrong in failing to see the force of a superior reason. In the sense that is relevant to practical matters, having good reason to hold a position does not just mean entertaining a relevant belief but means reaching the right on-balance conclusion; and even though we might recognize that the other has relevant beliefs, we still regard each other as lacking good reason for our respective on-balance positions. When a situation of deliberative disagreement exists, 'the best moral understanding that citizens can muster does not show them which position should be rejected from a deliberative perspective' (*ibid.*: 73). But who are *them*? 'They', from their different standpoints, may very well believe that moral understanding *has* shown which position is right, and the conflict will hardly be a significant one unless they do. We could, of course, introduce a separate agency which would do its best to decide impartially whether or not (and which) basic rights are involved, but that would be to abandon serious ground to constitutional rather than deliberative democracy – that is, to a form of democracy that would give weight to pre-politically taken values as well as to politically given conclusions.

In the here-and-now, contested issues are to be settled by a deliberatively informed procedure. Majorities decide, constrained by basic rights, as interpreted by themselves or by courts, or perhaps by both at different levels of abstractness. Majority decision is taken as a kind of proxy for an ever-receding reflectively right decision, which, as a regulative idea, sustains the whole procedure in a normative sense, although every procedural decision made in its name must be open to challenge. We are to regard (deliberatively informed) majority rule as proper because it expresses respect for citizens' status as moral equals. The issue of legitimacy, then, would seem to divide into two, depending on the question asked. If we ask what makes the whole democratic enterprise a good one, the answer is epistemic: it leads us towards, without reaching, the solutions that reasonable reflection would dispose us to accept. But if we ask what made last year's election outcome legitimate, we get a procedural answer: majority rule respects equality of status. That, however, is quite consistent with the possibility that *someone's* conception of basic rights was violated, and that private and public reasoning were violently at odds with one another.

Much like Habermas, Gutmann and Thompson treat majority rule as a sort of proxy for a rational consensus. This is, on the present argument, a clear mistake, because it misrepresents the nature of the majority principle by telescoping together two of its important but quite distinct features. As was argued in Chapters 2 and 3, majority rule has the virtue of encouraging the generalization of political argument, which is an important service to public reason; and it also has the virtue that because the counting of votes records a fact, it can yield the unequivocal answer that we need in order to have a political authority. Both of these justifications have weight even for the outvoted, and so can serve as bases for a political morality of democratic citizenship, addressable to anyone regardless of their political view. But the idea that democratic majorities are in some way authoritative, even temporarily, with respect to the issues that public reason debates, is one that minorities have no reason to accept. They have reason to accept reliance on the majority principle as a way of settling those issues, based on both the epistemic and the institutional considerations just stated: when something has become a topic of disagreement, then we want both an institution that will bring its various aspects to light, and a mechanism for giving it resolution. But minorities have no reason to accept that the majority's construction of the issues is the right one. Neither set of considerations compels that, for while they entitle majorities to settle issues, they confer no right to say what the issues *are* – that is, to issue authoritative rulings on how they should be construed. Hence the need for the kind of reservations about majority rule, and the limits to it, described in Chapters 4 and 5.

The source of the problem here is the asymmetry with which parties to a disagreement may interpret it. If you and I agreed that our disagreement was essentially metaphysical, or that it rested on disputed facts, or was simply a case of conflicting interests, resolution would not be far off. We could agree to differ, or launch a fact-finding inquiry, or strike a compromise. Politically, however, this prior agreement may be lacking, one party believing that a basic right is at issue, the other that it is just an issue of preference that majorities should decide. This is the feature which principally distinguishes political disagreement from other kinds. In interpreting a literary text, or approaching a problem in moral philosophy, one is entitled to adopt the theory that one believes best represents the truth of the matter, even if there are (and one knows there to be) theories of a different character which characterize the text or the problem quite differently. One can, if one wishes, or if it is necessary, address these other theories and seek to undermine them, but that is extraneous to one's own construction of the text or problem, and optional even if advisable. Politically speaking, however, the existence of other general views can hardly be extraneous to the definition of the problem; in fact, the problem may be, exactly, that rival and incompatible general views confront each other. We cannot simply assign to this range of views the statuses that they would enjoy within the general theory which we favour. That remains true even if we hold a general theory which tries to account for disagreements, for (politically speaking, again) we have to give weight to the self-understandings of those who disagree with each other, whether or not those self-understandings happen to have status within the theory of disagreement that we favour. A theory of disagreement imposes a standard conception of disagreement that the parties to actual political disagreement need not accept.

That objection applies even to one of the most provocative treatments of disagreement to be offered in the past few decades, W. B. Gallie's 'Essentially contested concepts', which contains, in fact, its own intriguing version of 'deliberative democracy' *avant la lettre* (Gallie, 1955–6). Gallie too sees dialogic contest as an epistemic instrument by means of which our understanding of such ideas as justice or democracy is extended and deepened. Such ideas, he claims, are internally complex, containing several elements which are essential to them, but which cannot be arranged in any agreed hierarchical order. Different schools of thought argue for the particular hierarchy that they favour – rather in the manner of athletic teams who favour a particular style of play – but never achieve more than a temporary sway over majority opinion, which will eventually be overthrown, and which will be contested by dissident minorities even while it lasts. 'Democracy', for example, contains ideas such as participation, accountability and equality; democratic theories give one or other feature a primary place, assigning subordinate positions to the other two, only to be replaced by some other constellation which in turn wins temporary approval. But the effects of all this are benign: because some group has an interest in promoting the theme of, say, 'participation' for all it is worth, we get to know more about that topic than we would if it never had to compete; and the same goes for the other features of democracy. Gallie paints a picture of agonistic enlightenment, through which public reason is constantly enriched by its own endemic internal divisions. Learning about this dynamic, moreover, breeds a liberal culture in which toleration is the norm: understanding that the views of one's rivals are always of potential critical value to the development of one's own, one will come to see the folly of regarding one's opponents as 'perverse, bestial or lunatic' (*ibid.*: 193).

As has been clear from the earliest critiques of Gallie's argument, there is a basic problem of perspective in the model of essential contestation (Gellner, 1968). Once we have learned that the idea of democracy, say, contains three elements which are all vital to it but which cannot be arranged in any stable order, what exactly is the point of continuing to insist that 'democracy really means maximum participation?', and not only insisting on it but insisting with the polemical vigour that the model requires of its participants? Democracy, one's saner self should say, 'really' means no such thing, and exclusive kinds of claim about an inherently complex idea are essentially dogmatic. If the two levels of understanding could somehow be kept distinct, with the participants urging their narrow-minded claims while a somewhat Hegel-like reason surveyed the scene in retrospect, we would have a workable (though morally suspect) theory; but as we have seen, reason is to become accessible to the participants themselves, leading them to a state of mind that seems curiously bifurcated between activist obsession and reflective mellowness.

Can one believe both that a concept is essentially contested in Gallie's sense *and* that one view (or 'conception') of it is better than others? One might claim, for example – as Andrew Mason does – that a range of different conceptions of it are reasonable, but that one particular conception is supported by stronger reasons than the others are (Mason, 1993: 53). But here we begin to tread upon the unstable ground that Gutmann and Thompson also try to occupy: it is very hard to find a stable point between the ideas of *relevant* and of *compelling* reasons, and hence between two possible senses of 'reasonableness'. In its weaker sense, to say that something is reasonable is just to say that one could advance reasons for it that have an intelligible connection with what is proposed; in its stronger sense, to say that something is reasonable is to claim that the balance of reasons, taken together, inclines in its favour. It would be difficult to claim that a concept were essentially contestable unless the stronger of these senses applied, for otherwise virtually anything could be said to be essentially contestable: there are reasons, in the weaker sense, to believe that the earth is flat, or that the Holocaust never happened. But the problem with taking the stronger sense to apply is that it is also in that sense that one believes it reasonable to prefer one contested conception to another. In ordinary speech, no doubt, we *do* often use 'reasonable' in a sort of intermediate sense, meaning that a certain position is supported not just by relevant reasons but by reasons that are quite solid, or that one is tempted to hold oneself; but it is hard to find a compelling basis for this usage of the word, and it seems in any event that one would not use it in this way except in cases in which one was less than confident about the conclusive superiority of the *better* reasons. None of this, of course, touches on the important recognition that those with whom one disagrees 'have their reasons' for what they think, a recognition which plays a role in how one should treat one's rivals, but which does not bring into play any epistemic judgements at all – it is just the recognition of a fact.[1]

There may be another way, though, to rescue the model. If 'there is no best conception' and 'there is a best conception' confront each other as, so to speak, discursive equals, there can be no reconciliation, without repealing the law of non-contradiction. But perhaps 'there is no best conception' might belong to the discursive realm of political philosophy and the history of ideas, while 'there is a best conception' is a pragmatic judgement tied to a here-and-now reality. At certain points in the nineteenth century, for example, it would have made sense to say that democracy 'means' the extension of the franchise, the point of the remark being that if we believe democracy is valuable, there is above all one thing that we have to do in order to promote or safeguard its future. Perhaps, too, at particular moments in the history of art or Christianity (two of Gallie's other examples) some important feature might have become so neglected or marginalized that it had become vital (to some) to restore it *for the sake of the whole enterprise*, so that to say 'Art really means ... ' is to make a claim that is at once partial – it refers to just one feature of art – and universal – its motivation is supplied by the project of sustaining the whole artistic enterprise. (Perhaps Marcel Duchamp's hanging a urinal on a gallery wall is a passable example.) Gallie himself appeals to pragmatic exigencies of something like this kind, and the value of drawing attention to them is that we are enabled to introduce dual and non-competing points of view into the idea.

Doing so also enables us to rescue Gallie from another critic, Christine Swanton (1985), who deploys the distinction between *concept* (justice, say) and *conception* ('justice as fairness', for example). Does it make sense to say that people who disagree with one another can share a concept while disagreeing about conceptions of it? If there were an uncontested way of describing the concept, why would this not enable us to distinguish among the competing conceptions of it, in terms of their accuracy and appropriateness? On the other hand, if there is no uncontested way of describing the concept, why regard the competing conceptions as being conceptions of the same thing? Picking the example of distributive justice, Swanton convincingly shows the impossibility of separating concept from conception, core meaning from interpretation. If we take contemporary theories of justice, for example, as interpretations of justice, the ideas of justice that they interpret are themselves different. 'Whatever distribution of a social advantage arises from a just situation is itself just' is different from 'A proper nonarbitrary balance among competing claims for social advantage is determined' and both in turn are different from 'There is a rendering unto each his/her share or amount of social advantage' (*ibid.*: 817).

Now maybe some admirer of the work of the Italian legal theorist G. del Vecchio might see some even more abstract vision of justice behind these already abstract formulas (del Vecchio, 1952). And then we would be back on the terrain of discussions about what is and is not 'the same'. But this seems, once again, too cognitive, and insufficiently connected to the requirements of political action. These different ideas of justice are competitors, not (necessarily) because they cannot be comprehended within some still more general definition, but because they (necessarily) have exclusive practical implications. To return to Swanton's three rival definitions: the state can let millionaires keep their non-fraudulently acquired millions; or it can tax them in order to improve the lot of the less fortunate; or it can redistribute them in the name of equality or overall need-satisfaction. But it cannot do all of them and it cannot do none of them, and the ideas of justice compete for that reason; they would compete even if their names were changed, or if their adherents accepted the label of 'justice' but with distinct subscript numbers. Although it is certainly true that contests, to be serious, must be 'contests over something', it does not, surely, follow that they have to be 'about the same concept' (Lukes, 1974: 187), for whether or not they are about the same concept – a matter on which in turn there may be unsettleable disagreements – they can be about the serious question of what to do.

This chapter has touched on some disparate theories and it may be wise to state its general point in conclusion. Various large perspectives compete for our attention when it comes to understanding 'difference'. They range from a Derridean version of scepticism to a neo-Enlightenment theory of rational deliberation, taking in essential contestability as a sort of mid-point on this spectrum. All three suffer from the same defect – that is, they want us to understand difference on the basis of a cognitive model which claims to tell us something decisive about the truth-content of the various positions whose rivalry constitutes politics. But this misunderstands politics. Political disagreement, as a topic, is at once less and more exigent. It is less exigent in that it does not require us to adopt a general theory about why people disagree – perhaps the missing theory which, within the social sciences, is furthest from our grasp. It is more exigent in that it requires us to give weight to the fact of disagreement, even if we give no weight to its source.

The idea of a political morality responds to this double consideration. It leaves intact our own beliefs, while compelling us to take seriously the fact that others do not share them, and thus to do what we can to find arrangements that derive not from common beliefs, which we cannot assume or impose, but from our common situation. Given that situation, one has to acknowledge that democratic majorities have the best claim to impose a political resolution of disputes: but one also has to acknowledge that the grounds on which they do so may be seen, by those who disagree, as wholly inadequate to the case. We will want an account of politics that gives weight to both of those considerations, and will therefore reject all three of the positions criticized in this chapter.

Note

1. See Raz (1990: 46) for the view that there is no epistemic basis for a 'middle way' between considerations that ought to convince people and those that ought not, but do.

CHAPTER 8

Neutrality and Community

The argument above has made a limited commitment to the idea of state neutrality,[1] and it is time to examine some critical issues that this poses. Initially, it was argued that a minimal idea of neutrality was contained in the very idea of democracy: matters can be settled openly through responsive public institutions only if those institutions are not wholly precommitted in terms of the outcomes that they produce or permit. It was then argued that this minimal sense of neutrality provided a basis for a move from neutrality to equality: only a condition of equal political status allows us to describe public institutions as neutral. Equal political status seems initially to involve the hopeless task of weighing exclusive or incommensurable ideals against each other; but it makes sense if we take it to mean that the ideal democratic political process will give the maximum chance of access to the best reasons, thus respecting everyone's status as a reasoning agent. Democratic institutions are justifiable to the extent that they provide for this.

It is impossible to claim that the best reasons will win in everyone's judgement. So, it was argued, we will want to constrain the process to the losers' benefit, so that even though their minority position prevents them from moulding the public environment as they would like, it does not prevent them from living their own lives according to the principles that they favour. The majority has an obligation to leave minorities a space in which they can adjust their lives to a public environment that they did not choose. There is an obvious sense in which we might regard this 'compensability' condition as providing an approximation to neutrality. Nothing can make contested public decisions neutral in their impact; but the idea of compensability provides that while some win and some lose, the losers preserve as much as they can hope to in a justifiable democratic system in which there is no systematic privilege, and no systematic disadvantage.

Finally, to complete this review, the 'perfectionism' of liberal democracy was rejected. Although, it was argued, democracy as conceived of here necessarily has a liberal character, its liberal character does not imply values commonly associated with liberalism, such as autonomy, let alone the even more specific values to be found in a liberalism such as Galston's. Of course, it rests on normative beliefs, such as beliefs in the value of equality and transparency. But, it was argued, these are beliefs arising from the very idea of political legitimation, rather than from a particular view of how life should be conducted; and, it was contended, there is a difference between accepting that political systems will embody normative beliefs and enforce behaviour which conforms with them, and maintaining that a political system ought to embody a certain ideal of life. For this reason, the liberalism defended here was distinguished from more robust and ambitious liberalisms which offer not just a political morality but a whole ethical programme. In this sense it has more in common – as its occasionally Lockean inspiration would suggest – with what is sometimes called 'Reformation' liberalism than with 'Enlightenment' liberalism; but it must not therefore be taken to be only a pragmatic or *modus vivendi* theory, for it is a view about the morally justifiable conditions on which political living can be carried on.

There are, then, a number of different but related senses in which neutrality can be claimed, and a number of ways in which limited claims to neutrality appear to make sense (though what is currently termed 'neutral*ism*' is rejected). That said, it can hardly be claimed that a liberal democratic polity is neutral in its effects. As already noted, the idea of complete effect-neutrality is hopeless. The very existence of political contestation rules it out. It is one thing to be neutral in the sense of not wanting to confer benefits on one side, and something else to act in a way which confers benefits differentially. But in between these two fairly clear ideas – one possible, the other impossible – there is a more awkward case, one of predictable but unintended effects. A political system may be recommended without any intention of distributing costs and benefits in any particular way, but it may be predictable that it will confer benefits on some general types of project and impose costs on others. It is a reasonable objection that liberal democracy would impose costs on those who value certain kinds of communities – a point very widely discussed, from many different perspectives, in recent political theory.

Now the whole project attempted here *intentionally* and necessarily excludes one kind of communitarianism – that is, a political theory which sees democracy as a way of protecting and imposing a community's character. The idea of political legitimation, taken as a starting point above, carries the further idea that the norms and beliefs which are to determine laws and policies are yet to be established, by public means. That makes no sense if it is generally supposed that all the important norms and beliefs are already given, together with our picture of what it means to belong to our community; and while it is in the nature of communities that *some* norms and beliefs are already given, and while it may even be true that democratic politics can operate only *when* some norms and beliefs are taken as given, all that means is that not everything can be democratic. But we could think about democracy in a fundamentally different way, in which communal norms and beliefs would not be limits on democracy but, rather, the point of the whole enterprise. This is what Habermas (perhaps eccentrically) calls 'republican' democracy, conceived of as the enterprise of giving realization to the aspirations of a 'people' defined as an historic entity with a particular and celebrated character.

Political 'community' in that sense, then, is ruled out by the premises of the argument here. But there remains the case of communities within liberal democratic society, groups which have no ambition to turn the polity into a vehicle of communal aspirations, but which want to maintain a way of living together that distinguishes them in important ways from the surrounding society. It can safely be predicted that liberal democracy will make life more difficult for them than for majorities which, just because they are majorities, have no need to be concerned with sustaining their own ways of doing things. For reasons offered in Chapter 7, the model of mutual incomprehension is rejected as a general theory of intercommunal relations; but all the same, it is surely beyond dispute that there is an argumentative gradient, so to speak, which works to accelerate some people's proposals and to decelerate others'. If contentious matters have to be brought before public judgement, even with the constraints outlined above, those closer to the majority's presuppositions will have a much easier time of it than those who are more distant.

In an episode given perceptive and sympathetic treatment by Calvin Trillin, a community of Orthodox Jews in north London encountered this problem, in what must be a paradigmatic way (Trillin, 1994). According to their beliefs, respecting the Sabbath requires that one should perform no work for the stated period, and 'work' embraces not only the activities recognized as such by the larger British society but also such things as pushing a baby carriage or carrying food when visiting family or friends. Such things would, however, be permissible if carried out within the space circumscribed by an *eruv*, or a boundary marking out the community's space. Established rules permitted this boundary to be marked out in a notional way, making use of existing physical features such as roads or railway lines. But the north London Orthodox Jewish community could not complete their *eruv* without filling in an unmarked space, which they proposed to do by erecting a row of posts connected with fishing line; and when they tried to do so, they met variously justified (and perhaps still more variously motivated) forms of local opposition. In the public wrangles which followed, the whole notion of and (complex) justifying argument for the *eruv* inevitably became an issue, and a spokesman for the Orthodox community – giving way to understandable frustration – said, 'You don't understand it, you won't understand it, and, quite honestly, you don't need to understand it. The point is that we want it, we consider it important, and we ask you to respect that' (*ibid.*: 62).

On the argument developed above, this is not a possible claim. 'You cannot understand' would simply close off the whole argumentative process, the existence of which is the only basis of a justifiable democracy. It cannot be a democratic solution to dispose of public space according to private and non-demonstrable beliefs. But the argument would be morally obtuse if it did not acknowledge the poignancy here. Here we have a group of people who throughout their lives have had to bend their understanding of things to take account of majority ways, ways which no doubt they often found to be bizarre or corrupt or lax or just plain different, but which, in any event, they had to accept whether they could make sense of them or not. But now, when *they* make a claim, all of a sudden there has to be complete transparency, and proposals have to be brought to the bar of public (read: 'majority') understanding.

There is a sort of radical unfairness in the burden of empathy.

Moreover, there is a further important way in which the effects of liberal democracy are non-neutral. Within communities, it is normally the case that conservative and adaptive trends of thinking coexist, often in considerable variety, if not in considerable tension. Conservatives are often formalists, attaching importance to the strict observance of codes of ritual or dress or diet, which they may see as matters of 'piety' (Scruton, 1980: 32–3). Adapters, by contrast, attaching more importance to what they see as the spiritual or ethical core of community life, are more willing to accommodate on forms. There is no question that conservative elements will find it much harder to share public space within a liberal democracy, and that the environment will tend persistently to have (in a different sense) a 'liberalizing' impact within communities, so that, for example, Muslim girls who want to wear headscarves in French schools will be under much greater pressure than others who are content merely to dress with relative demureness.

These consequences are problematic for the approach outlined here; in effect, they reach back to the beginnings of the argument. Not everyone is open to the appeal of the 'best reasons' case for democracy: people who have a settled view of the best way to live, or the best way for themselves to live at any rate, will not welcome the unsettling critical effects of political argument. To say that they should welcome it on the grounds that they would be better for it would of course be to turn the argument into a perfectionist one. We can avoid that by insisting that the grounds are non-perfectionist: that public resources must be disposed of according to a justifiable public process, and that only the 'best reasons' model gives a good account of that. But all the same, the predictably asymmetrical effects remain troubling. True, if we take international neutrality in wartime as a paradigm case, asymmetrical effects as such pose no problem; for geographical reasons among others, one's abstention is quite likely to benefit or handicap one party or another, without one's 'neutrality' being undermined. But as Peter Jones points out, we cannot take the international case as a paradigm in this respect, for the interstate and intrastate contexts are too different. In the case of international conflict, states which decide to remain neutral bear no responsibility either for the conflict or for the relative strengths of the warring states, and so it is implausible to hold them responsible for whatever effects their abstention has on the conflict – whereas a state has to defend its claim to neutrality in a context in which its own policy 'sets the terms' on which the various parties compete (Jones, 1989: 25).

It is of course something to be able to claim that state neutrality relieves groups of the risk of being officially branded as outcasts, even though the trend of policy may run against them. Rousseau believed that a hostile intention alone made losses oppressive. It is not the nature of things that maddens us, he thought, but only the presence of ill will: if we believed that the curtailments of freedom that we suffered were due to some person's will, they would have a character that they do not have if (as Rousseau believed) they result from the impersonal workings of an institution – if they are in that sense 'the will of no one'. This is at least an important point, and of course it is a crucial one if it is the best that we can do. It may just not be possible to distribute the burdens of coexistence evenly, and if so, then all we can do is distribute them without adding a further burden of official contempt. Perhaps that is as far as the argument can go; perhaps the theory has done all it can in promoting a political morality in which majorities must take account of the adjustments that minorities must endure. But before we are forced to this conclusion, one more avenue needs to be explored.

Much of the recent discussion of this issue has focused on what are termed 'cultural' groups, groups, that is, which embody a distinct and historically transmitted way of seeing the world and of living in it.[2] Just because it is a different way of life it is likely not to share in the 'economies of scale' which benefit the majority. And because it is historically transmitted, it is an acculturated way of life rather than a chosen one, and not comparable, therefore, to an expensive taste for which the person concerned might reasonably be expected to pay.

Both of these claims, however, have been contested in a persuasive way. First, what reason is there to think that culture is a more important source of 'difference' than other features of life may be – such as social class, or political belief, or physical characteristics? One's identity, as one critic points out, may owe as much to membership in a group of 'socially maladept anarchist poets', or of 'very thin and exceptionally myopic individuals' (Fierlbeck, 1996: 14, 16).

Second, what reason is there to think that attachments other than 'cultural' ones are *not* transmitted rather than chosen? Why should we suppose that being a Chinese Canadian, for example, is a status given by birth, while regarding a taste for opera or caviar or handmade shotguns by Purdy's as something freely cultivated? Both lines of objection are compelling, for the argument developed above concerns the (forward-looking) effects of being deprived of something rather than the (backward-looking) origins of the desire for it. Veterans' groups, no less than 'cultural' groups, are adversely affected by such things as the construction of public space. Opera lovers, no less than consumers of some ethnic foods, suffer from diseconomies of scale. An aristocratic lifestyle can be just as much an inherited feature of life as a religious belief is; and if there is a difference in that regard, it does not seem that we would want to make our different responses to the two cases turn upon that.

Third, as Jeremy Waldron asks, why, even if people need culture, do they need to have a *single* culture? (Waldron, 1991–2). People cannot indeed invent their lives out of nothing; they need the resources which have evolved over the years from human interactions. But it does not follow that these resources have to be drawn from a single source: someone

> may live in San Francisco and be of Irish ancestry, [but he] does not take his identity to be compromised when he learns Spanish, eats Chinese, wears clothes made in Korea, listens to arias by Verdi sung by a Maori princess on Japanese equipment, follows Ukrainian politics, and practices Buddhist meditation techniques. (*ibid.*: 754)

Moreover, given an individualist approach to justification, in which cultures are valued because they contribute to personal fulfilment, why would we need to provide *secure* cultures rather than letting them take their chances in the light of whatever it is that people reflectively find to be fulfilling? (*ibid.*: 786–7).

That is not, of course, the end of the various conceptual and empirical questions involved in this debate, and the case for liberal multiculturalism can be refined to respond to at least some of these kinds of criticism (Kymlicka, 1995). But the model of democracy adopted here suggests a different approach. The model emphasizes the stimulation and exchange of reasoning and evidence. It depends, therefore, on some standard agreement on what counts as a reason and what counts as evidence. It can tolerate some divergence from the norm, accepting, for example, that admitting something as a reason might involve moving to a deeper level of the reason-giver's belief system, and that admitting something as evidence might sometimes mean accepting a less than universal definition of it. But the further we move into this kind of territory, the more we risk straining the majority's credulity. What is termed 'cultural' difference is particularly strain-inducing. Members of the majority can give reasons and expect, in the normal case, to be understood, although not necessarily to win agreement; members of some cultural minorities can expect, in the normal case, not to be understood, and thus to be two steps away, not one, from winning democratic support. They cannot be guaranteed democratic support, for guarantees of that kind are undemocratic. But they can reasonably expect to be placed only one step away from it, as most members of the majority might generally be supposed to be.

We may, then, have a different reason for taking 'culture' seriously, not based on its surely far from unique importance as a source of identity, but as one of the most marked potential barriers to communication. It is reasonable to guess that as the most common source of people's earliest-acquired assumptions and symbols, it forms a semi-conscious layer which moulds one's perceptions, whether or not one values it, or identifies with it, or is identified with it by others. This is a guess and not an empirically supported claim, and if others want to claim that class and gender have these properties to the same degree, then they can make the necessary improvements to the argument here. The point is simply that culture is at least among those elements which impede mutual understanding, and that a democratic theory of the kind offered here must take it seriously for that reason, even if other proffered reasons are more questionable.

The theory offered here limits the legitimate power of majorities by means of the idea of uncompensable defeats. Some of these defeats can be blocked by rights, which require interpretation by courts. Others can be prevented only by the self-restraint of democratic majorities. Courts and voters and legislators, then, are called on to make judgements about what is and is not essential to others' lives; and if there are 'others' about whom they are particularly likely to get it wrong, there is the strongest possible case for some kind of group presence. This point goes back at least to Mill, who (writing of class barriers rather than cultural ones) asked:

Does Parliament, or almost any of the members composing it, ever for an instant look at any question with the eyes of a working man? ... On the question of strikes, for example, it is doubtful if there is so much as one among the leading

members of the House who is not firmly convinced that the
reason of the matter is unqualifiedly on the side of the masters
... how different, and in how infinitely less superficial a
manner the point would have to be argued, if the classes who
strike were able to make themselves heard in Parliament.
(Mill, 1910: 209–10)

The same argument is currently more usually made in the context of
culture and gender. The excluded must be made 'present' so that
their actual thoughts, as distinct from their presumed ones, can be
made known (Phillips, 1995). Just how the excluded are 'to make
themselves heard', or to be made 'present', is unsettleable by purely
theoretical means. Social circumstances, political institutions, and
the interaction between them will prompt or call for arrangements
of very different kinds. But a lack of *any* arrangements constitutes
disenfranchisement. Opponents of group representation draw
attention to various risks that the practice involves. It is, they fear,
'communo-pathic', giving prominence to difference while undermining the common ground which democratic dialogue should have
the merit of disclosing (Ward, 1991). Perhaps these risks might
even be decisive if group representation were an option; but under
certain circumstances, it may be required by one of the most basic
elements of democratic theory.

    One of the problems posed by group representation is a certain
inevitable flattening of intragroup diversities. There is an important
difference, as Kymlicka points out, between endorsing the present
substance of a culture and giving weight to a 'structure' with the
task of protecting it. The former is deeply conservative, enshrining
the status quo at the expense of critics or reformers within the group
(Kymlicka, 1989: 166–7). But even if we could manage,
institutionally, to create a structure which would not enshrine
substance, it is unlikely that the full range of internal diversity can
be reflected in the group's official positions, which must often be
taken on binary choices. What is the status of internal dissent
within officially recognized groups? According to one view, put
forward by Chandran Kukathas, dissenters from the group's way of
life, or from decisions made by whomever is taken to speak for the
group, have no claim to be given weight – provided that they can
leave (Kukathas, 1995). We should treat a group as being more or
less like a traditional liberal 'association', which will survive as long
as it meets its members' needs (at acceptable cost) and provides a

156

way of living that they find satisfactory, or will disintegrate if it fails to do so and its members drift away and assimilate into the larger society. Groups can, then, practise 'illiberal' ways of living, their continued existence being a sufficient sign that they are consented to.

To resist this conclusion might at first seem to imply some version of perfectionist liberalism, according to which people's real autonomy-based interests override their apparent interests. But actually, there is another approach. In terms of the distinctions made above, we can ask whether power-holders in such groups – those who have internal status and influence, and who claim to speak to others on the whole group's behalf – are subject to the constraints of political or of social morality. If the former apply, then those who act for the majority can, in the last resort, determine which (if any) of the minority's potential losses are compensable; and if they decide that a minority's claims are unreasonable, they can refuse to meet them. If the latter apply, on the other hand, the minorities themselves get to define which potential losses are uncompensable. Minorities may, then, make their own judgements about what is living and what is dead, essential and archaic, in their traditions; moreover, they could not be compelled to leave as the price of following their own judgements, for their preference, obviously, is to stay while adapting their traditions, and leaving involuntarily would be another uncompensable loss.

So everything hinges on which morality applies. And there seems to be no way, in general, to decide. 'Groups' will be very different in character. But if powerholders are to maintain that political morality applies, and that they, like states, can override minorities' judgements, then of course all the constraints of political morality come into play, just as they do in the case of the state. There will have to be ways of ensuring that all views are effectively heard, that the exchange of views is free, that no relevant information is suppressed, and so on. So the larger society would not be right to – in effect – devolve a political power to the leaders of minority groups, unless the internal relations of a group met a quite high standard of transparency. Just as in the case of the larger society itself, the standards of transparency would be particularly demanding when (potential) minorities were ascriptively defined – when, for example, men claimed to speak on behalf of women. If the subordinated do not know what is said on their behalf, or have incentives to concur, or are kept ignorant of alternatives, then their consent counts for nothing. This is not, it should be noted, to apply a higher standard to 'communities' than to the larger society; nor is it to adopt a 'perfectionist' attitude to the overriding value of the reasoned life. It is simply to recognize that a liberal democratic society can hardly avoid taking an interest in the uses of power, since its basis is the replacement of power by persuasion when and to the extent that this is possible.

The project of ensuring a community's very survival may pose special problems. As Charles Taylor points out, this is sometimes a sticking-point for liberals who demand scrupulously even-handed treatment and therefore resist demands for special arrangements designed to provide for a culture's transmission to future generations. But while this might be a sticking-point for some liberals, it may also be vital to members of the community in question. Writing of the case of Quebec, Taylor notes the desire to '[make] sure that there is a community of people here in the future that will want to avail itself of the opportunity to use the French language. Policies aimed at survival actively seek to *create* members of the community' (Taylor, 1994: 58–9). This is, as he points out, a different matter from simply demanding the accommodation of existing differences, which can be justified by taking only one short step beyond quite ordinary individualistic grounds.

In some cases, the intergenerational aspect of group survival projects may be a source of problems. These problems do not arise in the case of the desire to transmit a language. One necessarily transmits one language or another. Every language contains a set of cultural and social opportunities, and although some languages offer fewer social (and economic) opportunities than others on a global scale, that is not a reason to doom all but English, Russian, Mandarin and Spanish to extinction. But other kinds of transmission can limit the opportunities of future generations in quite severe ways. A deeply traditional community, for example, might want to provide for its survival by limiting educational opportunities for its children; or by limiting the horizons of young women; or by transmitting a way of life entailing poverty and marginalization.

Needless to say, all these things could also be described as the giving of opportunities – as initiation into a way of life the strength of which depends on imposing these limits. We cannot solve this dilemma in the same way as we can solve the issue of a group's treatment of adults – that is, by relying on ordinary social and political processes to inform people of their options and thus either to make consent to the status quo meaningful, or reform of the status quo possible. It cannot be solved in this way, because the very purpose of these modes of socialization is to form the standards by which children will eventually judge, and so it would be absurd to leave the matter to their judgement.

Some theories of liberal or democratic education take a strong line on this matter, insisting that children be given the capacity to make an eventual choice about the life they want to lead. In the case of Gypsy communities in the United Kingdom, for example, one writer complains that children 'are being denied the sort of education which would fit them to make a rational choice of lifestyle as adults', and demands that they be given a level of education which will remedy this (Poulter, 1987: 600–1). Criticizing this passage, Kukathas objects that 'there is no more reason to insist that Gypsy parents offer their children a "rational choice" of life-style through public education than there is to require that other parents offer their children the opportunity to become gypsies' (Kukathas, 1995: 248). But surely one cannot 'become' a Gypsy (except perhaps in the unusual sense in which we might say that Grey Owl had 'become' a native North American). One can decide to live a nomadic life on the fringes of society (or try to), and one would hope that public education would – perhaps through the study of literature – expose children to a wide range of possibilities, including defiant rejection of the work ethic. So the symmetry is not quite right. 'Becoming a Gypsy' is not in the normal case a choice at all, and the question is how far choice ought to be introduced into the process.

A more compelling reason for non-intervention in this particular case would be the marginal connection between Gypsy society and the larger society. It is hard to imagine what interest a democratic theory would take in a group of people who desire, apparently, just to be left alone, and are less a part of the larger society's life than many resident aliens are. Perhaps other groups also fit this pattern; in which case there, too, there may be no real middle ground between humane tolerance and inhumane integration (or expulsion). But it is quite a different matter when a community is integrated into the larger society by virtue of holding property under its legal system, of paying taxes, of voting or otherwise participating politically, or claiming some sort of recognition in a system of pluralist representation.

A similar distinction is made by David Miller, who contrasts the case of anomalous but 'self-contained' groups (such as ultra-Orthodox Jews who live in Israel but deny the legitimacy of the Israeli state) with that of groups which claim and exercise the rights of citizenship (Miller, 1995b: 145). The latter, he argues, must admit an obligation to prepare their children for effective citizenship.

That may be true, but there is also a still more basic norm involved here. It is a condition of democratic political morality that only fairly constituted majorities can substitute their judgement for others, when it is a matter of judging the compensability of losses; groups must accept their members' own estimations. In the case of children, that principle may need to be weakened, but it need not be wholly abandoned. We can presume that children will want full exposure to the culture in which their parents live. That it will entail losing other experiences is of no weight, since every process of acculturation is exclusive. But we cannot presume that they will want to be irreversibly committed to it. Physical mutilation, hostile prejudices which prevent any real receptiveness to other ways of living, the lack of basic skills sufficient to disqualify one from other ways of living; these are things that it is right to protect children against, not on the perfectionist grounds that a chosen life is better than an unchosen one, but on the grounds, important to the morality of democracy, that choice cannot be presumed. The net result, then, would seem to be some kind of compromise in which at least the minimum is done to protect both kinds of aim. This is not, however, a compromise of principle, but one resulting from the fact that we are trying to come to terms with inherently unknowable future desires and intentions, so that the reach of both principles is simply unsettleable.

It is a different matter, it should be noted, if a group's decisions issue from some procedure, such as internal democracy, which enjoys a degree of real consent. As noted earlier, in Chapter 4, in such a case there would be a stronger reason to accept the majority principle than in the case of public institutions: it is obviously better that people should actively participate in common life on terms which are approved of by more rather than fewer of their number. When that is so, the majority's preference serves not just as a formal test of legitimacy but as an actual predictor of a proposal's chances of success; and the minority has a reason to accept the majority's view which does not apply in the public case. The whole project, which the majority and the minority share, will go better that way. As a matter of prudence, however, the same consideration should warn majorities of the danger of relying too heavily upon it: for the shared project will also go better to the extent that the cooperation of minorities is willing rather than forced.

The other notable hard case is that of internal minorities (Green, 1994). Internal dissenters are people who identify with the group but not with its officially proclaimed position; internal minorities are not members of the group, but inhabit space in which the group predominates. Linguistic examples – such as pockets of non-Francophone speakers within a predominantly Francophone Quebec – are familiar ones. They exemplify dilemmas, of the kind mentioned in Chapter 4, in which one cannot help but impose a defeat upon one group or another, and in which the loss in both cases would be similarly uncompensable. Would the defeat be a moral one? Language is not of course immediately a moral issue: it is hardly disturbing to observe others speaking another language in the way that it is disturbing to observe things of which one disapproves, such as pornography in corner stores, or abortion clinics in public hospitals. But all the same, the right to use one's own language can become a morally charged issue, as when, for example, it comes to be connected with respectful treatment. Particularly in cases in which one language has been the typical language of success and power, users of other languages may come to feel that the use of their own language is essential to the recognition of their equality, and thus comes to be a moral requirement. They may also demand some form of legislative or even constitutional protection for their language, on the grounds that circumstances are weighted against its voluntary adoption by those who would prefer to use it. There might, for example, be free-rider problems, for while most members of the group might want to use the language, they might reasonably be unwilling for themselves (or their children) to suffer disadvantages if compliance fell short of a certain level. Or there might be issues about educational provisions that demand legislative resolution.

So let us accept that if the group were denied the provisions that can reasonably be regarded as necessary, they would suffer a moral defeat. The 'internal minority' problem is that by granting them the provisions, one would impose restrictions on a smaller group, who could protest, in turn, that they were now being defeated in *their* aim, that of living in their own language.

To treat this as an ordinary political issue and to resolve it by majority decision would lead to results that depend entirely on the distribution of opinion and the polity's institutional structure. In a federal system in which the local majority had constitutional status, it might win. In a unitary system, everything would depend on whether the local minority enjoyed majority support in the larger society. But if it is right to suppose that the issues involved are moral ones, then it does not seem right to leave matters there. It is reasonable to ask about the best outcome here, even if institutional forms are going to affect the outcome decisively.

As the example has been constructed, both parties deny that they can adequately adjust their lives to legislative or constitutional defeats, and the majority has no good grounds to reject either denial. As a way out of this impasse, a reversion to Locke's original version of the compensation model was suggested above: the idea of providing state compensation to the defeated, rather than that of self-compensation. Although the defeated (whoever they are) may rightly deny that they can undertake self-compensation, states may often be in a position to provide them with additional resources or opportunities when they have imposed a defeat upon them. If a local majority *or* a local minority were denied the legislative support or constitutional status that it demanded, it might still be provided with policies that contributed to its objective: cultural support policies, publication subsidies, special educational funding. It would be important, given the distinction between compensation and consolation made earlier in the book, that these provisions should actually contribute to the objectives of the defeated group, as opposed to palliating their defeat. If there were any asymmetry in the parties' position here – if, that is, one, if defeated, could be compensated, while the other, if defeated, could only be consoled – then that is something that could have reasonable weight in making a democratic judgement.

The guiding thought here is this. The justification of democracy is necessarily abstract. The very fact that a democratic polity, by definition, makes its decisions for itself means that we must make minimal assumptions in characterizing its features. The arguments made in the first four chapters of this book attempted to meet this condition: in their treatment of modernity, justifiability or compensation, they made no reference to all the institutional variations within real-world democracies that affect the practical meaning of such things. But these variations, as we have seen, will crucially affect what happens to the claims of local majorities and the local minorities within them. If we think of democracy as the forum in which the best reasons stand their best chance of being best expressed, then we will also want it to take account of the possibly irrational effects of its own mode of institutionalization. That it has to institutionalize itself in one way rather than another is beyond question, but the nature of its own justification may require it to take account of distortions which its basic principles cannot justify.

There is of course an important sense in which every democratic decision is an artefact of the decision rule adopted, as was noted in Chapter 2. And obviously a system must take as legitimate the artefacts of whatever set of electoral institutions it has (or else change it). It would be absurd to argue that every democratic decision had to be discounted in favour of another decision that might have been made by different institutions. But all the same, there are degrees of artifice, and to acknowledge this may be useful in distinguishing clear from unclear cases. The clearest case for a theory of democratic deliberation would be a single constituency dividing on some issue without regard to the effects of internal differentiation. Then some arguments for the majority principle, including the argument adopted above, are attractive. They become progressively less attractive as we approach the unclear end of the spectrum, and outcomes are effectively determined by the spatial distribution of votes, particularly when spatial location and other sources of ('communal') differentiation overlap. At a certain point we may lose meaningful contact with anything that makes the majority principle compelling, and splitting the difference comes closer to ordinary ideas of fairness. This argument from institutional effects provides a further reason for the apparently anti-majoritarian elements in the argument – 'apparently', because actually they follow from the very reasons which sustain the majority principle in the first place, and so do not really diminish that principle, correctly understood.

The above argument has concerned the political representation of groups, and has suggested that it might be required for democratic reasons; it may be the only way for some points of view to be heard. The matter of group *rights*, however, is somewhat different. By 'group rights' here I mean constitutionally protected entitlements enjoyed by named communities. Such devices seem quite appropriate in the case of the anomalous and self-contained communities mentioned by David Miller. They seem appropriate, too, in the case of at least some of what Will Kymlicka terms 'national minorities' – that is, groups with an historical claim to maintain some degree of independence, perhaps because they were forcibly incorporated into the state in question (Kymlicka, 1995: 19–20). Aboriginal communities are the clearest case: they may have or claim or acquire rights to self-government which differ from the standard case of liberal rights both because they are collectively exercised and because they are not universal.

Such rights do not seem to pose any particular conceptual problem. Indeed, as Peter Jones writes, 'Given the special moral significance that rights possess, it is difficult to see what could justify our confining that significance to things which matter only to individuals as separate individuals' (Jones, 1994b: 187). And if, to apply a well-known formulation, one has a right, provided that some aspect of one's well-being is a sufficient reason, to hold others to have a duty (Raz, 1986: 166), then to confine 'well-being' to cases of separate individual well-being would be arbitrary. It is true that even if a group has a collective interest that passes the threshold of significance, it is not always practical, or meaningful, to confer a right. For rights of this kind are valued and sought-after only if they carry something approaching peremptory force – if, that is, their beneficiaries are protected against calculations and weighings of competing interests that might work out against them. But very often the need to take account of the highly significant interests of several groups might make it impossible to give peremptory force to the interest of any one of them. In the case of aboriginal groups, for example, recognizing a collective right means that we have already concluded (presumably) that some aspects of their situation are unique, and that problems of competing group interests will therefore not come into play, at least not immediately.

The moral problem posed by group rights concerns what those rights might enable groups to do to their own members. Certainly groups would be entitled to charge their members with their fair share of the costs of maintaining the group's identity and survival, and would be entitled to penalize or expel free-riders. But can they likewise penalize or expel those who dissent from some group-sanctioned practice? Here two different considerations seem to be in play. On the one hand, if we regard group rights as being like treaty rights between nations – as in some respects they are, with the peculiarity that the nations in question are physically interspersed – then there is no more reason to intervene to protect internal dissenters than there is to invade other countries for the same purpose. On the other hand – to revert to an argument already introduced above – we cannot entirely analogize the domestic and international situations, since in the international situation, constrained (to the extent that it is) by considerations of sovereignty, one must take what comes, while in the domestic situation one has a degree of control over what others do. We might perhaps think that in compensation for this, the right of exit would be more effective in the domestic situation than in the international one, since it is easier to leave one domestic community for another than to emigrate. If so, it would follow that communities within states could be more demanding than states themselves could, since their members would have (to a higher degree) the alternative of exit. But this simply does not seem to correspond to the facts. It might actually be easier for a Russian Jew to emigrate to Israel than to assimilate into Russian society, or for a Czech Gypsy to emigrate to Canada than to be accepted by Czech society. Thus the right-of-exit argument might actually impose *more* stringent obligations on internal communities than on states. But it is hard to generalize, given that communities and states are so different, so let us just discount that argument for the present purpose.

This might seem to leave the argument at a stalemate, the analogy between the domestic and international situations tending in one direction, the disanalogy tending in another. But what may break the tie is one of the arguments basic to liberal democracy. The majority principle is best defended, as we saw above, as an instrument of public reason, creating incentives to generalize one's argument maximally. This is so, as we also noted, only when the majorities and minorities form in a relatively fluid way; and one of the major empirical obstacles to this approach is that it fails when groups are entrenched and simply pursue partial interests unreflectively. Enumerated group rights have an entrenching effect, tending to fix political affiliations along predefined group lines (Brodie, 1996). But other kinds of rights, such as (unenumerated) equality rights, can be one of the most potent means of inducing political formations which cut across groups, disturbing fixed lines of attachment: for they can be put to diverse and inherently unpredictable uses. Perhaps we have, then, a second important strategy against the problem of majoritarian self-interest. One is provided by the compensation principle, whether institutionalized in the form of protective rights or simply accepted as part of the democratic ethic. The other is the provision of abstract rights which can catalyse shifting political formations.[3]

Seyla Benhabib complains that some liberal political theorists mischaracterize rights as devices for keeping matters 'off the agenda'. 'Basic human civil and political rights,' she points out, 'are never really "off the agenda" of public discussion and debate.' Although they are sometimes constitutionally entrenched, 'we are always disputing their meaning, their extent, and their jurisdiction' (Benhabib, 1996: 79). Surely this is true, but perhaps it would be more complete to note that rights have two distinct aspects. On the one hand, we want some of them, or all of them sometimes, to have peremptory or 'trumping' effect, in order to avoid putting some crucially important things into the balance along with pressing but temporary needs. That would be true, for example, of the rights to security that Mill discusses in *Utilitarianism*. Without physical security, to take the most obvious example, no other good would be worth having, and if it were constantly set in the balance with expediency, life would not be worth living (Mill, 1910: 50). On the other hand, it is the distinct merit of rights that they can be subject to open-ended interpretation which can provide the basis for a deliberative politics. That would be true, for example, of the general right to equality which inspires Mill in *The Subjection of Women*, a right which figures as a point of recurrent reference in the critique of social institutions. It is the second aspect of rights that Benhabib stresses for her purposes, and this aspect naturally depends on rights having a degree of abstraction.

Not much separates the deliberative and the liberal positions (or some liberal positions, at any rate) here. Ronald Dworkin's version of liberalism is perhaps best known for advancing the idea that rights are important for their trumping capacity, or their power to impose peremptory closure. But he also insists upon the capacity of rights to provoke 'republican' deliberation more effectively, in some cases, than politics would do if not compelled to face basic questions of political morality (Dworkin, 1994). He cites the national debates about racial justice in the United States from the 1950s on, and, more recently, about abortion. Comparing the treatment of the abortion issue in the United States with its more summary political resolution in Ireland or France, Dworkin claims that thanks to the involvement of constitutional rights, there was wider debate, deeper disclosure of the complex issues involved, and a greater sense of the difference between matters of right and wrong and matters of state jurisdiction. No doubt Dworkin and the deliberative democrats take different views about the role of courts in the process, the latter tending to the view that localizing principled argument in a court might detract from, rather than stimulate, its democratic pursuit. But here the contested matters are partly empirical ones, and from even a slight distance the disagreement seems intramural rather than fundamental. Whatever the differences here, there is a shared understanding that rights have not only an agenda-closing but an agenda-setting power, and that this power can bring about alliances and oppositions which draw upon reflective rather than ascriptive commitments.

Notes

1. To be distinguished from the *political* neutralism rejected in Chapter 5; *state* neutrality refers to constitutional norms, *political* neutralism to the kinds of considerations that can be brought to bear in course of the democratic process.
2. The modern debate begins, effectively, with Kymlicka (1989).
3. See Waldron (1993: 419) for the importance of the abstractness of rights. Lefort (1986: 239–72) stresses the power of rights to unsettle political formations.

Conclusion: Liberalism, Democracy, Liberal Democracy

This book has argued that liberal democracy is neither an oxymoron nor a tense pragmatic compromise but a single political conception, which is defensible on minimal assumptions. These assumptions depend on taking a particular (but reasonable) view of our relation to our past, a view which picks out the contraction of non-political authority. If politics must generate its own authority, then political institutions must be neutral in the sense of public or unappropriated, which in turn implies an equal civic status. This is attainable through the majority principle, in the sense that it is a principle that expresses each citizen's respect for the others' need to be persuaded. But the same value also leads us to a certain protectiveness towards minorities, whether these are of a democratic or an ascriptive kind. Moreover, one can arrive at liberal democracy in this manner without the vulnerable commitments that some liberal and democratic theories make. We do not, for example, have to defend autonomy as a primary value (a task often imposed on liberals – sometimes self-imposed), and we do not have to make needlessly strong claims for democratic deliberation, claims which greatly understate the depth of political conflicts, or even mistake their character.

But how does liberal democracy, thus interpreted, stand, in relation to other versions of liberalism or of democracy? And, as a construct of an abstract kind, what relation does it bear to actual institutions termed 'liberal democratic'?

CONCLUSION

One conclusion of this book is that it is important to distinguish between liberal democracy and liberalism. Liberal democracy is a constitutional theory which serves to justify political systems that rest on a certain combination of practices, namely the accountability and the restraint of government. Liberalism is a trend of moral thinking that seeks to influence the laws and policies of liberal democratic (or other) political systems. Liberal democracy cannot make such far-reaching claims as liberalism can; but liberalism cannot impose itself with constitutional force, as liberal democracy claims to do. On the argument of this book, it is a mistake to try to combine the moral ambitions of the former with the compulsory status of the latter. Critics of liberalism are often on the mark in complaining about the false universalization of liberal beliefs, or of some of them at any rate.

It is possible to be a liberal but not a liberal democrat, as defined in the argument above, in at least three ways. First, one might hold a perfectionist version of liberalism, resting on grounds which are, as it were, democracy-neutral. It might be one's absolute priority to cultivate what Mill termed 'individuality' – that is, the creative power to overturn convention, to develop one's natural capacities to the full, and (since Mill's doctrine is not a narcissistic one) to stimulate and foster the same power in other people. Whether or not this view allies itself with democracy depends on empirical factors. Mill himself connects individuality with a particular kind of democracy – that is, local self-government. In the final paragraph of *On Liberty*, he says the practice of taking part in local administration can '[call] forth the activity and powers of individuals' (Mill, 1910: 169), instead of turning them into passive clients of bureaucracy. But here the classic pitfalls of any perfectionist approach come to light: the commitment to developing an end-state goal, such as a certain kind of personality, can carry embarrassing implications if the background empirical assumptions turn out not to hold. In one of the earliest critiques of *On Liberty*, James Fitzjames Stephen pointed out that some kinds of repressive or disciplinarian communities (such as Calvinist churches) can be quite good at fostering 'individuality', and that liberty might not turn out, after all, to be the best means (Stephen, 1993: 29–32). The connection between individuality and local democracy is equally vulnerable, or more so. Suppose local self-government is not very good at promoting individuality; or does it only very selectively; or is less cost-effective (in the broadest sense) than some other means; or leads

169

to poor outcomes? Since Mill's link would not hold, or would not be strong enough to take the strain, the individualist would have to stop being a democrat, unless there were some other instrumental argument to turn to.

Although not necessarily committed to democracy in the way that a liberal democrat is, the liberal individualist would want no doubt to play a part or exert influence *in* democratic politics, as a way of defending or promoting his or her values. Individualist liberals would, to take an important example, have distinctive views about the right approach to non-liberal minorities within democratic society. There is perhaps something of a tendency to exaggerate this problem. Will Kymlicka has pointed out how confrontational it is to assume that religious or ethnic minorities are going to treat their own members in an illiberal way, ignoring the fact that most such minorities are by and large content with liberal constraints, even if their normative (religious, cultural) starting points are not the same as the liberal's (Kymlicka, 1995: 171–2). But no doubt there are awkward cases: cases that fall somewhere in between the isolated groups which really need to stand in a kind of treaty relation to the liberal democracy which surrounds them, and groups which can be fully functional in liberal democratic society. It may be that in the light of the compensability criterion, a liberal democrat would decide to leave them alone rather than undermine their ways of living; whereas the liberal individualist would presumably feel more strongly impelled to change them for the better.

This difficult issue has been carefully discussed by political theorists, however, and it is far from clear what the liberal individualist should actually *do*, as opposed to feeling impelled to do. If imposing individualist practices would destroy insular communities without providing an alternative that their members were capable of adopting, the liberal individualist might reasonably decide that the project was purely destructive and self-defeating: better to leave illiberal minorities alone, surely, than to reduce them to anomie (Raz, 1986, 423–4). So the liberal individualist and the liberal democrat might not end up far apart. But all the same, the individualist's threshold for protection is significantly higher than the liberal democrat's: for presumably the individualist would feel that no loss had occurred if the members of illiberal minorities *were* likely to make the transition to a new and better way of life, while the liberal democrat would insist that the members of minorities must be able to regard their way of living, if it is to be changed by the majority, as significantly continuous with the way of life with which they began.

A case that might bring out the difference here is the traditional practice of arranged marriages, favoured by some members of some immigrant communities from South Asia (Kukathas, 1995). If there is a good case for believing the practice to be interwoven with other aspects of family life in the culture, in such a way that the whole ideal of family life would be distorted were it to be forbidden, then one would hope that liberal democrats, given their political morality, would accept the practice, whatever their personal morality suggested about the matter. Liberal individualists, however, would from their point of view be right to see the practice as a relic of an authoritarian past, and a serious obstacle to the ideal of a developed and autonomous life. Given the nature of the case, they could hardly prohibit the practice (without massive invasions of privacy, which they should find objectionable on other grounds), but they could make arranged marriage contracts unenforceable – as Mill proposed to make slavery contracts unenforceable. Or, without going to those lengths, they could use the resources of the educational system to discredit it. The one consideration that should stop them – that it would prevent South Asians from leading any sort of meaningful life – is wholly implausible.

Second, some liberals will part company with liberal democrats on the issue of rights. The liberal democrat arrives at the adoption of rights by a conditional route. Actually, the theory above provides two routes, which are complementary. One is that the limits of public persuasion point towards areas of vulnerability where minorities' moral views need recognition. The other is that by grounding the power of overriding minorities' judgements on the distinct requirements of public action, one implicitly denies anyone that power in private relations. We cannot, in our dealings with one another as individuals and neighbours, override each other's views of what we need – as we can in our dealings with one another as citizens. Both routes are conditional on the background conditions for a liberal democratic polity. But liberals of one kind (let us call them ethical liberals) will believe that rights should be provided and enforced universally, not just where the conditions of liberal democracy happen to apply.

The ethical liberal view is hardly resistible if we think of certain kinds of rights, particularly those connected with basic security. It becomes much less compelling as we move down the list in the direction of the full individualist programme. A universal right to Millian 'individuality' looks like less good a candidate than a universal right to physical security (as Mill himself would surely have agreed, for he is emphatic on the point that individuality is possible only within advanced or 'civilized' societies, whereas security is fundamental to any life at all). Up to a certain point on the list – a point which I make no attempt to define here – a liberal democrat might have good reason to think that the recognition of some entitlements is an inescapable part of moral belief itself; that a set of beliefs which denied them was not within the pale of morality. Then the liberal democrat and the ethical liberal would be in agreement on a set of basic human rights. But one would hope – and both of them, presumably, would hope – that recognizing such rights would not depend on beginning from their own premises. One would hope that basic human rights would be discernible from within a variety of non-liberal, non-liberal-democratic and non-democratic ideologies and traditions because one hopes, after all, that they can become effective under all kinds of political regimes driven by all kinds of moral beliefs or ideologies. At this humanitarian level, one would want to seek points of convergence with non-Western traditions, and to locate the functional equivalents of rights there (de Bary and Tu Weiming, 1998). Doing so would reflect a view about the basic facts of human vulnerability (Shue, 1980). It would reflect an assessment of what any life needs, and it would accept that while it is a failure of imagination to deny that lives of decency and dignity can be lived in traditional societies in which liberalism and democracy are not valued, it is a still worse failure of imagination *not* to deny that the victims of systemic brutality and deprivation enjoy decent and dignified lives.

All of this can be accepted within the theory developed here. Where the liberal democrat differs from the ethical liberal is not in denying the existence of rights, but in claiming that the imperfectness of obligations comes into play.[1] In their political action, co-citizens rely on a scheme of institutions which creates mutual expectations, and meeting others' expectations is a condition of benefiting from them. There are considerations, then, that make respecting others' rights perfectly obligatory. Where the obligation falls in the case of the rights of other nationals is the topic of a large and complex literature that cannot be explored here.[2] But the liberal democrat will insist that the reciprocity among co-citizens must make a difference. The question will be whether it makes a difference at the same level as basic rights, so that the obligation to meet the basic rights of non-citizens is imperfect, or if it makes a difference above the level of basic human rights, those rights being treated as a minimum or threshold. It does not seem that a theory of liberal democracy is usefully discriminating at this point, just because, as a theory of democracy, it gives weight to the mutual expectations of co-citizens. Beyond the ground covered by those, it simply has to give way to a broader moral inquiry.

A third possible kind of non-democratic liberal is a sceptical kind of liberal who may possibly accept the importance of persuasion, as the liberal democrat is claimed here to do, but who found the liberal democrat's expectations seriously unrealistic. Those expectations are demanding: we have to be able to think of politics as, potentially, a forum in which good arguments are developed and valid evidence uncovered, so that rival views become as persuasive as they can be, and our interests as reasoning persons are therefore respected. There is no easy defence against the objection that this is to hope for too much. The liberal democrat understands, it was argued above, that public persuasiveness is less easily achieved than private persuasiveness, that Locke's 'civil communication' is a more approximate affair than, say, philosophical discourse. But a sceptical liberal would take the point further: it is not just more difficult, it is downright impossible. Civil communication, one might believe, is a realm of rhetoric and deception in which the lowest common denominator of belief is sovereign. It is hopeless to expect levels of transparency of the kind that the reflective life can achieve, or even perhaps comparable to it. So our priority must be to protect individual reflectiveness from the idiocies of mass opinion: we will want a much more extensive and more unconditional scheme of rights than the liberal democrat envisages. A 'liberalism of fear' would see liberal democracy as irresponsibly incautious.

Some degree of political scepticism – to be clearly differentiated from general philosophical scepticism – seems essential to basic political literacy. It is hard to take seriously the views of people who have no sense of the shadow that falls between the principled intention and the political act, as well as between the principled act and its actual consequences. How far it should be taken is in general an unsettlable matter. But in the case of the sceptical liberals, there

173

is one line of approach that may help. If they take their political scepticism to the point of denying that democracy is in any way better than other (available) forms of collective decision-making, there may be nothing further to be said. But if they recognize any (comparative) merit in democracy at all, then we can ask why. If, as maintained above, the standard arguments lead us back in one way or another to the value of persuasion, then the liberal democrats might gain some ground. The issue becomes one of degree, a matter of conducting institutional assessments and predictions, of the kind that theory cannot hope to settle; but it will have been justified in its claim that that is the domain of questions that is decisive.

The sceptical liberal may perhaps maintain, as William Riker (1982) does, that liberal values lay the basis for no more than cautious and modest democratic claims, reminiscent perhaps of Madison's. Ambitious democracy, the 'populism' of his book's title (*Liberalism against Populism*), is a set of beliefs which lays claim to the existence of a popular will that democratic processes can reflect, enjoying legitimacy to the extent that they do. Social choice theory has entirely discredited the very idea of such a will, and so the populist legitimation of democracy fails. The 'liberalism' of the title is an alternative and, Riker claims, more successful set of beliefs. Essentially, it values democracy as a defensive strategy against tyrannical governments. Being sustained by this more negative kind of value, it therefore does not depend on social-choice-theory-violating premises about the existence of common 'wills' (or preference functions). It is hard, however, to find an answer to Joshua Cohen's objection that this defence of democracy assumes some coherence in democratic outcomes, 'enough, at any rate, to provide potential tyrants with incentives to refrain from grosser violations of liberties' (Cohen, 1986: 30). To suppose that majorities can reliably identify tyranny is to make or imply a claim of an epistemic kind. Paradoxically, Rikerian sceptical liberalism depends (if only implicitly) upon *stronger* claims for the validity of democratic outcomes than does the theory of liberal democracy sketched above, which makes no claims for the validity of *those* outcomes at all, as opposed to the epistemic outcomes of the procedures which are motivated by majority rule.

Can a democrat not be a liberal democrat? The argument developed above, for all its conditional nature, is a universal one. Although the conditions for its application are not always present, its claims hold whenever the conditions *do* apply. So whenever we have circumstances in which political legitimation is needed (in the sense outlined in Chapters 2 and 3), the theory demands liberal democracy as a response. The theory has not said anything about the desirability of those background conditions, and would be hard pressed to do so without giving up on its minimalist pretensions. If a society seeks legitimation of a non-political kind, the theory offers no objection, although in many cases it might prompt one to ask if the consensus assumed by non-political legitimation is really as complete as its defenders pretend (and if this can be convincingly shown in the absence of democracy). There are huge incentives to self-interested pretence here (Sen, 1999). For the background conditions of liberal democracy do in fact apply quite widely, in a world in which the existence of alternatives is hard to keep secret. Of course, the whole point of imposing authoritative rather than political legitimation *is* to keep alternatives secret, or at least to invalidate them as alien or evil. It is hard to see how the liberal democrat (as opposed to the liberal individualist, or ethical liberal) can consistently object: if one's normative position rests on background conditions, one can hardly demand on normative grounds that those conditions should be brought into being. But the liberal democrat (or indeed anyone) could object if, as will sometimes be the case, the exclusion of alternatives has to be accomplished by means which are prohibited at a deeper moral level, as violations of basic human rights.

The background conditions of liberal democracy include an already-constituted political community, which undergoes a contraction of authority, with the results hypothesized above. It does not, then, allot any primary importance, within political morality, to community-building, for, taking community for granted, it limits itself to setting out the terms on which its continued existence will be legitimate. As a result, liberal democracy will have disagreements with versions of democratic theory that take seriously the ethics of nationality, allotting normative space to the creation and defence of particularist identity. Democratic positions of this kind may represent the model's most important, and questionable, exclusion. It would not be of much importance if all that was excluded was 'republicanism' as defined by Habermas – that is, a view of democracy as a process to be valued because it allows the assertion of a particular national character. That is something of a caricature of the republican position anyway, but even if it were

175

widely held, it would not be a position carrying much moral attractiveness. Much more serious, however, is the exclusion of an 'ethics of nationality' which, exactly inverting Habermas's idea of republicanism, presents national identity as an important precondition for democracy.

Several strong arguments are available in support of such ethics; here I list some drawn broadly from David Miller's *On Nationality* (Miller, 1995b: 49–80). One concerns what we may call the burdens of altruism. Given widely shared assumptions about ordinary human nature, we cannot just suppose that obligations will be met simply because they are justified. It is not easy for most people to forgo advantages or bear costs beyond a certain point, a point which the usual circumstances of political life will certainly surpass. But the burdens will be more easily borne if one sees them as contributions to an ongoing shared form of life from which one benefits oneself.

Another concerns the conditions of deliberative trust. Real deliberation is possible only if the participants feel themselves bound to apply the principles that they invoke in like cases in the future, even when those principles might work to their disadvantage: but participants are unlikely to do so when they regard coparticipants as strangers or enemies, and more likely to do so if bound to them by other relations of trust and cooperation.

A third argument, perhaps the most compelling of all, concerns the capacity to sustain redistributive solutions. A politics of social justice requires the relatively advantaged to accept transfers of resources to the relatively disadvantaged; but transfers will be resisted if there is no sense of solidarity transcending social position, a solidarity which nations can provide as few other formations can. (In the years since German reunification, to pick one prominent recent example, the taxpayers of the former West Germany have accepted huge transfers to the former East Germany on a scale greater than that provided to fifteen European countries by the United States' post-war Marshall Plan. Even under the exceptional conditions of national reunification, the redistribution was not accomplished without resistance and complaint; and the idea that massive redistributions can be accomplished *between* nations remains untested.)

Arguments of this kind establish the importance, to democratic politics, of some shared background of common identity. Where no such background exists, it would be a legitimate democratic project to try to create one. One would then have a variety of nation-building democracy that might depart in significant ways from liberal democracy. It might be justified in (emotively) 'persuading' as opposed to (rationally) 'convincing', to borrow Rousseau's succinct (if not entirely standard) distinction, for we cannot expect the effect to precede the cause, or 'the social spirit which must be the product of institutions ... to preside over the setting up of those institutions' (Rousseau, 1968: 87). Measures might be taken to create a civic culture with a distinctive solidarity-building character. One might be less protective towards minorities than a liberal democrat would demand (though concern for future solidarity would itself obviously dictate prudence here). But whether or not such departures from liberal democracy are justifiable in a *constituted* polity is another matter.

One reason for doubting it is that established societies enjoy such immense non-political resources for preserving their character. The process of socialization largely escapes governmental control, as do folklore and mythmaking; the massive influence of the majority language carries a cultural as well as a linguistic content; and public space inevitably reflects the tastes and mores of the majority of its users. Surely all this is enough. It is true that we cannot regard the attainment of national solidarity as a once-and-for-all achievement, and that the symbols and practices that represent it must retain their power; but they do not *all* have to retain their power, and it would be an odd situation in which enough of them could not retain their power, or undergo a sufficiently gradual transformation, through the various influences of civil society itself.

Another reason derives from the instrumental nature of the argument for taking nationality seriously. We cannot, as Rousseau points out, require the eventually expected 'spirit' to attend the conditions of its founding; but we must require the conditions of its founding to retire once it is created. For example, it would have been unhelpfully pedantic, during the years of Canada's founding, to cast doubt upon the mythic story of Laura Secord, a Canadian[3] woman who is believed to have led her milking cow past American sentries, during the war of 1812, in order to warn a British post – which she reached with the help of friendly Indians – of an impending attack. This story has received, over the years, numerous embellishments. Neither the cow nor the friendly Indians, expressing in their different ways a Canadian pastoral and pacific self-image, figure in its earliest versions, and their addition testifies to the story's use as a focus for national self-interpretation. But however helpful the Secord myth – taught to generations of Canadian schoolchildren – might once have been, surely there can be no case for resisting a system of public education which will expose it and other national myths to entirely uninhibited scrutiny. That follows from the mode of justification which is explored here.

It might, of course, be hard to find a democratic nationalist who would disagree, or who would not be equally critical of forms of conservative nationalism which are protective of mythology (Miller, 1995b: 124–30). Many national traditions have absorbed elements of liberal democracy at a basic level, so that reproducing these traditions is entirely harmonious with those elements. That makes purely theoretical discussion of this issue largely indeterminate, once we get beyond the rather bald statement that the reproduction of tradition will have a lower priority in liberal than in nationalist democracy. Determinacy is also limited by the fact that different national traditions, all with perfectly good claims to incorporate liberal democratic politics, are liberal democratic in different ways. The French, American and British traditions, for example, contain different articulations of civic and particular identity (Levinson, 1997). But Miller's discussion of nationalist ethics offers a fundamental challenge to universalist theories that demands consideration at a theoretical level. Even if, as a reader might well feel, versions of democratic nationalism evolved in liberal societies will share a good deal of political ground with some theories of liberal democracy, the democratic nationalist, Miller contends, is better able to give an intelligible account of his or her project; for universalist political theories cannot give a convincing explanation of why national boundaries count, in our practical reasoning, at all (Miller, 1995b: 64).

Miller deals effectively with some strategies that a universalist – such as a liberal democrat as defined above – might use to explain why nationality has any weight in our moral reasoning. One is the idea of nationality as a 'useful convention', the other of nationality as a 'voluntary creation' (ibid.: 51–2, 58–65). The former tells us that while moral obligations are in principle universal, they are more effective if they are locally applied, and people are in the first instance obliged to take care of their co-nationals. The second tells us that we have special obligations to co-nationals in rather the same way as we have special obligations to people with whom we have made contracts or from whom we have received benefits. For the reasons that Miller gives, neither strategy works, and so, it would seem, we should take more seriously the claims of ethical particularists, who begin by giving due weight to the memberships and attachments that people have, as factors which should weigh in their moral reasoning. A particularist, unlike a universalist, can validly offer 'because he is my brother' as a reason for an act of generosity or loyalty (*ibid.*: 50), and likewise an ethics of nationality allows us to say 'because they are Canadian' if asked why a piece of legislation gives preference to co-nationals over citizens of another country.

Since the first, at least, of those reasons seems such a natural one to give, this critique threatens to undermine the universalist project. The issues arising here are large, and I shall simply indicate one way in which the universalists might attempt to defend themselves. Miller's argument depends on our accepting that national obligations fall into the particularist category along with family obligations and the like. But it is not entirely clear that they belong there. In fact, it is not entirely clear that 'because he is my brother' belongs there either. 'Because he is Tom' or 'because he is my favourite brother' is an authentically particularist declaration, as is Montaigne's famous 'Because it was I, and it was he' as an explanation of the strongest friendship of his life. 'Because he is my brother' may already have entered the realm of moral generalization ('brothers should help each other'): and 'because they are Canadian' is a statement that requires a historical background to which many powerful abstractions have already contributed, such as duty, honour, gratitude, sacrifice and (according to Samuel La Selva, 1996) *the idea of* fraternity, an idea with the features of a humanist and universal morality. It seems very much an open question whether obligations to co-nationals are particular in nature, and thus a challenge to the universalist, or whether they are the work of universalizing efforts, repeated over the centuries, in which co-nationals figure as tokens or proxies for humanity. 'Do unto others', after all, is usually learned as a rule about how to deal with neighbours – the annoying child in the next row of desks – rather than people whom one has never met at all, or even heard of. And it is a familiar fact that nations should represent their ambitions – especially when aggressive – as universal ones; that they should see themselves as the agents of reason or revelation or culture or civilization or democracy or socialism, as though even in its own self-understanding the national idea resisted moral particularization, seeming inadequate for respectable legitimizing purposes. The bible for this line of thinking might be Henri Bergson's recently very neglected book *The Two Sources of Morality and Religion* (1935), which interestingly claims that societies require a practical amalgam of family- or tribe-based imperatives and a universalizing morality that speaks in abstractions; that just as the latter could never have attained motivating power without drawing on the former, so too the former could never have adapted itself to large societies without borrowing from the latter. If this line of speculation has any merit, then the universalist may be committed not to 'heroic' but to utopian schemes of world community, but may accept nations as relatively stable containers for human reciprocity.

The third and final topic – that of the critical potential of liberal democracy – is potentially inexhaustible, and again I can only indicate directions. First in line for attention, perhaps, is the apparent absence of any economic or redistributive dimension in the argument above – an absence that may provoke suspicions that the argument lacks egalitarian bite. If those suspicions were justified, it would be regrettable, for since T. H. Green's day, liberal political theory has taken on a socially as well as a politically egalitarian project. This has been sustained by various considerations: Green's own view of the need to take account of socio-economic as well as political 'hindrances' to freedom, T. H. Marshall's argument about the conditions necessary for the effective exercise of citizenship, Rawls's 'difference principle', or Dworkin's 'equality of resources' approach. Even the narrowest version based on 'negative freedom', it is argued, can be made to yield a redistributive potential (Waldron, 1993: 309–38). If liberal democracy, as defined here, had nothing to say about the matter, it would be a retrograde step.

In distancing itself from end-of-history triumphalism, the case made here began by separating liberal democracy as a political conception from economic liberalism, or from capitalist economies. That political emphasis has characterized the argument throughout, at the cost, perhaps, of seeming indifferent to precisely that realm in which current liberal democracies are most vulnerable to critical appraisal. Here, though, a distinction must be made. As far as economic organization is concerned, the idea of liberal democracy defended here contains nothing that will direct us to any particular solution. It also remains my view (simply asserted here) that the various possible solutions, whether capitalist, socialist or mixed, do not basically differ in the kinds of political systems that they require. Nevertheless, the core argument adopted above has strong if as yet indeterminate distributive implications. People have an underlying interest in conducting their lives on the basis of considerations that they find persuasive, and so deserve a political system in which the considerations that are to dominate will be given as persuasive a form as institutional factors can provide for.

But the capacity of people to respond to persuasive considerations is not entirely a cognitive matter; it is partly to do with the costs to them of doing so. One has to be able to afford to respond as one thinks is best; and it is a reasonable guess that the main obstacle here is competing personal interest of an urgent kind. If I believe that environmental considerations are compelling from an impersonal point of view, but that responding to them will cost me my job; that public support for some valuable cultural project is desirable, but that tax increases would be personally unsustainable; that increased immigration quotas are required by international justice, but that competition from immigrants will tend to diminish my family's welfare; that affirmative action policies for women or minorities are justified, but that they will prevent me or my sons from finding work; then I am to that extent much less likely to see things from the impersonal point of view that is the regulative idea of public reason. It follows that if the argument developed above is to work, a liberal democratic society will have to take steps to reduce the most important vulnerabilities of its members. Its justifying theory does not support equality of resources; its requirements are cast, rather, in terms of an absolute threshold above which it should try to move everyone, and beyond that it leaves further redistributions to democratic decision.[4] Nor does it support giving special weight to the claims of the worst-off; it is not, as far as the distribution of opportunities goes, a theory of fairness. As abstractly stated, it does not tell us enough to make policy choices, for these depend on judgements about the relative importance of kinds of vulnerability, judgements unsupported by any of the argument developed above. To the achievements of progressive liberalism and social democracy in areas such as health, education and welfare, one needs to add concern with security in employment, or equivalents to that, in order to take account of an especially pervasive source of anxiety.

But although it is obviously in need of development, the argument does allow us to say that a society that does nothing to diminish vulnerability, and thus to promote its members' capacity to respond to the best considerations as they see them, cannot benefit from the case for liberal democracy. Governments which knowingly pursue policies that actually increase citizens' vulnerability, and diminish their capacity to act as general concerns would incline them to, benefit from no known theory of political justification at all. They rest on economic fashion and political illiteracy, and their appropriation of the term 'liberal' is deeply mystifying.

This case perhaps most closely resembles T. H. Marshall's (1965)[5] among the earlier liberal cases for redistributive policies: one cannot be a citizen unless one is guaranteed the conditions for one's personhood, taken here to include the capacity to follow one's judgements. This may attract another line of criticism. If we demand a range of positive entitlements or 'social rights', are we – as Richard Bellamy argues – reverting to some form of perfectionism, since any set of positive entitlements will have importance only in some views of life, and will be rejected in others? (Bellamy, 1992: 255). We would seem, after all, to be discriminating, in a way that sits uncomfortably within liberalism, between important and unimportant elements in people's lives. Now that might be so if the starting point were a field of possible 'rights', together with their associated lives, from which we had to make a justified choice. But that was clearly not the avenue adopted here. What justifies the rights in question is a consideration drawn, mediately, from the basic legitimating argument of liberal democracy, and not the values that they enable people to realize in conducting their lives. They depend not on an idea about how people should live, but on a view of the legitimate basis on which they can politically coexist.

As for the more directly political requirements, much has already been said by theorists of deliberative democracy, with many of whose practical conclusions one can agree despite reservations, set out above, about their starting point. This book tried to offer a more minimal starting point, less demanding in its expectations about democracy, less vulnerable to sceptics, and more hospitable to people who share liberal intuitions. The idea of democracy developed above has placed a premium on the cultivation of open and informed public reasoning, as something required by the principle of equality. Under conditions of disagreement, it was argued, all that principle can require is that we respect one another in our capacity as moral reasoners, and adopt public institutions that express that respect, abandoning a 'better answer' theory. These institutions must, to the greatest practicable extent, motivate the generalization of principle, the transparency of argument, and the discovery of evidence.

Some concrete proposals of a very general kind were made above. The discourse of equality rights might play a particularly valuable role in disturbing ascriptive majority/minority divisions, and provoking unanticipated and principled coalitions. The constitutional representation of ascriptive minorities might compel a greater transparency of argument, and would certainly motivate the discovery of evidence relevant to public decisions. One would also expect questions of media control and party financing, and sometimes electoral systems,[6] to arise in connection with this approach to justifying democracy. James Fishkin's discussion of (and experiments with) deliberative polling is particularly valuable, if one believes that the deliberative deficit is caused principally by institutional failures which impede the flow of reliable information, thus permitting the manufacturing of consent (Fishkin, 1991, 1995). Other political scientists who are more sceptical about the short-term prospects for deliberation have made valuable suggestions for institutional reform (Stokes, 1998; Johnson, 1998). Of course, the problems may lie at a deeper level. No doubt one needs, beyond institutions, a general culture in which tentativeness and openness to evidence are encouraged, rather than one in which a norm of 'discursive machismo' leads participants to cling to their initial positions at all costs (Gambetta, 1998). Where these cultures come from, and how you change them if you happen to have them, are themselves good examples of questions calling for tentativeness and openness to evidence.

The argument of this book has, however, suggested that political deliberation has its limits even if we could find a way past the obstacles set by institutions and political culture. Fishkin's interesting proposal provides an opportunity to summarize these considerations. What he proposes is a kind of small replica of deliberative politics which the larger society can observe and learn from. A random sample of citizens are given the opportunity to study and discuss an issue in depth, with the aid of expertly prepared briefing materials which state the case for various alternative points of view; their attitudes to the issue are polled before and after their deliberation, and others can then observe what typical fellow-citizens would conclude under ideal deliberative conditions. It is not to diminish the interest of this idea to point out that the sense in which it might be said to *improve* political decisions is unclear. It will make them more informed, and in certain cases – such as the Manchester experiment that Fishkin (1995: 177–81) reports on – we may infer that this prevents them from supporting policies that are actually against their own interests; and we will think this a good thing when voters' interests are legitimate. But we cannot conclude that informed decisions are in general better, for several reasons: more informed decisions sometimes conflict;[7] more information sometimes leads different people in different directions (*ibid*.: 181); and decisions involve processes of weighing and prioritizing that information can enlighten, certainly, but not determine. We do not face these difficulties, however, if we take the view that deliberative polling and other devices are valuable if they encourage elites to make their reasoning persuasive, or if they encourage voters to reflect on the reasons that they hold. The bare fact that *others* (the sample polled) have found certain reasons to be persuasive, however, would not be of interest from a liberal democratic point of view – except in those cases in which, information being decisive, another's being persuaded is a reason for me to be persuaded too.

There is one further point of dissent between the demands of liberal democracy and the proposals of deliberative democracy (in some of its versions); and this point may involve a major critical objection to the position developed above. The theory offered here is state-centred, in the sense that it bears on the formal institutions of public decision-making, central, regional or local. Some deliberative theorists, however, attach great importance to a democratized civil society, calling for a proliferation of sites of public debate, as something integral to the political ethos that they favour (Cohen and Rogers, 1995). This gives them common ground with other democratic theorists who call for an extension of participation on different grounds, as well as with feminists concerned about the oppression latent in the private–public distinction, and others who for related reasons favour the 'decentring' of political life. The Italian socialist Norberto Bobbio, a finely critical sympathizer, regarded the failure to democratize civil society as one of the major broken promises of liberal democracy (Bobbio, 1987). From these various points of view, the state-centred character of liberal democracy may be its single most unappealing feature.

There are, of course, many distinct ideas in play here, which call for different kinds of comment. As for the sites of politics, liberal democracy necessarily takes a restrained view, initially at least. It offers itself as a solution to the problem of political legitimation. Given that starting point, it cannot consistently demand the multiplication of the sites at which political legitimation is required. It asserts itself where politics exists, but cannot demand the existence of politics. Moreover, taking politics as a background condition of a factual kind, it would see no particular value in further politicization. That is not to say that it actually excludes a 'civic humanist' idea of politics as the central activity of life; but it maintains, reasonably (surely), that this is not an attitude of the sort that can impose itself as a constitutional requirement, whatever normative appeal it may have – here, tastes differ (Miller, 1995a: 448).

But the issue of what is and is not political is one whose importance has often been greatly inflated. For one thing, it seems to derive much of its appeal from recurrent ambiguities. Sub-state institutions might be called 'political' on any of a number of different grounds. They might be called political because they contain their own micropolitics; or because they contain relations of internal domination; or because they 'allocate values' for a wider public; or because they might be the subject of public contestation; or because their decisions have implications for the state; or because their procedures provide a site of learning for attitudes that are transferred to higher levels. One or more of these is virtually certain to apply, and so the universality of 'politics' gets to be confirmed; but the point is gained at the great cost of obscuring these different meanings and the different (even contradictory) implications that they might have for political organization.

Second, though, how much actually *does* follow from what looks like basically a semantic point? Perhaps it is supposed that if things are political they ought to be democratized, and that only things that are political ought to be democratized; but neither of these follows, and the question of what to do about sub-state institutions seems independent of the issue of what to call them. In a democracy, there might be political matters (such as diplomatic negotiations) which ought not to be handled in a fully democratic way. Conversely, one might reject all the reasons just listed for calling factories 'political' yet still favour their democratization, because, for example, it might favour efficiency, or social harmony. Altogether too much is made to hinge on definitional matters.

If the primary value appealed to were 'autonomy', then there might be at least a plausible case for democratizing sub-state institutions, on the grounds that the value ought to be reflected in every organization in which hierarchy could be diminished and autonomous self-government enhanced. And if the way for collective autonomy to be exercised is through democratic deliberation, then deliberation ought to be practised in civil society as well as in the state. The one reservation that one might have concerns the interdependence of levels: if sub-state institutions are to have important things to deliberate over, then to that extent the jurisdiction of the state itself would have to be limited, and the reach of collective autonomy at that level would be constrained. But this can be resolved by trading off, or by principles of 'subsidiarity', which might tell us where responsibilities ought to lie. The main objection, however, concerns the starting point. To take 'autonomy' as a primary value is to adopt a strong but very exclusive point of departure, which one has no reason to believe to be appealing. Liberals are rightly taken to task for giving it a degree of weight that it does not have in many people's lives, and surely the same objections apply with no less force to its collective or democratic version. The alternative route, adopted above, was to take the fact of self-government, in its collective sense, as a background condition, not as a value. The primary value – the only possible one, it was argued, given that background condition – was equality.

Now equality, an idea with virtually limitless potential, could of course lead us back to many or even all of the democratizing projects mentioned above. Once it comes into play (as Tocqueville pointed out in *Democracy in America*), it has the capacity to overturn hierarchies large and small. And within liberal democracy, there can be no objection to its pursuit. Liberal democracy does not directly sanction any ideas of property that might impede the democratization of, say, the workplace. It does not adhere to any private–public distinction, except the distinctions that arise from its own deliberated and temporary conclusions. So nothing in it precludes further democratization. But it could be thought to require further democratization only on the grounds that this would be instrumental to its own conception of equality – that, for example, the skills and sense of efficacy necessary to citizenship would need to be learned and developed at other levels of organization. And then all the questions become empirical; we would need to know that participation at other levels would indeed strengthen a sense of civic values, rather than tending to dissolve citizenship into more highly cultivated particular affiliations.[8]

One of the useful tasks of political theory in general is to sort out what is a matter of fact, or of definition, or of principle. But the discussion of liberal democracy seems especially in need of discriminations of this kind. It has been shrouded in many misunderstandings. Some of these arise from grounding its values in a particular 'Western' moral and religious tradition, instead of in a re-articulation of the relation between political and extra-political authority. Others arise from failing to distinguish a principled and critical theory from a description of contemporary facts. Others arise from confusing a political morality, constrained by the need to take account of disagreement, with a unilateral and moralistic liberalism. Yet others arise from stale oppositions which for one reason or another assume enmity between liberal democracy and 'stronger' democratic forms, turning empirical questions into principled ones. Against this background of misunderstandings, it seems important to try to work out what the principled requirements of liberal democracy are, so that we can then think about two matters: how, empirically speaking, its principles might be realized; and whether its principles, morally speaking, are enough. This book has stopped short of tackling the former question. As for the latter, it has confined itself to describing the grounds on which one would find liberal democracy attractive. A work of advocacy would have taken a different form. But obviously, my assumption has been that liberal democracy is more readily defensible when one recognizes what it is, and my view has been that too many critiques of liberal democracy have missed the point.

Notes

1. Some rights create 'perfect' obligations – that is, they clearly establish who it is that has the obligation to meet the right. Other rights create only 'imperfect' obligations – that is, they establish that someone (the right-bearer) has a compelling need, but they do not establish that anyone in particular has an obligation to meet it. A right to 'charity' is the standard example.
2. Effectively, this literature begins with Beitz (1979).
3. Formerly an American Loyalist.
4. This argument rests on the importance of being persuaded rather than the importance of persuading others, and so leads to results that differ from James Bohman's (Bohman and Rehg, 1997: 321–48). However, Bohman's proposals for equalizing political influence are a good example of the kind

of stronger democratic demand that might be put forward within liberal democracy, and which is entirely consistent with its values.

5. See also Hobhouse (1964: 117): liberalism 'assumes that the individuals whom it would enfranchise can enter into the common life and contribute to the formation of a common decision by a genuine interest in public transactions'.

6. Guinier (1994) discusses electoral reform and redistricting policies, with a view to improving the prospects of inter-racial discussion and coalition. Her proposals are of particular interest, if the idea of liberal democracy developed here is adopted, when racial demographics make pure majority rule inappropriate.

7. Commenting on the MX missile acquisition question, Fishkin (1995: 89) outlines several conflicting options and then maintains, 'Any of these options reached after widespread knowledge of the arguments and a collective engagement in the debate might have brought us a public opinion worth having.' It is not explicit what makes informed choices better, but since the informed options conflict it cannot be that information makes them right.

8. Compare, for example, Young (1997) and Offe (1995).

Bibliography

Appiah, A. K. (1997), 'The multiculturalist misunderstanding', *New York Review of Books*, 9 October, 30–6.

Arblaster, A. (1984), *The Rise and Decline of Western Liberalism*. Oxford: Blackwell.

Aristotle (1953), *The Ethics of Aristotle*, J. A. K. Thomson ed. and trans. Harmondsworth: Penguin.

Banning, L. (1986), 'Jeffersonian democracy revisited: liberal and classical ideas in the new American republic', *William and Mary Quarterly*, 43, 3–19.

Barnard, F. M. (1991), *Pluralism, Socialism and Political Legitimacy*. Cambridge: Cambridge University Press.

Barry, B. M. (1970), *Sociologists, Economists and Democracy*. London: Collier-Macmillan.

Barry, B. M. (1973a), *The Liberal Theory of Justice*. Oxford: Oxford University Press.

Barry, B. M. (1973b), 'Wollheim's paradox: comment', *Political Theory*, 1, 317–22.

Barry, B. M. (1982), 'Is democracy special?', in B. Barry and R. Hardin (eds), *Rational Man and Irrational Society?* Beverly Hills, CA: Sage, 325–40.

Barry, B. M. (1990), 'How not to defend liberal institutions', in R. B. Douglass, G. M. Mara and H. S. Richardson (eds), *Liberalism and the Good*. New York: Routledge, 44–58.

Barry, B. M. (1995), *Justice as Impartiality*. Oxford: Clarendon Press.

Baum, B. (1997), 'Feminism, liberalism and cultural pluralism',

Journal of Political Philosophy, 5, 230–53.

Beetham, D. (1992), 'Liberal democracy and the limits of democratization', *Political Studies*, 40, 40–53.

Beiner, R. (1992), *What's the Matter with Liberalism?* Berkeley: University of California Press.

Beitz, C. (1979), *Political Theory and International Relations*. Princeton, NJ: Princeton University Press.

Beitz, C. R. (1989), *Political Equality*. Princeton, NJ: Princeton University Press.

Bellamy, R. (1992), *Liberalism and Modern Society: A Historical Argument*. University Park, PA: Pennsylvania State University Press.

Bellamy, R. (1997), 'The construction of Europe: rights or democracy?', in R. Bellamy, V. Bufacchi and D. Castiglione (eds), *Democracy and Constitutional Culture in the Union of Europe*. London: Lothian Foundation Press, 153–75.

Benhabib, S. (1996), *Democracy and Difference*, Princeton, NJ: Princeton University Press.

Bergson, H. (1935), *The Two Sources of Morality and Religion*, R. Ashley Audra and Cloudesley Brereton trans. New York: Henry Holt.

Berlin, I. (1969), *Four Essays on Liberty*. London: Oxford University Press.

Black, A. (1997), 'Christianity and republicanism: from St. Cyprian to Rousseau', *American Political Science Review*, 91, 647–56.

Bobbio, N. (1987), *The Future of Democracy*, Richard Bellamy ed., Roger Griffin trans. Minneapolis: University of Minnesota Press.

Bohman, J. and Rehg, W. (1997), *Deliberative Democracy*. Cambridge, MA: MIT Press.

Boucher, D. and Kelly, P. (eds) (1994), *The Social Contract from Hobbes to Rawls*. London: Routledge.

Brennan, G. and Lomasky, L. (1993), *Democracy and Decision: The Pure Theory of Electoral Preference*. Cambridge: Cambridge University Press.

Brodie, I. (1996), 'The market for political status', *Comparative Politics*, 28, 253–71.

Castoriades, C. (1997), 'Democracy as procedure and democracy as regime', *Constellations*, 4, 1–18.

Charvet, J. (1992), 'The idea of an international ethical order', *Studies in Political Thought*, 1, 59–72.

Christiano, T. (1993), 'Social choice and democracy', in D. Copp,

J. Hampton and J. E. Roemer (eds), *The Idea of Democracy*. Cambridge: Cambridge University Press, 173–95.

Cohen, J. (1986), 'An epistemic conception of democracy', *Ethics*, 97, 30.

Cohen, J. (1989), 'Deliberation and democratic legitimacy', in A. Hamlin and P. Pettit (eds), *The Good Polity*. Oxford: Blackwell, 17–34.

Cohen, J. (1996), 'Procedure and substance in democratic theory', in S. Benhabib (ed.), *Democracy and Difference*. Princeton, NJ: Princeton University Press, 95–119.

Cohen, J. (1998), 'Democracy and liberty', in J. Elster (ed.), *Deliberative Democracy*. Cambridge: Cambridge University Press.

Cohen, J. and Rogers, J. (eds) (1995), *Associations and Democracy*. London: Verso.

Coleman, J. and Ferejohn, J. (1986), 'Democracy and social choice', *Ethics*, 97, 6–25.

Constant, B. (1988), *Political Writings*, B. Fontana ed. and trans. Cambridge: Cambridge University Press.

Cooke, M. (1996), 'Are ethical conflicts irreconcilable?', *Philosophy and Social Criticism*, 23, 1–19.

Dagger, R. (1997), *Civic Virtues: Rights, Citizenship, and Republican Liberalism*. Oxford: Oxford University Press.

Dahl, R. A. (1989), *Democracy and Its Critics*. New Haven, CT: Yale University Press.

de Bary, T. and Tu Weiming (eds) (1998), *Confucianism and Human Rights*. New York: Columbia University Press.

De Marneffe, P. (1994), 'Contractualism, liberty and democracy', *Ethics*, 104, 764–83.

del Vecchio, G. (1952), *Justice*. trans. Lady Guthrie. Edinburgh: Edinburgh University Press.

Derrida, J. (1974), *Of Grammatology*. Gayatri Spivak trans. Baltimore: Johns Hopkins University Press.

Dunn, J. (1990), *Interpreting Political Responsibility*. Oxford: Polity.

Dworkin, G. (1975), 'Non-neutral principles', in N. Daniels (ed.), *Reading Rawls*. Oxford: Blackwell, 124–40.

Dworkin, R. (1977), *Taking Rights Seriously*. Cambridge, MA: Harvard University Press.

Dworkin, R. (1978), 'Liberalism', in S. Hampshire (ed.), *Public and Private Morality*. Cambridge: Cambridge University Press, 113–43.

Dworkin, R. (1985), *A Matter of Principle*. Cambridge, MA: Harvard

University Press.

Dworkin, R. (1990), 'Foundations of liberal equality', *The Tanner Lectures on Human Values*, vol. 11. Salt Lake City: University of Utah Press, 1–119.

Dworkin, R. (1994), 'Mr. Liberty', *New York Review of Books*, 11 August, 17–22.

Elster, J. (ed.) (1986), *The Multiple Self*. Cambridge: Cambridge University Press.

Elster, J. (1998), *Deliberative Democracy*. Cambridge: Cambridge University Press.

Elster, J. and Hylland, A. (eds) (1986), *Foundations of Social Choice Theory*. Cambridge: Cambridge University Press.

Engels, F. (1972), 'Letter to Joseph Bloch, September 21–22, 1890', in R. C. Tucker (ed.), *The Marx–Engels Reader*. New York: Norton.

Estlund, D. (1997), 'Beyond fairness and deliberation'. In J. Bohman and W. Rehg (eds), *Deliberative Democracy*. Cambridge, MA: MIT Press, 173–204.

Fay, B. (1996), *Contemporary Philosophy of Social Science*. Oxford: Blackwell.

Feinberg, J. (1973), *Social Philosophy*. Englewood Cliffs, NJ: Prentice-Hall.

Fierlbeck, K. (1996), 'The ambivalent potential of cultural identity', *Canadian Journal of Political Science*, 29, 3–22.

Fishkin, J. (1979), *Tyranny and Legitimacy*. Baltimore: Johns Hopkins University Press.

Fishkin, J. (1985), *The Voice of the People: Public Opinion and Political Democracy*. New Haven, CT: Yale University Press.

Fishkin, J. (1991) *Democracy and Deliberation: New Directions for Democratic Reform*. New Haven, CT: Yale University Press.

Foucault, M. (1972), *Histoire de la folie à l'âge classique*, 2nd ed. Paris: Gallimard.

Freud, S. (1965), *New Introductory Lectures on Psychoanalysis*, J. Strachey ed. and trans. New York: Norton.

Friedman, J. (ed.) (1996), *The Rational Choice Controversy*. New Haven, CT: Yale University Press.

Fukuyama, F. (1992), *The End of History and the Last Man*. New York: Free Press.

Gallie, W. B. (1955–6), 'Essentially contested concepts', *Proceedings of the Aristotelian Society*, 56, 167–98.

Galston, W. (1991), *Liberal Purposes: Goods, Virtues and Diversity in the Liberal State*. Cambridge: Cambridge University Press.

Gambetta, D. (1998), 'Claro! An essay on discursive machismo', in J. Elster (ed.), *Deliberative Democracy*. Cambridge: Cambridge University Press, 19–43.

Gellner, E. (1968), 'The concept of a story', *Ratio*, 10, 49–66.

Gewirth, A. (1978), *Reason and Morality*. Chicago: University of Chicago Press.

Green, D. P. and Shapiro, I. (1994), *Pathologies of Rational Choice Theory*. New Haven, CT: Yale University Press.

Green, L. (1994), 'Internal minorities and their rights', in J. Baker (ed.), *Group Rights*. Toronto: University of Toronto Press, 100–17.

Guinier, L. (1994), *The Tyranny of the Majority*. New York: Free Press.

Gutmann, A. and Thompson, D. (1990), 'Moral conflict and political legitimacy', in R. B. Douglass, G. M. Mara and H. S. Richardson (eds), *Liberalism and the Good*. New York: Routledge, 125–47.

Gutmann, A. and Thompson, D. (1996), *Democracy and Disagreement*. Cambridge, MA: Harvard University Press.

Habermas, J. (1994), 'Struggles for recognition in the democratic constitutional state', in A. Gutmann (ed.), *Multiculturalism*. Princeton, NJ: Princeton University Press, 107–48.

Habermas, J. (1995), 'Reconciliation through the use of public reason: remarks on John Rawls's *Political Liberalism*', *Journal of Philosophy*, 92, 109–31.

Habermas, J. (1996), *Between Facts and Norms*, W. Rehg trans. Cambridge, MA: MIT Press.

Harrison, R. (1993), *Democracy*. London: Routledge.

Hart, H. L. A. (1955), 'Are there any natural rights?', *Philosophical Review*, 64, 175–91.

Hart, H. L. A. (1963), *Law, Liberty and Morality*. Stanford, CA: Stanford University Press.

Hobhouse, L. T. (1964), *Liberalism*. New York: Oxford University Press.

Holmes, S. (1995), *Passions and Constraint*. Chicago: University of Chicago Press.

Honderich, T. (1982), '*On Liberty* and morality-dependent harms', *Political Studies*, 30, 504–15.

Horton, J. (1985), 'Toleration, morality and harm', in J. Horton and S. Mendus (eds), *Aspects of Toleration*. London: Methuen, 113–35.

Isaac, J. C. (1988), 'Republicanism vs. liberalism: a reconsideration', *History of Political Thought*, 9, 349–77.

Ivison, D. (1997), *The Self at Liberty*. Ithaca, NY: Cornell University Press.

Johnson, J. (1998), 'Arguing for deliberation: some skeptical considerations', in J. Elster (ed.), *Deliberative Democracy*. Cambridge: Cambridge University Press, 161–84.

Jones, P. (1989), 'The ideal of a neutral state', in R. E. Goodin and A. Reeve (eds), *Liberal Neutrality*. London: Routledge, 9–38.

Jones, P. (1994a), 'Bearing the consequences of belief', *Journal of Political Philosophy*, 2, 24–43.

Jones, P. (1994b), *Rights*. Basingstoke: Macmillan.

Kekes, J. (1997), *Against Liberalism*. Ithaca, NY: Cornell University Press.

Kukathas, C. (1995), 'Are there any cultural rights?', in W. Kymlicka (ed.), *The Rights of Minority Cultures*. Oxford: Oxford University Press, 228–56.

Kymlicka, W. (1989), *Liberalism, Community and Culture*. Oxford: Clarendon Press.

Kymlicka, W. (1995), *Multicultural Citizenship*. Oxford: Clarendon Press.

La Selva, S. (1996), *The Moral Foundations of Canadian Federalism*. Montreal: McGill-Queen's University Press.

Lefort, C. (1986), *The Political Forms of Modern Society*, Eng. trans. Cambridge, MA: MIT Press.

Levine, A. (1978), 'A conceptual problem for liberal democracy', *Journal of Philosophy*, 75, 302–8.

Levinson, M. (1997), 'Liberalism versus democracy? Schooling private citizens in the public square', *British Journal of Political Science*, 27, 333–60.

Locke, J. (1823), *A Third Letter for Toleration*, in Works, vol. 6. London: Tegg.

Locke, J. (1975), *An Essay concerning Human Understanding*, P. H. Nidditch ed. Oxford: Clarendon.

Locke, J. (1983) *A Letter concerning Toleration*, J. H. Tully ed. Indianapolis: Hackett.

Lukes, S. (1974), 'Relativism: cognitive and moral', *Proceedings of the Aristotelian Society*, 48, 187.

Lukes, S. (1989), 'Making sense of moral conflict', in N. L. Rosenblum (ed.), *Liberalism and Moral Life*. Cambridge, MA: Harvard University Press, 127–42.

Lyotard, J.-F. (1984), *The Postmodern Condition*, Eng. trans. Minneapolis: University of Minnesota Press.

MacCormick, N. (1982), *Legal Right and Social Democracy*. Oxford: Clarendon Press.

MacIntyre, A. (1967), *Secularization and Moral Change*. London: Oxford University Press.

Macpherson, C. B. (1965), *The Real World of Democracy*. Toronto: Canadian Broadcasting Corporation.

Macpherson, C. B. (1973), *Democratic Theory*. Oxford: Clarendon Press.

Macpherson, C. B. (1977), *The Life and Times of Liberal Democracy*. Oxford: Oxford University Press.

Manin, B. (1987), 'On legitimacy and political deliberation', *Political Theory*, 15, 338–68.

Marshall, T. H. (1965), *Class, Citizenship and Social Development*. New York: Anchor.

Mason, A. (1993), *Explaining Political Disagreement*. Cambridge: Cambridge University Press.

May, K. O. (1952), 'A set of independent necessary and sufficient conditions for simple majority decision', *Econometrica*, 20, 680–4.

Mill, J. S. (1910), *Utilitarianism, Liberty, Representative Government*, London: Dent.

Mill, J. S. (1965), *Essays on Literature and Society*. New York: Collier.

Miller, D. (ed.) (1991), *Liberty*. Oxford: Oxford University Press.

Miller, D. (1992), 'Deliberative democracy and social choice', *Political Studies*, 40, 54–67.

Miller, D. (1995a) 'Citizenship and pluralism', *Political Studies*, 43, 432–50.

Miller, D. (1995b), *On Nationality*. Oxford: Clarendon Press.

Nagel, T. (1987), 'Moral conflict and political legitimacy', *Philosophy and Public Affairs*, 16, 215–40.

Nagel, T. (1991), *Equality and Partiality*. New York: Oxford University Press.

Nielsen, K. (1978), 'Class and justice', in J. Arthur and W. H. Shaw (eds), *Justice and Economic Distribution*. Englewood Cliffs, NJ: Prentice-Hall, 225–46.

Offe, C. (1995), 'Some skeptical considerations on the malleability of representative institutions', in J. Cohen and J. Rogers (eds), *Associations and Democracy*. London: Verso, 114–32.

Parekh, B. (1992), 'The cultural particularity of liberal democracy', *Political Studies*, 40, 160–75.

Parekh, B. (1995), 'The Rushdie affair: research agenda for political philosophy', in W. Kymlicka (ed.), *The Rights of Minority Cultures*. Oxford: Oxford University Press, 303–20.

Passmore, J. A. (1978), 'Locke and the ethics of belief', *Proceedings of the British Academy*, 64, 185–208.

Patten, A. (1996), 'The republican critique of liberalism', *British Journal of Political Science*, 26, 25–44.

Pennock, J. R. and Chapman, J. W. (eds) (1983), *Liberal Democracy*. New York: New York University Press.

Pettit, P. (1992), 'Habermas on truth and justice', in G. H. R. Parkinson (ed.), *Marx and Marxisms*. Cambridge: Cambridge University Press, 207–28.

Pettit, P. (1997), *Republicanism*. Oxford: Oxford University Press.

Phillips, A. (1992), 'Must feminists give up on liberal democracy?', *Political Studies*, 40, 68–82.

Phillips, A. (1995), *The Politics of Presence*. Oxford: Oxford University Press.

Popper, K. (1970), 'Normal science and its dangers', in I. Lakatos and A. Musgrave (eds), *Criticism and the Growth of Knowledge*. Cambridge: Cambridge University Press, 51–8.

Poulter, S. (1987), 'Ethnic minority customs, English law, and human rights', *International and Comparative Law Quarterly*, 36, 589–615.

Proast, J. (1984), *The Argument of the Letter concerning Toleration Briefly Consider'd and Answered*, P.A. Schouls ed., *Letters concerning Toleration*. New York: Garland.

Proudhon, P.-J. (1868), *L'Idée générale de la révolution au XIXe siècle*. Paris: Internationale.

Przeworski, A. (1988), 'Democracy as a contingent outcome of conflicts', in J. Elster and R. Slagstad (eds), *Constitutionalism and Democracy*. Cambridge: Cambridge University Press, 59–80.

Rawls, J. (1971), *A Theory of Justice*. Cambridge, MA: Harvard University Press.

Rawls, J. (1993), *Political Liberalism*. New York: Columbia University Press.

Rawls, J. (1995), 'Reply to Habermas', *Journal of Philosophy*, 92, 170–80.

Raz, J. (1984), 'Right-based moralities', in J. Waldron (ed.), *Theories of Rights*. Oxford: Oxford University Press, 182–200.

Raz, J. (1986), *The Morality of Freedom*. Oxford: Clarendon Press.

Raz, J. (1990), 'Facing diversity: the case of epistemic abstinence', *Philosophy and Public Affairs*, 19, 3–46.

Rees, J. C. (1985), *John Stuart Mill's 'On Liberty'*. Oxford: Clarendon Press.

Richardson, H. S. (1997), 'Democratic intentions', in J. Bohman and W. Rehg (eds), *Deliberative Democracy*. Cambridge, MA: MIT Press, 351.

Riker, W. H. (1982), *Liberalism against Populism*. San Francisco: W. H. Freeman.

Rosemont, H. (1998), 'Human rights: a bill of worries', in T. de Bary and Tu Weiming (eds), *Confucianism and Human Rights*. New York: Columbia University Press, 54–66.

Rousseau, J.-J. (1968), *Social Contract*, M. Cranston ed. and trans. Harmondsworth: Penguin.

Rousseau, J.-J. (1974), *The Essential Rousseau*, trans. L. Bair. New York: Mentor.

Scanlon, T. M. (1975), 'Preference and urgency', *Journal of Philosophy*, 72, 660.

Scruton, R. (1980), *The Meaning of Conservatism*. Harmondsworth: Penguin.

Sen, A. K. (1999), 'Human rights and Asian values', in J. H. Rosenthal (ed.), *Ethics and International Affairs*, 2nd ed. Washington, DC: Georgetown University Press, 170–93.

Shapiro, I. (1996), *Democracy's Place*. Ithaca, NY: Cornell University Press.

Shue, H. (1980), *Basic Rights: Subsistence, Affluence and U.S. Foreign Policy*, part 1. Princeton, NJ: Princeton University Press.

Siedentop, L. A. (1989), 'Liberalism: the Christian connection', *Times Literary Supplement*, 24–30 March, 308.

Skinner, Q. (1991), 'The paradoxes of political liberty', in D. Miller (ed.), *Liberty*. Oxford: Oxford University Press, 183–205.

Skinner, Q. (1998), *Liberty before Liberalism*. Cambridge: Cambridge University Press.

Spitz, E. (1984), *Majority Rule*. Chatham, NJ: Chatham House.

Spragens, T. A. (1990), *Reason and Democracy*. Durham, NC: Duke University Press.

Stephen, J. F. (1993), *Liberty, Equality and Fraternity*. Indianapolis: Liberty Fund.

Stokes, S. C. (1998), 'Pathologies of deliberation', in J. Elster (ed.), *Deliberative Democracy*. Cambridge: Cambridge University Press, 123–39.

Sunstein, C. R. (1998), 'Beyond the republican revival', *Yale Law Journal*, 97, 1539–89.

Swanton, C. (1985), 'On the "essential contestedness" of political concepts', *Ethics*, 95, 811–27.

Taylor, C. (1967), 'Neutrality in political science', in P. Laslett and W. G. Runciman (eds), *Philosophy, Politics and Society*, 3rd series. Oxford: Blackwell, 25–57.

Taylor, C. (1982), 'The diversity of goods', in A. K. Sen and B. Williams (eds), *Utilitarianism and Beyond*. Cambridge: Cambridge University Press, 129–44.

Taylor, C. (1994), 'The politics of recognition', in A. Gutmann (ed.), *Multiculturalism*. Princeton, NJ: Princeton University Press, 25–73.

Trillin, C. (1994), 'Drawing the line', *New Yorker*, 12 December, 50–62.

Van de Veer, D. (1979), 'Of beasts, persons and the original position', *The Monist*, 62, 368–77.

Vernon, R. (1986), *Citizenship and Order*. Toronto: University of Toronto Press.

Vernon, R. (1996), 'John Stuart Mill and pornography: beyond the harm principle', *Ethics*, 106, 621–32.

Vernon, R. (1997), *The Career of Toleration*, Montreal: McGill-Queen's University Press.

Vernon, R. (1998), 'Liberals, democrats and the agenda of politics', *Political Studies*, 46, 295–308.

Waldron, J. (1988), 'Locke: toleration and the rationality of persecution', in S. Mendus (ed.), *Justifying Toleration*. Cambridge: Cambridge University Press, 61–86.

Waldron, J. (1991–2), 'Minority cultures and the cosmopolitan alternative', *University of Michigan Journal of Law Reform*, 25, 751–93.

Waldron, J. (1993), *Liberal Rights*, Cambridge: Cambridge University Press.

Waldron, J. (1997), 'Participation: the right of rights', Conference for the Study of Political Thought, Columbia University, New York.

Walzer, M. (1997), *On Toleration*, New Haven, CT: Yale University Press.

Ward, C. V. (1991), 'The limits of "liberal republicanism": why group-based remedies and republican citizenship don't mix', *Columbia Law Review*, 91, 581–607.

Webster, R. (1990), *A Brief History of Blasphemy*. Southwold (Suffolk): The Orwell Press.

Williams, B. (1973), *Problems of the Self*. Cambridge: Cambridge University Press.

Williams, B. (1981), *Moral Luck*. Cambridge: Cambridge University Press.

Wollheim, R. (1962), 'A paradox in the theory of democracy', in P. Laslett and W. G. Runciman (eds), *Philosophy, Politics and Society*, 2nd series. Oxford: Blackwell, 71–87.

Wootton, D. (1989), 'John Locke: Socinian or natural law theorist?', in J. E. Crimmins (ed.), *Religion, Secularization and Political Thought*. London: Routledge, 39–67.

Young, I. M. (1989), 'Polity and group difference: a critique of the ideal of universal citizenship', *Ethics*, 99, 250–74.

Young, I. M. (1990), *Justice and the Politics of Difference*, Princeton, NJ: Princeton University Press.

Young, I. M. (1997), 'Difference as a resource for democratic communication', in J. Bohman and W. Rehg (eds), *Deliberative Democracy*, Cambridge, MA: MIT Press, 383–406.

Index